Neil J. Anderson

ACTIVE
Skills for Reading: Book 4

THOMSON

★

™

HEINLE

Australia · Canada · Mexico · Singapore · Spain · United Kingdom · United States

THOMSON
HEINLE

Active Skills for Reading, Student Book 4

Neil J. Anderson

Publisher, Global ELT: Christopher Wenger
Editorial Manager: Sean Bermingham
Development Editor: Maria O'Conor
Contributing Writers: Arlen Gargagliano,
   Kristin Johannsen
Production Editor: Tan Jin Hock
ELT Directors: John Lowe (Asia), Jim Goldstone
(Latin America—ELT), Francisco Lozano (Latin
America—Academic and Training, ELT)

Director of Marketing, ESL/ELT: Amy Mabley
Marketing Manager: Ian Martin
Interior/Cover Design: Christopher Hanzie, TYA Inc.
Illustrations: Cue Art & Design Associates
Composition: Stella Tan, TYA Inc.
Cover images: PhotoDisc, Inc.
Printer: Seng Lee Press

Printed in Singapore
2 3 4 5 6 7 8 9 10   06 05 04 03

For permission to use material from this text or
product, contact us in the United States:
Tel   1-800-730-2214
Fax   1-800-730-2215
Web   www.thomsonrights.com

For more information, contact Heinle, 25 Thomson
Place, Boston, Massachusetts 02210 USA, or you
can visit our Internet site at http://www.heinle.com

ISBN 0-8384-2647-6

Photo Credits

Unless otherwise stated, all photos are from
PhotoDisc, Inc. Digital Imagery © copyright 2002
PhotoDisc, Inc.

Photos on pages 64, 71, 78, 106, 120, 190, 211 (top
right), and 218 are from Associated Press. Photo on
page 197 is from Index Stock Imagery. Photo on page
211 (bottom right) is from Associated Press/POOL
NEWSDAY. Photo on page 211 (left) is from Associated
Press/KEYSTONE.

Microsoft®, Visual C#™, .Net™, Outlook®, and
Windows® (page 23) are either registered trademarks

or trademarks of Microsoft Corporation in the United States
and/or other countries. Cranium® (page 120) is a registered
trademark of Cranium, Inc. Pictionary® (page 121) is a
trademark of Pictionary, Inc. Scrabble® (page 121) is a
registered trademark of Hasbro, Inc. in the United States
and Canada. Scrabble rights elsewhere in the world are
held by J.W. Spear and Sons, PLC.

Every effort has been made to trace all sources of
illustrations/photos/information in this book, but if any have
been inadvertently overlooked, the publisher will be
pleased to make the necessary arrangements at the first
opportunity.

Dedication & Acknowledgments

I dedicate this book to Maria O'Conor. As my editor, she worked diligently to keep this project on schedule. We have worked well together.

In May 2000, I was sitting at a swimming pool in Melaka, Malaysia, with my colleagues and friends David Nunan and John Lowe. We started talking about my interest in reading, and in the lack of a good EFL reading series. That's when the idea for *ACTIVE Skills for Reading* began. I thank the other incredible staff at Heinle/Thomson who have worked with me on this level of the series: Chris Wenger, Sean Bermingham, David Bohlke, Stephanie Schmidt, and Tan Jin Hock, as well as Arlen Gargagliano and Kristin Johannsen for their contributions. I also thank the people at TYA for making this book look so wonderful: Christopher Hanzie and Stella Tan.

Kathy, Cameron, Todd, Kara, Miranda, Amy, Tyler, Ryan, and Douglas are my very best friends. They provided support and encouragement to complete this project.

My hope is that EFL teachers around the world can use this series as a way to engage their learners in the active and strategic skills of reading. I hope that learners become better readers, and are able to use their improved skills to accomplish their life goals, using English as their tool.

I appreciate enormously the input we received from teachers in Korea, Taiwan, and Japan. We also received valuable input from teachers in the United States, Canada, Mexico, and Turkey. Many thanks to those teachers listed below.

Neil J. Anderson

Penny Allan	Languages Institute, Mount Royal College, Alberta, Canada
Jeremy Bishop	Ehwa Women's University, Seoul, Korea
William E. Brazda	Long Beach City College, California, U.S.A.
Michelle Buuck	Centennial College, Ontario, Canada
Chih-min Chou	National Chengchi University, Taipei, Taiwan
Karen Cronin	Shinjuku, Tokyo, Japan
Marta O. Dmytrenko-Ahrabian	Wayne State University, English Language Institute, Detroit, Michigan, U.S.A.
James Goddard	Kwansei University, Osaka, Japan
Ann-Marie Hadzima	National Taiwan University, Taipei, Taiwan
Diane Hawley Nagatomo	Ochanomizu University, Tokyo, Japan
Carolyn Ho	North Harris College, Houston, Texas, U.S.A.
Feng-Sheng Hung	National Kaohsiung First University of Science and Technology, Kaohsiung, Taiwan
Yuko Iwata	Tokai University, Foreign Language Center, Kanagawa, Japan
Johanna E. Katchen	National Tsing Hua University, Department of Foreign Languages, Hsinchu, Taiwan
Peter Kipp	Ehwa Women's University, Seoul, Korea
Julie Manning	Ritsumeikan Uji High School, Kyoto, Japan
Gloria McPherson	English Language Institute, Seneca College, Ontario, Canada
Mary E. Meloy Lara	John F. Kennedy Primary School, Puebla, Mexico
Young-in Moon	English Language and Literature Department, The University of Seoul, Korea
Junil Oh	Pukyong National University, Pusan, Korea
Serdar Ozturk	Terraki Vakfi Okullarj, Istanbul, Turkey
Diana Pelyk	Ritsumeikan Asia Pacific University, Oita, Japan
Stephen Russell	Meiji Gakuin University, Tokyo, Japan
Consuelo Sañudo	Subsecretaria de Servicios Educativos para el Distrito Federal, Mexico
Robin Strickler	Kansai Gaidai University, Osaka, Japan
Liu Su-Fen	Mingchi Institute of Technology, Taipei, Taiwan
Cynthia Cheng-Fang Tsui	National Chengchi University, Taipei, Taiwan
Beatrice Vanni	University of Bahcesehir, Istanbul, Turkey
Kerry Vrabel	LaGuardia Community College, New York, U.S.A.
Aysen Yurdakul	Buyuk Kolej, Ankara, Turkey

Contents

Are You an ACTIVE Reader?

Before you use this book to develop your reading skills, take a minute to think about your reading habits, and your strengths and weaknesses when reading in English.

1. Do you enjoy reading in your native language? ☐ Yes ☐ No

2. How much time do you spend each day reading in your native language? _____

3. What types of material do you read in your native language?

   ☐ newspapers ☐ textbooks ☐ magazines

   ☐ poetry ☐ fiction ☐ nonfiction

   ☐ e-mails ☐ web sites ☐ letters from friends or family

   ☐ Other: _____

4. Why do you read these materials?

   ☐ Pleasure ☐ I have to ☐ Both

5. Do you enjoy reading in English? ☐ Yes ☐ No

6. How much time do you spend each day reading in English? _____

7. What types of material do you read in English?

   ☐ newspapers ☐ textbooks ☐ magazines

   ☐ poetry ☐ fiction ☐ nonfiction

   ☐ e-mails ☐ web sites ☐ letters from friends or family

   ☐ Other: _____

8. Why do you read these materials?

   ☐ Pleasure ☐ I have to ☐ Both

9. Assess your reading. Circle one of the two choices for each of the reading areas below.

   a. speed   fast   slow   _____

   b. comprehension   good   not so good   _____

   c. vocabulary   good   not so good   _____

   d. use of reading skills good   not so good   _____

10. Which of the areas above would you most like to improve? Outside of class, look through the first unit of the book and, on the lines above, write down the section(s) of the unit that you think will help you improve each of the above areas. As you work through the book, pay attention to those areas that will help you to improve your reading skills.

Looking for Work

Getting Ready

Discuss the following questions with a partner.

1. *Where, or how, would you look for a full-time job in your country?*
2. *Is there a shortage of workers in any field or occupation? Why do you think this is?*
3. *What is the employment situation like in your country at the moment? Is it difficult for graduates to find jobs or not?*
4. *What kind of information would you expect to find on a résumé? Do you have an up-to-date résumé?*

Before You Read:
Preparing the Right Résumé

(A) How much do you know about working overseas? Do you think that résumés in your country are different from résumés in other countries? In what way? Read each statement below and decide if it is true (T) or false (F).

	T	F
1. Interest in working overseas has decreased over the last few years.		
2. There are numerous reasons why professionals seek career experience abroad.		
3. In the United States, there are set guidelines for preparing a résumé that do not change.		
4. When sending a résumé to an employer in the United States, you should always attach a photo.		
5. If you e-mail a résumé, you should also mail a 'hard' or paper copy, too.		
6. Your résumé should show you are familiar with the language and the culture of the country in which you want to work.		
7. The fastest way to be hired abroad is to get a work permit.		
8. A résumé and a curriculum vitae are the same thing.		✓

(B) The following words can all be found in the reading. How do you think they relate to the topic of résumés?

initiative (ad) (n)   terminology   certify

expertise   recipient

(n)

Reading Skill:
Scanning

> When we need to read something to find specific information, we move our eyes very quickly across the text. When we 'scan' like this, we do not read every word or stop when we see a word we do not understand; we read quickly and pause only to find the particular information we are looking for.

(A) Scan the reading to find out if the statements above are really true or false.

(B) Read the passage again, then answer the questions that follow.

Creating a Global Résumé _____

The following reading is adapted from *Global Résumé and CV Guide* by Mary Anne Thomson © 2000. This material is used by permission of John Wiley & Sons, Inc.

Interest in pursuing international careers has soared in recent years, enhanced by chronic personnel shortages that are causing companies to search beyond their home borders for talent.[1]

Professionals seek career experience outside of their home countries for a variety of reasons. They may feel the need to recharge their batteries with a new challenge. They may want a position with more responsibility that encourages creativity and initiative. Or they may wish to expose[2] their children to another culture, and the opportunity to learn a second language.

The terms 'résumé' and 'curriculum vitae' (CV) generally mean the same thing: a one or two-page document[3] describing one's educational qualifications and professional experience. However, guidelines for preparing a résumé are constantly changing. The best advice is to find out what is appropriate regarding the corporate[4] culture, the country culture, and the culture of the person making the hiring decision. The challenge will be to incorporate two or more cultures into one document. The following list is a good place to start.

• In many countries, it is standard procedure to attach a photo or have your photo printed on your résumé. Do not attach a photograph to your résumé if you are sending it to the United States; the employer will dispose of it.
• Educational requirements differ from country to country. In almost every case of 'cross-border' job hunting, just stating the title of your degree will not be an adequate description. Provide the reader with details about your studies and any related experience. The same advice is true for experienced professionals who have participated in numerous training or continuing education courses.
• If you have specific[5] training, education, or expertise, use industry-accepted terminology in your description.
• Pay attention to the résumé format you use—chronological or reverse-chronological order. Chronological order means listing your 'oldest' work experience first. Reverse-chronological order means listing your current or most recent experience first. Most countries have preferences about which format is most acceptable. If you find no specific guidelines, the general preference is for the reverse-chronological format.
• The level of computer technology and accessibility to the Internet varies from country to country. Even if a company or individual lists an e-mail address, there is no guarantee that they will actually receive your e-mail. Send a 'hard' or paper copy of your résumé, as well as the e-mailed copy, just to make sure that it is received.
• The safest way to ensure that your résumé is 'culturally correct' is to review as many examples as possible. Ask employers or recruiters for examples of résumés that they thought were particularly good.
• If you are submitting your résumé in English, find out if the recipient uses British English or American English because there are variations between the two versions. For example, university education is often referred to as 'tertiary education' in the United Kingdom, but this term is almost never used in the United States. A reader who is unfamiliar with these variations may presume that your résumé contains errors or typos.[6]
• Although English is widely accepted today as being the universal language of business, most multinational companies will expect you to speak the

language of one of the countries in which they do business, in addition to English. Have your résumé prepared in both languages, and be ready for your interview to be conducted in both languages. Most companies will want to see and hear proof of your language skills.

60 • If you can, ask someone who is a native speaker of the language in which your résumé is written to review your document. One goal of your résumé should be to show your familiarity with the culture by using culturally appropriate language.

• Be aware that paper sizes are different dimensions in different countries.
65 The United States standard is 8½ by 11 inches, whereas the European A4 standard is 210 by 297 millimeters. When you send your résumé via e-mail, reformat your document to the recipient's standard. Otherwise, when it is printed it out, half of your material may be missing!

• Most employers who want to hire from abroad must be able to certify to
70 their local government that they are unable to find locals with the required skills necessary to do the job. The fastest way to be hired abroad is either to seek a country where there is a shortage of people with your skills or to be an 'intra-⁷company' transfer to another country. Be aware that obtaining a work permit can take a few months.

75 To be successful, and to enjoy your experience abroad, you must be flexible, open-minded, and both eager and willing to learn new ways of doing things. People everywhere appreciate individuals who are interested in getting to know them and learn about their ways of doing things. Enormous cultural faux pas⁸ are forgiven of individuals who are making honest attempts to fit
80 in.⁹ Be patient and observant. Ask questions to demonstrate your interest in learning and broadening your horizons. Remember that you represent your country to everyone you meet.

---

¹ **talent** skilled people
² **expose (to)** to put in contact with something, usually a form of reality
³ **document** a paper, such as a letter, contract, or report
⁴ **corporate** related to a business, especially one that is incorporated
⁵ **specific** particular, special, or unique
⁶ **typos** typographical errors; mistakes in print
⁷ **intra-** prefix meaning 'within'
⁸ **faux pas** /foʊpɑz/ mistakes; French expression literally translated as 'false steps'
⁹ **fit in** become accepted in a new environment

Reading Comprehension: What Do You Remember?

Decide if the following statements about the reading are true (*T*) or false (*F*). If you check (✔) false, correct the statement to make it true.

		T	F
1.	The increase in hiring individuals from overseas is partly due to a lack of qualified personnel in the home country of some companies.	V	
2.	The biggest challenge when preparing your résumé will be to find out about a company's corporate culture.	V	
3.	Vocabulary specific to your area of expertise should be used on your résumé.	V	
4.	Be aware that variations exist between North American and British English when preparing your résumé.	V	
5.	Reverse-chronological order lists your oldest work experience first.		✓
6.	If you send your résumé electronically, reformat the document to the recipient's standard paper size.	V	
7.	As English is the universal language of business, companies will only be interested in knowing about your English language ability.		✓
8.	Getting a work permit is quick and easy.		✓

Vocabulary Comprehension: Words in Context

Ⓐ The words in *italics* are vocabulary items from the reading. Read each question or statement and choose the correct answer. Compare your answers with a partner.

1. Every field of study has its own *terminology*, which means it has _____.

   a. its own specific language   **b.** its own rules for behavior

2. If you were going to *seek* assistance, you would _____ it.

   a. find   **b.** look for

3. You could show that you *appreciate* someone by _____.

   a. not answering their calls   **b.** writing him/her a thank-you note

4. 'I *presume* they're coming,' means _____.

   a. I think they're coming   **b.** I don't think they're coming

5. How could you show your boss that you were taking *initiative*?

   a. wait for him/her to tell you what to do

   b. ask or figure out what needs to get done and do it

6. What would mean the opposite of *broadening one's horizons*?

   a. keeping a narrow-minded outlook

   b. asking questions and reading as much as possible

7. The first *recipient* of the Nobel Peace Prize was the first person to ____.

   a. award the prize   **b.** get the prize

8. If you are watching an *enhanced* picture on television, it ____.

   a. looks worse   **b.** looks better

9. When you are required to *certify* a document, you must _____.
   a. get an official to sign and stamp it   **b.** make a copy of it
10. Arzu's *expertise* is in the culinary arts. This means _____.
    a. she doesn't know much about it   **b.** she is very knowledgeable about it

Ⓑ Now think of other examples using the vocabulary from A. Share your ideas with a partner.

1. Give some examples of computer *terminology*.
2. What qualities do you *seek* in an ideal boss?
3. What are some things that you *appreciate* about your family?
4. Do you think we should *presume* people are innocent until proven guilty?
5. Do you show *initiative* at school or work? Explain your answer.
6. What do people mean when they say "travel abroad is a good way of *broadening your horizons*"?
7. Have you ever been the *recipient* of an award or prize? What was it for?
8. Name two ways that you can *enhance* your English language learning skills.
9. Give an example of something that needs to be *certified*.
10. What would you like your field of *expertise* to be in?

Vocabulary Skill:
The Prefixes *inter-* and *intra-*

In this chapter you read the words 'interview' and 'intra-company.' 'Inter-' is a prefix that means 'between,' 'among,' or 'together.' 'Intra-' is a prefix meaning 'in,' 'within,' or 'interior.' For example, 'international' means 'between different countries,' whereas 'intra-company' means 'within a particular company.' Knowing these prefixes, and the differences between them, will help you to understand many more words in English.

Ⓐ For each word below, study the different parts. Then, write the part of speech and a simple definition. Use your dictionary to help you. Share your ideas with a partner.

Vocabulary	Part of Speech	Definition
1. intrapersonal	adjective	within the individual self or mind
2. interpersonal		
3. Internet		
4. intranet		
5. intermingle		
6. intravenous		
7. interactive		
8. interfere		
9. interject		
10. intermarriage		

Ⓑ Now complete the following sentences using some of the words from A. Be sure to use the correct form of each word.

1. Most employers look for people who have good _____ skills as they want employees who can work well with each other.
2. The _____ system within the White House is considered top secret.
3. A 'busy-body' is someone who likes to _____ in other people's lives.

4. Lawyers are usually quite good at being able to _____ when their opponents are speaking.

5. In certain cultures _____ is frowned upon because they believe it interferes with the traditions and culture of the people.

6. Very sick patients in the hospital receive food and water through an _____ tube.

7. Because of the ease and prevalence of the _____, people have virtually no excuse for not keeping in touch with each other.

8. _____ activities in the classroom are fun because everyone gets involved.

C Write two sentences of your own using the remaining words from A. Share your ideas with a partner.

1. _____

2. _____

Think About It Discuss the following questions with a partner.

1. *What kinds of jobs are most popular for graduates in your country at the moment?*

2. *When do college and university students in your country start looking for jobs? Are there any special resources to help them?*

3. *Would you like to go and work in another country? What challenges do you think you would face?*

4. *Do you think job-hunting is difficult? What can you do to make it easier?*

Before You Read:
You're Hired!

Discuss the following questions with a partner.

1. Have you ever had a job interview? What job was the interview for?

2. Did you feel nervous before the interview? If so, what did you do to calm your nerves?

3. How are job interviews in your country structured? Are there different types of interviews? What are they, and when are they used?

4. How do you think the following words and phrases relate to the topic of job interviews?

rapport   inconsistencies   concise

complement   think on your feet   clarification

Reading Skill:
Developing Reading Fluency

By building your reading fluency you will be able to read faster in exams. If you improve your reading fluency, you'll probably improve your exam scores.

Time yourself as you read through the passage. Try to read as fluently as you can. Record your time in the Reading Rate Chart on page 234.

Job Interview Types

The following reading is adapted from *Job Interview Types*. Reprinted with permission from www.careerbuilder.com © 2001.

If you are going to apply for a job in the United States, be prepared in advance for the types of interviews you can expect during the hiring process. Here are the major ones and tips on how to handle them.

Screening[1] Interview

5 A screening interview is meant to weed out[2] unqualified candidates. Interviewers will work from an outline of points they want to cover, looking for inconsistencies in your résumé and challenging your qualifications. Provide answers to their questions, and never volunteer any additional information. That could work against you. One type of screening interview is the telephone
10 interview.

Telephone Interview

Telephone interviews are merely[3] screening interviews meant to eliminate poorly qualified candidates so that only a few are left for personal interviews. You might be called out of the blue,[4] or a telephone call to check on your résumé might turn into an interview. Your mission[5] is to be invited for a personal face-to-face interview.

Here are some tips for telephone interviews:

Anticipate the dialogue. Write a general script with answers to questions you might be asked. Focus on skills, experiences, and accomplishments. Practice until you are comfortable.

Keep your notes handy.[6] Have any key information, including your résumé and notes about the company, next to the phone. You will sound prepared if you don't have to search for information. Make sure you also have a notepad and pen so you can jot down[7] notes and any questions you would like to ask at the end of the interview.

Be prepared to think on your feet. If you are asked to participate in a role-playing situation, give short but concise answers. Accept any criticism with tact and grace.[8]

Avoid salary issues. If you are asked how much money you would expect, try to avoid the issue by using a delaying statement or give a very broad range. At this point, you do not know how much the job is worth.

Push for a face-to-face meeting. Sell yourself by closing with something like: "I am very interested in exploring the possibility of working in your company. I would appreciate an opportunity to meet with you in person. I am free either Tuesday afternoon or Wednesday morning. Which would be better for you?"

Try to reschedule surprise interviews. If you were called unexpectedly, try to set an appointment to call so you can be better prepared by saying something like: "I have a scheduling conflict right now. Can I call you back tomorrow after work, at 6 p.m.?"

One-on-One Interview

In a one-on-one interview, it has already been established that you have the skills and education necessary for the position. The interviewer wants to see if you will fit in with the company, and how your skills will complement the rest of the department. Your goal in a one-on-one interview is to establish rapport with the interviewer and show him or her that your qualifications will benefit the company.

Lunch Interview

The same rules apply in lunch interviews as in those held at the office. The setting may be more casual, but remember, it is a business lunch and you are being watched carefully. Use the lunch interview to develop common ground[9] with your interviewer. Follow his or her lead in both selection of food and in etiquette.

Committee Interview

Committee interviews are a common practice. You will face several members of the company who have a say in[10] whether you are hired. When answering questions from several people, speak directly to the person asking the question; it is not necessary to answer to the group. In some committee interviews, you may be asked to demonstrate your problem-solving skills. The committee will outline a situation and ask you to formulate a plan that deals with the problem. You don't have to come up with the ultimate solution. The interviewers are looking for how you apply your knowledge and skills to a real-life situation.

Group Interview

A group interview is usually designed to uncover the leadership potential of prospective managers and employees who will be dealing with the public. The front-runner[11] candidates are gathered together in an informal, discussion-type interview. A subject is introduced and the interviewer will start off the discussion. The goal of the group interview is to see how you interact with others and how you use your knowledge and reasoning powers to win others over.[12] If you do well in the group interview, you can expect to be asked back for a more extensive interview.

Stress Interview

Stress interviews are a deliberate attempt to see how you handle yourself. The interviewer may be sarcastic or argumentative, or may keep you waiting. Expect this to happen and, when it does, don't take it personally.[13] Calmly answer each question as it comes. Ask for clarification if you need it and never rush into an answer. The interviewer may also become silent at some point during the questioning. Recognize this as an attempt to unnerve you. Sit silently until the interviewer resumes[14] the questions. If a minute goes by, ask if he or she needs clarification of your last comments.

---

1 **screening** looking carefully at someone/something in order to evaluate them/it
2 **weed out** to remove what is not needed or wanted
3 **merely** only; just
4 **out of the blue** without warning; suddenly
5 **mission** object or goal
6 **handy** ready to hand; nearby (for reference)
7 **jot down** write something down quickly and in brief
8 **grace** good will
9 **common ground** agreement or understanding between two people
10 **have a say in** have a role in deciding something
11 **front-runner** a leading contender for a job or competition
12 **win others over** gain the approval or backing of other people
13 **take something personally** react as if one's skill, ability, or character has been attacked
14 **resume** begin something again

Ⓐ The following statements are all about the reading. Complete each one using the information you have read.

1. A variety of _____ types are used by employers in the United States.

2. One purpose of a screening interview is to identify inconsistencies in your _____.

3. Your goal during a telephone interview is to be invited for a _____ interview.

4. One purpose of a one-on-one interview is for the employer to see how your _____ will complement those of the other employees.

5. A _____ interview may appear casual, but remember you are being _____ carefully.

6. During a committee interview, _____ _____ (two words) to the person asking the question.

7. One purpose of a group interview is to identify your _____ potential.

8. A _____ interview is an attempt to see how you _____ yourself under pressure.

Ⓑ Check your answers with a partner. Count how many you got correct—be honest! Then, fill in the Reading Comprehension Chart on page 234.

Ⓐ For each group, circle the word that does not belong. The words in *italics* are vocabulary items from the reading.

1. variances	*inconsistencies*	similarities	conflicts
2. act spontaneously	react quickly	plan ahead	*think on your feet*
3. *concise*	wordy	succinct	brief
4. diplomacy	insensitivity	*tact*	courtesy
5. *complement*	supplement	enhance	clash
6. harmony	disagreement	*rapport*	understanding
7. perfect	*ultimate*	ideal	latest
8. *deliberate*	purposeful	hasty	planned
9. jeering	mocking	*sarcastic*	pleasant
10. disorganization	*clarification*	disorder	misunderstanding

B Now complete the sentences below using the words in *italics* from A. Be sure to use the correct form of the word.

1. I thought Carlos was serious when he told me he used to be a chef. Once I tasted his soup I realized he was being _____. It was terrible.

2. Leon was very embarrassed in the board meeting as his report contained a lot of _____.

3. The reason Cynthia got the job was because she had an excellent _____ with the interviewer.

4. If you are asked to criticize anything in an interview, be sure to use _____. You don't want to appear rude or insensitive.

5. Being able to _____ is a necessary skill for many managerial jobs.

6. Jae-woo felt he had achieved _____ success when his business was floated on the New York Stock Exchange.

7. As soon as Serena was hired, she took the initiative to work on the office organization. She immediately began with the _____ of systems and procedures.

8. Parker's _____ attempt to ruin Jun's chances of promotion was apparent to everyone in the office.

9. Our office consists of a small and varied group of people, but we all have skills that _____ each other very well.

10. Martin's presentations are so well organized and _____ that his customers are continually asking for him to train their staff.

Vocabulary Skill:
Homophones

In this unit, you read the word 'complement.' There is another word, 'compliment,' that is pronounced the same as 'complement,' and is spelled almost the same, but has a different meaning. Words like these are called 'homophones,' and there are many of them in English.

A Compare the words *complement* and *compliment*. Use each in the sentences below. Be sure to use the correct form of each word.

complement /kɑmpləmənt/ *n.*	Something that completes, makes up a whole, or brings to perfection.
compliment /kɑmpləmənt/ *n.*	An expression of praise, admiration, or congratulation.

1. The famous painters Diego Rivera and Frida Kahlo were excellent partners because they truly _____ each other.

2. Sometimes just by _____ people, you can make them feel very good about themselves.

B Look at the words below. For each pair of homophones, look up the definitions in a dictionary and write them down. Then, write a sentence that uses each word correctly.

1. a. council: _____
   use: _____
   b. counsel: _____
   use: _____

2. a. faze: _____
   use: _____
   b. phase: _____
   use: _____

3. a. profit: _____
   use: _____
   b. prophet: _____
   use: _____

4. a. led: _____
   use: _____
   b. lead: _____
   use: _____

What Do You Think?

Discuss the following questions with a partner.

1. *Many people do jobs that they do not particularly like. Career counselors often advise people to find a job that they like doing in order to have a happier life. What is your ideal job? Do you think you will one day be able to work in this occupation?*

2. *What job would you least like to do? Why?*

3. *Around the world, attitudes towards work differ. We use the phrase 'work ethic' to talk about these attitudes. Phrases such as 'live to work' and 'work to live' are used to describe different work ethics. What do you understand by these phrases? What is the difference in meaning between them?*

4. *What is the work ethic in your country? Do you think this is good? Do you know of any countries where the work ethic is very different from that of your country?*

Real Life Skill

Reading Job Ads

The most common place to find job ads is in newspapers and magazines. Because advertising is expensive and space is limited, the ads often contain many abbreviations. It is important to understand the meaning of these abbreviations when looking for a job that fits your experience, skills, and educational background.

Ⓐ Read this job advertisement.

BOOKKEEPER

Imm opening in large medical office. Exp only. Req strong background in payroll, invoices, w/ knowledge of BookkeeperPro or similar software. Flexible PT sched, some wknds req. Excellent salary (neg) plus full benefits. **Call Sara at 555-0011.**

Ⓑ Match each abbreviation with its definition.

1. neg _____
2. exp only _____
3. imm _____
4. wknds _____
5. w/ _____
6. req _____
7. PT _____
8. sched _____

a. Saturdays and Sundays
b. working hours
c. not full-time
d. this is necessary
e. we will discuss this
f. right now
g. only people who have done this work before
h. having

Ⓒ With a partner, discuss what the exact meaning of each abbreviation is.

> e.g.: *exp only* stands for 'experienced only'

Ⓓ Read the following ad and try to figure out the meaning of each abbreviation.

INTERNATIONAL SALES:

Office Equipment

For Asia/Australia/NZ. Extensive travel.
Base salary (up to $30K neg) + excellent commission. Req four-yr degree, computer literate, excellent spoken/written English (other langs a plus). Imm start. Send res to: phil@globalhireonline

---

NZ _____   langs _____

K _____   res _____

yr _____

Ⓔ Do you think this would be a good job for you? Tell your partner why or why not.

Computer Culture

Getting Ready

Discuss the following questions with a partner.

1. *How essential are computers to your life and work?*
2. *What are some common technical problems associated with using computers? What are some computer problems caused by humans?*
3. *What type of person do you think would hack into a computer system?*
4. *What mental image do you have of a computer virus writer?*

Chapter 1: Unmasking Virus Writers and Hackers

Before You Read:
Criminal or Cool?

Discuss the following questions with a partner.

1. What do you understand by the word 'stereotype'? In your country, is there a stereotypical image of someone who is a computer expert? Describe this image.

2. Why do you think people hack into computers or write computer viruses?

3. What is your personal view of computer hackers and virus writers?

4. Is it a criminal act in your country to hack into a computer or spread any kind of computer virus? If so, do you agree with this law? Why or why not? If it is not law, do you think it should be made law?

5. Look at the title of the reading. The following words can all be found in the passage:

| malicious | abusive | assert |
| mischief | intimate | geeky |

Is each word positive or negative? How do you think they relate to the topic of the reading? Use your knowledge of prefixes, suffixes, and word roots, as well as your dictionary, to help you determine the meaning of each of these words.

Reading Skill:
Understanding Inference

Information in a reading passage can be found in two ways: by what is stated directly and written clearly on the page, or by what we can infer. When we infer, we use the information that is stated directly to draw conclusions about events, or the writer's opinion or purpose. Knowing how to infer can help you to better understand the writer's purpose and ideas. It is a useful skill to know when reading for pleasure, and can help you better understand reading passages in exams.

Ⓐ Read through each of the following statements carefully. Scan through the reading passage and decide if each statement is stated (*S*) or inferred (*I*). Check (✔) the correct column.

	S	I
1. Most people think that the majority of virus writers and hackers are male.		
2. One stereotypical image of virus writers is that they are introverted loners.		
3. Although hackers and virus writers tend to be grouped together as similar, they differ greatly in their knowledge of computers and motivation for what they do.		
4. Hacking into a computer tends to require a higher level of skill than virus writing.		
5. Hackers tend to be people who like to have control over what they do in life.		
6. Young virus writers like to think they can bring about social change.		
7. Computers act as a barrier that can cause us to become desensitized to others' feelings.		
8. Virus writing was once considered an exciting and trendy pursuit.		

Ⓑ Check your answers with a partner. Discuss the reasons for your answers by making reference to the relevant parts of the reading.

Ⓒ Now read the passage again and answer the questions that follow.

Unmasking Virus Writers and Hackers _____

The following reading is adapted from *Unmasking Virus Writers and Hackers* by Sarah Gordon. First published by Symantec Corporation April 24, 2002. Copyright © 2002 Symantec Corporation. Reprinted with permission.

When we think of the people who make our lives miserable by hacking into computers, or spreading malicious viruses, most of us imagine an unpopular teenage boy, brilliant but geeky, venting his frustrations[1] from the safety of a suburban bedroom.

Actually, these stereotypes are just that—stereotypes—according to Sarah Gordon, an expert in computer viruses and security technology, and a Senior Research Fellow with Symantec Security Response. Since 1992, Gordon has studied the psychology of virus writers. "A hacker or a virus writer is just as likely to be the guy next door to you," she says, "or the kid at the checkout line bagging[2] your groceries. Your average hacker is not necessarily some Goth[3] type dressed entirely in black and sporting a nose ring: she may very well be a 50-year-old female."

The virus writers Gordon has come to know have varied backgrounds; while predominately male, some are female. Some are solidly[4] academic, while others are athletic. Many have friendships with members of the opposite sex, good relationships with their parents and families; most are popular with their peers. They don't spend all their time in the basement. One virus writer volunteers in his local library, working with elderly people. One of them is a poet and a musician, another is an electrical engineer, and others work for a university quantum physics[5] department. You wouldn't pick them out of a lineup as being the perpetrator.

Hackers and virus writers are actually very different, distinct populations. "Hackers tend to have a more thorough knowledge of systems and a more highly developed skill set," Gordon says, "whereas virus writers generally take a shallower approach to what they're doing." Hackers tend to have a much deeper knowledge of individual applications and are still regarded as being somewhat 'sexy' in today's counterculture,[6] while virus writing is looked down upon, mostly for its random damage and lack of required skill.

Their motivations[7] may also differ. While both hackers and virus writers are initially attracted by the technical challenge, hacking is more about power and control. When you're hacking and you get into a system, you remain involved with that system—you take it over and dominate it. On the other hand, once a virus writer releases a program into the wild, the virus goes off and keeps on making copies of itself independently of the author. It's not as intimate or connected a relationship as between a hacker and the computer—the virus writer relinquishes control and becomes disassociated from the actual activity he or she has set in motion.

Gordon explains that people write viruses for a number of reasons. Some may perceive it as a technical challenge, even though writing a virus is actually very

40 easy. It can take two minutes or less, depending on the application you're using. And the part of the program that makes it viral, i.e., that makes it replicate itself, is generally very simple—just one or two lines of code.[8] It's much more complicated to write a useful application than it is to write a virus.

45 Younger virus writers like to be part of a group. They look for peer identity, which is important to them. Or it may be a way to make a social statement. If you're a young person who doesn't have a lot of power and you can assert yourself with a political statement in a virus that travels all around the world, you might think you're making a difference, imagining yourself a modern-day social activist.[9] Gordon says, "It's a big deal to them when they see it on CNN.
50 They feel like they've reached the world."

"Furthermore," Gordon says, "most virus writers don't understand the damage they do. Most of them just don't make the connection between actions and their consequences." This is understandable to a degree because the computer has introduced a shift in the way we communicate. Desensitization[10] occurs; you
55 miss all the visual cues, the contextual clues, and you don't see the impact you're having on another person. We've all gotten e-mail from people who are actually abusive in writing when they'd never speak to us that way in person.

People who make mischief with their computers seem to distance themselves from their actions. They justify their behavior with the rationale that "It's not
60 really wrong, it's not illegal." Or they may tell themselves, "Well, everybody has antivirus software so if I send this out it won't really hurt anybody."

Fortunately, social pressure is changing the impressions people have of hackers and virus writers. Their own peers are beginning to say to them, "This is not cool." And, while it is still widely legal to make viruses publicly available,
65 Gordon's research has shown a decrease in acceptance of online publication of virus source code. Gordon says the media used to promote virus-writers as being geniuses and heroes. But now the press has changed its tune.[11] They no longer portray virus writers as brilliant and misunderstood. "We're seeing the media start to turn around," she says, "We're getting the message out to young people
70 that writing viruses really isn't cool."

---

[1] **venting (his) frustrations** getting rid of feelings of anger or resentment
[2] **bagging** putting something in a bag
[3] **Goth** abbreviation of Gothic—of or relating to the Middle Ages; in modern terms, of or relating to a style emphasizing mystery and darkness, characterized by dark or black clothing and dark make-up
[4] **solidly** definitely; firmly
[5] **quantum physics** science of measuring energy
[6] **counterculture** a culture, usually prevalent among young people, with values that oppose those of the establishment
[7] **motivations** incentives or drives to do something
[8] **code** set of numbers, characters, or symbols that provide instructions to a computer
[9] **social activist** person who campaigns or takes action to bring about changes in society
[10] **desensitization** process of becoming less sensitive towards something
[11] **changed (its) tune** changed the view or opinion of something usually in a spoken or written form

Choose the best answer for each question or statement. Compare your answers with a partner.

1. The average hacker tends to be _____.
  a. a stereotypical geek
  b. more often male
  c. socially frustrated
  d. scientifically inclined

2. What does the reading tell us about the social backgrounds of virus writers?
  a. They come from many different backgrounds.
  b. Most of them work in grocery stores.
  c. Female virus writers like to dress in black.
  d. They are very antisocial.

3. Which of the following statements is NOT true about the differences between hackers and virus writers?
  a. Hackers tend to possess more technical knowledge.
  b. Virus writers take a shallower approach to what they do.
  c. Hackers have more knowledge of program applications.
  d. Hackers are more attracted by the technical challenge of what they do.

4. One main motivation that drives a hacker is _____.
  a. power and control
  b. fame
  c. it is easier than writing a virus
  d. intimacy

5. All of the following are reasons given for writing a virus except _____.
  a. it is a technical challenge
  b. it is easy to write
  c. peer identity
  d. replicating it is simple

6. What do younger virus writers hope to achieve?
  a. financial wealth
  b. social acceptance
  c. political power
  d. social change

7. Which of the following is given as a reason for the disassociation between action and consequence?
  a. Virus writers do not communicate with hackers.
  b. Virus writers have changed the way we communicate.
  c. It is easier to be abusive in e-mail messages.
  d. Computers distance us from other people's feelings.

8. How is social pressure changing the view of hackers and virus writers?
  a. By making it appear cool to be a hacker.
  b. By making it appear not cool to spread viruses.
  c. By promoting hacking and virus writing in the media.
  d. By increasing the acceptance of hackers and virus writers.

Vocabulary Comprehension:
Word Definitions

Ⓐ Look at the list of words from the reading. Match each one with a definition on the right.

1. malicious	_____
2. predominately	_____
3. perpetrator	_____
4. distinct	_____
5. dominate	_____
6. intimate	_____
7. relinquishes	_____
8. replicate	_____
9. assert	_____
10. rationale	_____

a. very closely associated or familiar

b. mostly; being the most noticeable or largest in number

c. to influence or control something or someone

d. someone who commits a crime or harmful act

e. to copy or repeat something

f. gives up or surrenders something

g. wanting to cause harm to others

h. reasoning or justification for something

i. to express oneself in a bold or forceful way

j. individual; distinguishable from others

Ⓑ Now complete the sentences below using the vocabulary from A. Be sure to use the correct form of each word.

1. One of the main reasons that people seek therapy is because they have a fear of _____ relationships.

2. For years the workforce in this company was _____ by men, now there are roughly equal numbers of men and women.

3. Though top executives in many international corporations are still _____ male, an increasing number of women are attaining high level positions.

4. In most ball games, one player or team wins when their opponent _____ control of the ball.

5. When people see my daughter, they often comment that she looks like a perfect _____ me!

6. After spending years being shy and introverted, Ling decided to _____ herself and asked Michael out on a date; he accepted, too!

7. Although he has lived in England for over thirty years now, Kieran still has a very _____ Irish accent.

8. Some people thought Carly's attempts to get promoted over Sunil were purely _____. However, others viewed her actions as healthy competition.

9. As a teenager, I never understood my parents' _____ when they prohibited me from staying out after midnight.

10. Some psychologists say that if you stare into the eyes of the _____ of any crime for long enough, you will be able to see if he or she is guilty or not.

Vocabulary Skill:
The Root Word
plic

A For each word, study its different parts. Use your knowledge of prefixes, suffixes, and word roots to write the part of speech and a simple definition. Use your dictionary to check your answers. Share your ideas with a partner.

Vocabulary	Part of Speech	Definition
1. implicate	_____	_____
2. inexplicable	_____	_____
3. explicit	_____	_____
4. pleat*	_____	_____
5. pliable	_____	_____
6. multiply	_____	_____
7. multiplex	_____	_____
8. implicit	_____	_____

*Some words can have more than one part of speech.

> In this chapter, you read the words 'replicate,' which means 'to repeat' or 'to copy,' and 'complicate,' which means 'to make more difficult.' The root word 'plic,' also written as 'ply,' 'plex,' or 'pli,' comes from the Latin word 'plicare,' meaning 'fold,' 'bend,' 'layer,' or 'entwine.' This root is combined with other prefixes and suffixes to form many words in English.

B Now complete the following sentences using the words from the chart. Be sure to use the correct form of each word.

1. Carl is quite particular about how his pants are pressed; the _____ have to be starched and ironed as straight as possible.

2. Does anyone want to see a movie at the new _____ tonight?

3. Joanne gave me very _____ directions to her house, but I still managed to get lost.

4. This new type of molding clay feels much more _____. It can be molded into shape more easily; the children love it.

5. The crowds outside the theater quickly _____ when word spread that free concert tickets were being given away.

6. As Jason had been seen hanging out with known thieves, the police _____ him in the robbery of the convenience store.

7. Even though Sara and Jin Soo do not believe in the supernatural, they had to admit to some _____ occurrences in their house.

8. Juliana and Keith had an _____ agreement not to discuss family issues around the dinner table.

Think About It Discuss the following questions with a partner.

1. *Do you think the reading presents virus writers and hackers in a positive or negative light? Explain your answer drawing on examples from the passage.*

2. *Has anything about this reading changed your view of virus writers and hackers? If so, what has changed?*

3. *How serious do you think the problem of virus writing and computer hacking is, (a) in your home country and (b) around the world? Can you name any specific viruses that have caused problems?*

Before You Read:
Prodigy
Programmer

Discuss the following questions with a partner.

1. Based on your knowledge of computer virus writers, how common is it for them to be female?
2. At what age do you think most virus writers would become interested in computers?
3. What damage can computer viruses cause?
4. Look at the title of the reading. The following words and phrases can all be found in the passage:

(prodigy)   (stand up for)   (mangles)
(declines)   (play along)

How do you think they relate to the topic of the reading? Use your knowledge of prefixes, suffixes, and word roots, as well as your dictionary, to help you determine the meaning of each of these words.

Reading Skill:
Developing
Reading
Fluency

> *By focusing on general ideas while you are reading, and not on specific vocabulary, you will become a more fluent reader.*

Time yourself as you read through the passage. Try to read as fluently as you can. Record your time in the Reading Rate Chart on page 234.

Female Virus Writer Packs Punch _____

The following reading is adapted from *Female Hacker Packs Punch* by Rick Lockridge, reprinted with permission of *TechTV* © 2002.

She can kick you in the pants *and* wipe your hard drive cleaner than a dog's dinner plate. So when the young kickboxer and virus writer known as 'Gigabyte' tells you she doesn't want her face on TV, well, you play along.

"I'll just shoot[1] you from behind," I say, carrying my TV camera across the large mat that covers the health club's gymnasium floor. It's almost time for the 6 P.M. kickboxing class, and Gigabyte is the only woman there. Of course, she's used to that. In the male-dominated world of virus writers, she stands out. And not only because of her gender. She is also something of a virus-writing prodigy, having started programming at age six. "I figured out how to write a few lines of code on my uncle's Commodore 64,"[2] says Gigabyte. "Later, I wanted to learn more about programming, so I went to the store and asked for books. The salespeople were surprised. It was like, 'Why do you want a book? Why don't you just buy a game and go play?' But games are not very interesting to me. I wanted to learn how to write real executable[3] programs."

So she did.

At age fourteen, she wrote her first computer worm,[4] which took over the shutdown screens of infected users. Two years later, she wrote a powerful virus that mangles MP3 files. More recently she became only the second person to write a virus in C#™[5], the language of Microsoft's® new .Net™ platform.[6] Her so-called 'Sharpei' worm, which comes in an e-mail attachment, spreads via Microsoft's Outlook® e-mail program and infects certain files in computers where the .Net™ framework is present.

The morning after kickboxing class, I arrive at Gigabyte's house at 6:30. She's having tea with her grandmother in the kitchen of a tiny, immaculate cottage. She has lived with her grandparents most of her life, for reasons she declines to discuss. We catch the public bus downtown to her school. Although the bus is packed with other teenagers, she speaks to no one.

We walk a few blocks to her school, where I meet her computer teacher. "She is a good young programmer," she says. "But I do not approve of her virus writing. I know she says she is not causing any harm, and it is true that she does not intentionally spread these viruses, but I do not think it is appropriate, and viruses can cause a lot of damage." Nevertheless, teacher and student are cordial to each other throughout the long morning class. Later that afternoon, Gigabyte walks around the computer room her grandparents have set aside for her, flicking on[7] no fewer than four Windows® machines. She's comfortable here, and full of opinions.

On being some sort of feminist icon, she says, ". . . I'm a virus writer. If I wanted to make a [feminist] statement, don't you think it would be part of the viruses I've written? I mean, yeah, I do want to admit I'm female because there is nothing to hide about it. The world should know there are female virus writers out there. But it's certainly not my motivation for virus writing. I do this for myself, not for the whole world. Other females don't need me to stand up for them, they can do it for themselves."

On the ethics of writing viruses: "I'm not responsible for stupid people who open e-mail attachments that erase their files."

"Hey," she says, "let's go outside. I want to show you something."

I'm led out into the backyard garden, which is beautifully groomed. There are painted gnomes, and a small pond, and then, suddenly, there is a ferret;[8] Gigabyte's pet ferret, out for a little afternoon walk. How right they are for each other, I think, looking at the ferret and the virus writer. Both are cunning and quick, and you wouldn't want either of them to bite you.

"Virus writing is so aggressive, and most reasonable people consider it an act of vandalism,[9] or at least potential vandalism," I say. "Would you spray paint graffiti on somebody's wall?"

"We are not coming inside anyone's walls," she said. "The users are running the virus. They are the ones clicking on it."

"So you think the people who execute these programs are responsible for the damage that your viruses do?" I ask.

"Actually," she says, "I think stupid people should have to have some sort of license to get on the Internet."

There's a pause in the conversation. The ferret is turning somersaults[10] in the grass at our feet. "Do you think of what you do as art?" I ask.

"I want to do something original, that not everyone does," she says. "If you write something that's new or funny or special in a way, then I think it is a form of art, yes."

I ask her if she wants to work with computers for a living. When she grows up, I mean.

"Yes. But not with an antivirus company," she says. "I will never do antivirus."

That would run counter to her code.

---

1 **shoot** film; colloquial term used to mean 'take a photo' or 'record film'
2 **Commodore 64** brand of early desktop computer manufactured in the 1980s
3 **executable** effective; able to perform and do the job for which it was designed
4 **worm** a type of computer virus that replicates itself and destroys information or interferes with software
5 **C#** pronounced 'C sharp'
6 **.Net platform** (dot net) software technology that allows various hardware devices such as computers, mobile phones, and servers to connect with each other via the Internet
7 **flicking on** switching on
8 **ferret** small, brown, furry animal kept as a pet and often trained to hunt rats and rabbits
9 **vandalism** the act of destroying property for fun
10 **somersaults** rolling the body over headfirst to land on the feet

Reading Comprehension: How Much Do You Remember?

(A) The following questions are all about the reading. Answer each one using the information you have read. Try not to look back at the reading for the answer.

1. Why is Gigabyte considered a virus-writing prodigy?
2. How old was Gigabyte when she wrote her first computer virus?
3. How does Gigabyte's Sharpei worm spread from one computer to another?
4. What can we infer from the reading about Gigabyte's relationship with her parents?
5. Does Gigabyte's computer teacher like her?
6. Is Gigabyte proud to be considered a feminist icon?
7. What is Gigabyte's view of people whose computers become affected by viruses?
8. What comparisons does the author make between Gigabyte and her pet ferret?

(B) Check your answers with a partner. Count how many you got correct—be honest! Then, fill in the Reading Comprehension Chart on page 234.

Vocabulary Comprehension: Words in Context

(A) The words in *italics* are vocabulary items from the reading. Read each question or statement and choose the correct answer. Compare your answers with a partner.

1. If someone is playing a joke on someone, and he or she asks you to *play along*, that person wants you to _____.
   a. say what the joke is   **b.** act as if the joke is real

2. When someone is called a *prodigy*, it's because he or she is _____.
   a. very smart   **b.** very quick

3. If someone *mangles* the engine in their car, it will _____.
   a. work better   **b.** not work at all

4. If your desk is *immaculate*, it is _____.
   a. disorganized and messy   **b.** very neat and tidy

5. If somebody *declines* to comment on a topic, it means they _____.
   a. want to speak about it   **b.** don't want to speak about it

6. A *cordial* letter is one that is _____.
   a. pleasant and friendly   **b.** malicious

7. You should *stand up for* your rights means that you should _____.
   a. stand up when you speak   **b.** assert yourself

8. Well-*groomed* is an adjective used to describe someone who is _____.
   a. well-traveled   **b.** neat in appearance

9. A *cunning* person would be more _____ towards others.
   a. deceptive   **b.** sincere

10. Where would you most likely find *graffiti*?
    a. on a dinner menu   **b.** on the walls of public bathrooms

Ⓑ Now think of other examples using the vocabulary from A. Share your ideas with a partner.

1. Talk about a time that you *played along* with a joke.

2. Give an example of a child *prodigy* whom you know, or have heard of. What are they good at?

3. Give another example of something that can be *mangled*. How would this object most likely end up in this state?

4. If somebody were to look around your bedroom or house right now, would they say it is *immaculate*? If not, what adjectives would they use?

5. When was the last time you *declined* an invitation to go out? What circumstances usually cause you to do this?

6. What is an example of a *cordial* greeting? Give an example of a greeting that is not so cordial.

7. Talk about someone you know, or someone in history, who is known for *standing up for* his or her rights, or the rights of others. What did they achieve by doing this?

8. On what occasions in your culture is it especially important to be well-*groomed*?

9. Do you know anyone who you could describe as *cunning*? Explain why you would describe this person as *cunning* using examples.

10. Do you see a lot of *graffiti* in your country or in your neighborhood? Do you consider *graffiti* to be a form of vandalism, or a form of art? Explain your answer.

Vocabulary Skill:
The Root Word
graph/graphy

In this chapter, you read the word 'graffiti,' a variation of the Greek word 'graphein,' meaning 'to write' or 'record' something. The root 'graphy' also refers to 'the study of something.' The root words 'graph' and 'graphy' are combined with prefixes and suffixes to form many words in English.

Ⓐ Look at the word stems in the box below, then read the list of definitions that follow. Add the root *graph* or *graphy* to each word stem to make words that match the definitions. Use your dictionary to check your answers.

| biblio | photo | para | bio | carto |
| mono | autobio | demo | seismo | choreo |

1. the life memoirs of a person, written by that person _____

2. a short section of a text, made up of one or more sentences, that deals with the same idea throughout _____

3. a written account, such as a book or scholarly pamphlet, on a particular and usually limited subject _____

4. the study of the characteristics of human populations, for example: size, growth, density, distribution, and vital statistics _____

5. the art and science of making maps or navigational charts _____

6. an image of an object, person, or landscape recorded digitally or on special film or paper _____

7. an instrument for automatically detecting and recording the duration, intensity, and direction of an earthquake _____

8. a list of writings related to a given subject, or referenced within a particular written work _____

9. the art of creating and arranging dance sequences _____

10. a written account of a person's life _____

Ⓑ Now go back to the word stems in A, and decide which form of the root *graph* or *graphy* each one uses, and which can use both. Complete the chart below. Use your dictionary to check your answers.

graph	both	graphy
_____	_____	_____
_____	_____	_____
_____	_____	_____
_____	_____	_____
_____	_____	_____

Ⓒ Now complete the sentences below using words from the chart; not all the words are used. Be sure to use each word in its correct form.

1. The standard academic essay in English is made up of at least five _____.

2. Many pop stars work with _____, who create original dances and develop new dance moves for them.

3. It's important to include a _____, citing all referenced works, as part of your research project.

4. In order to write someone's _____ you have to conduct an extensive amount of research on them.

5. As Della was a well-known chef, her _____ contained numerous recipes along with her memoirs.

6. Jun believes that living in Tokyo and experiencing numerous earthquakes as a young child inspired him to become a _____.

7. Though Annelise originally studied color _____, she recently learned more about using monochrome film and now works primarily in that mode.

8. Sebastian has been unable to find much published material on his chosen field of study except for a dated _____ in the reference library.

9. Anybody who studies _____ trends will know that the continual dramatic increase in global population is creating a huge strain on the environment.

10. Hyun Suk hopes that by getting a bachelor's degree in geography, he will eventually be able to enter the field of _____.

What Do You Think?

Discuss the following questions with a partner.

1. *What kind of person do you think Gigabyte is? How would you describe her to someone who has never met her?*
2. *Would you like to be Gigabyte's friend? Why or why not?*
3. *Is Gigabyte similar to anyone you know? If so, describe how this person is similar to Gigabyte.*
4. *If you could write Gigabyte an e-mail message, what would you say to her?*

Real Life Skill

Reading Computer Advertising

If you want to buy a computer system, it's important to compare the specifications (technical details) of different computers, as well as their prices. Advertising for computers often contains a lot of abbreviations for technical terms, as well as computer jargon. Being familiar with these terms can help you better understand exactly what it is you are buying.

Ⓐ Read the following advertisements for computers.

The Techron MZ4000 Desktop System features:
- 200 MB RAM at 133 MHz
- Big 60 GB HD
- DVD-ROM Drive
- 32X max CD-RW drive
- 6 USB ports
- Doorways Forever OS
- One year free ISP service

New low prices!

The Techie AZ2000 Laptop features:

New low prices!
- 180 MB RAM at 133 MHz
- 20 GB HD
- DVD-ROM Drive
- 3 USB ports
- Doorways Unlimited OS
- Free word processing & spreadsheet software

Ⓑ Write the abbreviations in the ads that stand for the following:

1. operating system—the basic software in the computer _____
2. hard drive—the part of the computer that stores information _____
3. Internet service provider—the company that gives you access to the Internet _____
4. digital video disk read-only memory—use this to watch movies on your computer _____
5. universal serial bus—a type of plug that allows you to connect devices such as a printer or mouse to your computer _____
6. random access memory—the part of the computer that enables the programs to work _____
7. a unit of computer memory capacity that measures one million bytes _____
8. compact disk rewritable—use this to listen to recordings and save information _____
9. megahertz—controls the speed at which the computer can carry out instructions _____
10. a unit of computer memory capacity that measures one billion bytes _____

Ⓒ Imagine you want to buy a computer. What do you need it for? What specifications do you need? Talk to a partner and discuss which features you would want or need to have in your computer. Which of the computers featured in the advertisements above would you buy?

Travel Adventures

Getting Ready

Complete the survey below. Then, share your answers with a partner.

What Kind of Traveler Are You?

Choose the best answer for each question below.

1. How often do you go on trips abroad?
   - **a.** once a year
   - **b.** a few times a year
   - **c.** when you can afford it

2. How often do you travel around your home country?
   - **a.** once a year
   - **b.** a few times a year
   - **c.** when you can afford it

3. Who do you like to travel with?
   - **a.** alone or with a friend or partner
   - **b.** family
   - **c.** a big group of friends

4. How do you like to travel?
   - **a.** in comfort
   - **c.** on an organized package tour
   - **b.** you like to figure it out yourself

5. Which of the following is the primary reason you go on vacation?
   - **a.** rest and relaxation
   - **c.** adventure
   - **b.** education and cultural learning
   - **d.** spend time with family or friends

6. Which of the following holidays appeals to you most?
   - **a.** island hopping in the South Pacific
   - **c.** backpacking across Europe
   - **b.** city tours of Australia
   - **d.** resort holiday with plenty of amenities

7. How do you usually pay for your vacation?
   - **a.** max out your credit card
   - **b.** find the cheapest way to get there and budget carefully
   - **c.** spend no more than a couple of weeks' salary
   - **d.** save all year for your big trip

Now, enjoy studying this unit and reading about some travel adventures!

Chapter 1: Into the Heart of a Family in Casablanca

Before You Read:
A Traveler's Tale

Discuss the following questions with a partner.

1. When was the last time you went on a trip? Where did you go? For what purpose was this trip?
2. What did you do while you were on the trip?
3. Did any unusual or interesting events happen on this trip? If so, what?
4. Did you meet, or talk to, anyone interesting on this trip? If so, who? Have you kept in touch with this person?
5. The following words can all be found in the reading:

decipher   cautiously   resemble   jaded   radiant

How do you think they relate to the topic of travel? Use your knowledge of prefixes, suffixes, and word roots, as well as your dictionary, to help you determine the meaning of each of these words.

Reading Skill:
Identifying Chronological Events

Dates and times, as well as words such as 'then,' 'next,' 'later,' 'soon,' and 'eventually' are often used in text to indicate the order in which certain events happened. Being aware of how a reading is organized can help you to understand it better, and enable you to find specific information in a passage more easily.

(A) Read through the sequence of events below and think about the correct order in which they probably happened.

A Traveler's Time Line	
	Abdelatif wrote down his address.
	Miguel and the writer found their friend.
	The family members took turns sitting with Miguel and the writer.
	Miguel, Abdelatif, and the writer worked as volunteers in Kenitra.
	The taxi driver asked for directions.
	Miguel and the writer realized they had made a mistake.
	The family gave Miguel and the writer some couscous and chicken to eat.
	A policeman and a young boy helped Miguel and the writer.
	They took photos and exchanged addresses.

(B) Now scan through the reading passage and put the events above into the correct order.

(C) Which words or expressions helped you to put these events in the correct order? Go back over the reading and circle any words or information that helped you.

Into the Heart of a Family in Casablanca __

The following reading is adapted from *Looking for Abdelatif, an Unexpected Journey into the Heart of a Family in Casablanca* by Tanya Shaffer. Reprinted with permission from Salon.com © 1999.

Here's what I love about travel: strangers can often amaze you. Sometimes a single day can bring a beautiful surprise, a simple kindness that opens your heart and makes you a different person by the time you go to sleep—more tender, less jaded than you were when you woke up.

This particular day began at seven in the morning in Casablanca. My friend Miguel[1] and I were going to visit Abdelatif, a young man we'd worked with on a volunteer project in Kenitra, an industrial city on the Moroccan coast. He'd been expecting us to arrive in Casablanca for a few days now, and since he had no telephone, he'd written down his address and told us to just show up—his mother and sisters were always at home. As my plane was leaving from Casablanca the following morning, we wanted to get an early start so we could spend the whole day with him.

Apparently[2] the address Abdelatif had written down for us was hard to understand, and when we got into the neighborhood, our taxi driver started asking directions. Eventually, with the help of a policeman and then a little boy, we were led to a house down a winding[3] road. Our driver went to the door and inquired. He came back to the cab saying Abdelatif's sister was in this house visiting friends and would come along to show us where they lived.

Soon a girl of about sixteen emerged from the house. Surprisingly, she didn't resemble Abdelatif at all. Still, I'd seen other families where children didn't look alike, so I didn't give it too much thought. We waited in the yard while the sister went in and returned accompanied by her mother, sisters, and brother-in-law, all of whom greeted us with cautious warmth. We were shown into a pristine home with multicolored tiles lining the walls. The mother told us in broken[4] French that Abdelatif was out, but would be home soon. We sat on low, cushioned seats in the living room, drinking sweet mint tea and eating sugar cookies, while the family members took turns sitting with us and making shy, polite conversation that frequently lapsed into uncomfortable silence. As anything was said, Miguel would say, "What?" and I would translate the simple phrase for him: "Nice weather today. Tomorrow perhaps rain."

An hour passed, and as the guard kept changing, more family members emerged from inner rooms. I was again struck[5] by the fact that none of them looked a thing like our friend. How did Abdelatif fit into this picture? Was he adopted? I was very curious to find out.

After two hours had passed with no sign of Abdelatif, the family insisted on serving us a meal of couscous[6] and chicken. "Soon," was the only response I got when I inquired as to what time he might arrive. But at last, we heard the words we had been waiting for. "Please," said the mother, "Abdelatif is here."

"Oh, good," I said, and for a moment, before I walked into the living room, his face danced in my mind—the brown eyes, the smile filled with radiant life. We entered the lovely tiled room we'd sat in before and a young man came forward to shake our hands with an uncertain expression on his face.

"Hello, my friends," he said cautiously.

45 "Hello," I smiled, slightly confused. "Is Abdelatif here?"

"I am Abdelatif."

"But . . . but . . ." I looked from him to the family and then began to giggle[7] nervously. "I - I'm sorry. I'm afraid we've made a bit of a mistake. I - I'm so embarrassed."

50 "What? What?" Miguel asked urgently. "I don't understand. Where is he?"

"We've got the wrong Abdelatif," I told him, and then looked around at the entire family who'd spent most of the day entertaining us. "I'm afraid we don't actually know your son."

For a split second[8] no one said anything, and I wished I could disappear right
55 there on the spot. Then the uncle exclaimed heartily, "It's no problem!"

"Yes," the mother joined in. "It doesn't matter at all. Won't you stay for dinner, please?"

I was so overwhelmed by their kindness that tears rushed to my eyes. "Thank you so much," I said fervently. "It's been a beautiful, beautiful day, but please
60 . . . could you help me find this address?"

I took out the piece of paper Abdelatif had given me back in Kenitra, and the new Abdelatif, his uncle, and his brother-in-law came forward to decipher it. "This is Baalal Abdelatif!" said the second Abdelatif, recognizing the address. "We went to school together! He lives less than a kilometer from here. I will
65 bring you to his house."

And that is how it happened. After taking photos and exchanging addresses and hugs and promises to write, Miguel and I left our newfound family and arrived at the home of our friend Abdelatif as the last orange streak of the sunset was fading into the dark night. There, I reached out and hugged him
70 with relief, exclaiming, "I thought we'd never find you!"

---

1 **Miguel** /mɪgɛl/ Spanish man's name; equivalent of English 'Michael'

2 **apparently** clearly; obviously; according to what is easy to see

3 **winding** /waɪndɪŋ/ twisting or curving

4 **broken** non-fluent

5 **struck** hit by an idea or awareness

6 **couscous** /kuskus/ a North-African pasta

7 **giggle** to laugh in a silly, uncontrolled way, usually when nervous or amused

8 **split second** tiny period of time

Reading Comprehension: What Do You Remember?

Decide if the following statements about the reading are true (*T*) or false (*F*). If you check (✔) false, correct the statement to make it true.

	T	F
1. Abdelatif gave friends his address and phone number.		
2. The writer and Miguel planned to stay with Abdelatif for a few days.		
3. The taxi driver had a difficult time finding the address.		
4. The taxi driver found Abdelatif's sister who showed them to the house.		
5. The writer was surprised as Abdelatif's sister looked so much like him.		
6. The family entertained the guests while they waited for Abdelatif.		
7. The writer was relieved when he met the first Abdelatif.		
8. Because of the mistake, the guests did not eat dinner with the family.		

Vocabulary Comprehension: Word Definitions

A Look at the list of words from the reading. Match each one with a definition on the right.

1. jaded _____
2. inquired _____
3. emerged _____
4. pristine _____
5. lapsed _____
6. radiant _____
7. exclaimed _____
8. heartily _____
9. fervently _____
10. decipher _____

a. warmly and sincerely
b. very clean; pure
c. to read or interpret; to decode
d. slipped gradually into a less favorable condition; passed by
e. appeared by coming out of something
f. tired or worn out, usually after overexposure to something
g. asked for information
h. filled with emotions of love or happiness; glowing or beaming
i. in a way that shows great emotion or warmth
j. cried out or spoke suddenly

B Complete the sentences below using the words from A. Be sure to use the correct form of each word.

1. If you are planning to take a trip overseas, you should _____ about the accommodations, climate, and culture of the country you are going to visit.

2. Even though I cannot _____ the language, I think it's fun to look at hieroglyphics and imagine what they might say.

3. Martin was shocked to see his girlfriend _____ from a restaurant with another man.

4. It is said that most New Yorkers are _____ with celebrities. They don't react to them like most tourists do.

5. The woman stood in the middle of the supermarket and _____ that her son was missing.

6. At her wedding, you couldn't help noticing how _____ Sheena was smiling.

7. After leaving the hospital, Dean wrote such a _____ letter of thanks to the nurses who cared for him that I almost cried when I read it.

8. The crowd cheered _____ when their team scored the first goal of the match.

9. After seeing how much his exam scores had _____ since last term, Eric's father grounded him for the rest of the year.

10. I have no idea how Marianne keeps her home so _____ with five children running around.

Vocabulary Skill: Adverbs of Emotion

In this chapter you read the adverbs 'fervently,' 'heartily,' 'urgently,' and 'cautiously.' They all describe the way in which the speakers in the reading passage expressed their feelings. Adverbs are often used in written texts to convey the emotions of a speaker. Knowing how these adverbs work, and what they mean, can help you to better understand readings that contain them.

Ⓐ Look at the list of adverbs below. For each one, write the feeling you think a person would be expressing if they spoke in this way; the first one has been done for you. Use your dictionary to help you.

Adverb	Feeling
1. furiously	*very angry about something*
2. cautiously	
3. urgently	
4. pensively	
5. firmly	
6. tactfully	
7. flatly	
8. humbly	
9. confidently	
10. joyously	

Ⓑ Now complete each sentence below using the correct adverb from A. Share your answers with a partner.

1. The waiter _____ apologized for the delay in showing us to our table. We had, after all, made reservations weeks ago.

2. Mario had to _____ explain to his boss that he had made a very significant mistake in her calculations.

3. The school principal _____ insisted that all students hand in their mobile phones to teachers during school hours.

4. Although the suspect was interrogated by the police for three hours, he still _____ denied having anything to do with the incident.

5. I knew immediately that Kumiko's father was very ill by the way she
_____ asked us to come over.

6. Sam screamed _____ at the man who crashed into her car; her
baby was in the car with her.

7. When news of the stock market crash reached the office, Ed immediately got
on the phone and _____ requested an update on his financial
portfolio.

8. Alicia phoned and _____ told us about the birth of her first
grandchild yesterday.

C Now write your own sentences using two of the adverbs from A. Share
your ideas with a partner.

1. _____

2. _____

Think About It **Discuss the following questions with a partner.**

1. *What images of the place the writer was visiting does the reading conjure up in
your head? Which words bring these images to mind?*

2. *If you had been the writer, how would you have felt when you realized you
were in the wrong house? Would you have reacted the same way?*

3. *Do you think the title of the passage, 'Into the Heart of a Family in Casablanca,'
is a suitable one for this story? Explain your answer.*

4. *Have you ever taken a trip to a foreign city or country to visit a friend? If so,
where did you go and when? Did you travel independently? Were you
comfortable doing this, or did you feel nervous?*

Before You Read:
Tourism with a Difference

Discuss the following questions with a partner.

1. What do you understand by the term 'eco-tourism'?
2. Would you like to go on an eco-tour? Why or why not?
3. Do many tourists visit your country each year? Which places do they usually go to?
4. Are eco-tours offered to any of the main tourist areas in your country? If so, what do they involve?
5. The following words can all be found in the reading:

incredulous   excursions   endemic
awe-inspiring   exhilarating

How do you think they relate to the topic of travel and tourism? Use your knowledge of prefixes, suffixes, and word roots, as well as your dictionary, to help you determine the meaning of each of these words.

Reading Skill:
Developing Reading Fluency

Before you begin reading, set a reading rate goal for yourself. This may be 150 or 200 words per minute. If you do not achieve your goal this time, then set a lower goal for yourself next time and slowly build up. Go at your own pace and you will achieve your goals more easily.

Time yourself as you read through the passage. Try to read as fluently as you can. Record your time in the Reading Rate Chart on page 234.

Canaima—Eco-tours with Angels and Devils

The following reading is adapted from *Canaima: Where Angels and Devils Collide* by Brad Weiss © 2001. Reprinted from IgoUgo with permission of the author; http://www.igougo.com/experience/archive43.html

I threw my bags into the back, went around to the passenger side, and slid into the front seat. Moments later the wheels started turning and our journey to Canaima National Park began. We climbed to a cruising altitude[1] of around 5,000 feet.[2] At this height, the jungle looked like a gigantic green carpet, except for the red rivers snaking through it. Our pilot followed the path of the Churún River, and as it approached the edge of the mesa,[3] the plane took a dramatic dive along the trajectory[4] of the mighty Angel Falls—the longest waterfall in the world—as it plummeted down into Devil's Canyon.

A half hour later, we landed on a dirt strip alongside six mud huts that

constitute the Pemón Indian village of Uruyen. As the trip continued, I became 10
increasingly amazed at the lack of tourists. Nowhere was it more surprising
than in Devil's Canyon, the principal vantage point[5] at the base of the 3,200-
foot (975-meter) Angel Falls. It was one of the most awe-inspiring sights I have
ever beheld,[6] but almost equally incredulous was the fact that we were the only
ones there! 15

How could this be? After all, you can barely move for crowds even on
overcast[7] days at Niagara. Canaima's remoteness is one reason; there is no road
access so you must charter a flight from Puerto Ordaz, a one-hour journey
from the Venezuelan capital of Caracas. Flights are limited and the trip is
expensive. Another major factor is that until recently, the Venezuelan 20
government did not promote tourism to Canaima and Angel Falls. Of the few
tourists who come here, most fly directly into Canaima village, which gives
easiest access to the Falls via a three-hour boat ride, and a moderately
challenging two-hour hike.

The tour operators at Angel Eco-Tours take an interesting approach in that 25
they emphasize the park and its people more than Angel Falls. In doing so, they
create an experience that I found to be truly unique. This is in large part due to
the close interaction we had with the Pemón Indians, to whom Angel Eco-
Tours donates 5 percent of its earnings. In previous stays at indigenous villages,
I had often gotten the sense that tourists were well received primarily because 30
they contribute significantly to the village's income. But the Pemón are
extremely gracious hosts. From the moment we arrived, it was clear that they
were genuinely excited to share their culture and learn about us.

We slept in their huts, played soccer with them, tried traditional dishes such as
cassava bread dipped in a beetle-based hot sauce, and even learned a few 35
phrases in the Pemón language (although most speak at least some Spanish).
My fondest memory is of spending an evening watching three generations of
Pemón, decked out in their traditional garb,[8] perform a ceremonial dance. The
show became increasingly amusing as Pemón and tourists alike drank more
and more of their homemade cassava beer. Our inhibitions quickly disappeared 40
and before we knew it, we were dancing alongside the Pemón.

Through our interactions with the Pemón, we gained a very special
understanding of the land they inhabit. They were our guides on hiking
excursions, bringing us to some of their most sacred spots. These included
caves with eerie rock formations resembling human faces, towering waterfalls 45
where we swam underneath the powerful spray, a spot in the river that formed
a natural Jacuzzi, and a riverbank with pink sandstone that can be used for
natural facials. As we walked through the forest, they pointed out the many
trees and plants that they use for medicinal or ceremonial purposes. Given the
other-worldliness of the park, I was not surprised to hear that a large number 50
of the flora, including several carnivorous[9] plant varieties, are endemic to the
region.

The Pemón also introduced us to their system of beliefs and spirituality. I had heard that the planet's major energy meridians,[10] which connect spiritual centers
55 such as Machu Picchu and Stonehenge, all run through Canaima. After a few days, I didn't doubt it. Nearly everyone in our group reported having extremely lucid dreams. Mysteries seemed commonplace; the sky at night constantly flickered with lightning, although there was never any thunder or rain. Supposedly, there are more UFO sightings here than anywhere in the world.
60 Sightings or not, by the end of the trip, everyone in the group felt that their batteries had been totally recharged.

As much as I found the trip exhilarating, I would not say it is for everyone. Eco-tourism means responsible, low-impact travel, and generally involves some degree of 'roughing-it.' This trip is no exception. Three of the five nights were
65 spent in hammocks,[11] which did not suit everyone's natural contours. You must not be averse to sun, sweat, mosquitoes, or bathing in rivers with little or no privacy. At $1,500 per person for the week-long trip it's an excellent deal, but still prohibitively[12] expensive for some people. If you can afford it, and don't mind a few ants in your pants, this trip will provide you with an incredibly
70 unique experience that I guarantee you will never forget.

---

1 **cruising altitude** height at which airplanes travel
2 **5,000 feet** equal to 1,524 meters
3 **mesa** Spanish word meaning 'plateau'; a flat-topped mountain
4 **trajectory** moving path
5 **vantage point** strategic or advantageous position for viewing something
6 **beheld** seen
7 **overcast** cloudy
8 **garb** distinctive clothing
9 **carnivorous** flesh-eating
10 **meridian** invisible line or circle on the earth's surface that passes through certain points
11 **hammock** lounger or bed made of netting, supported at each end usually by a tree
12 **prohibitively** causing something to be impossible

Reading Comprehension: How Much Do You Remember?

(A) How much do you remember from the reading? Choose the best answer for each question or statement.

1. Devil's Canyon is situated _____.
   a. at the bottom of Angel Falls
   b. in a popular tourist spot
   c. near Niagara Falls
   d. along the path of the Churún River

2. Angel Falls is _____.
   a. too far from Caracas to visit
   b. the longest waterfall in the world
   c. a spiritual mecca for eco-tourists
   d. as popular as Niagara Falls

3. Not many tourists visit Canaima National Park because _____.
   a. it is too expensive to travel there
   b. there is no access to it
   c. there are red snakes in it
   d. it is located in such a remote place

4. The writer considers the trip to Canaima National Park to be _____.
   a. very easy for most eco-tourists
   b. challenging, but well worth the effort
   c. inexpensive considering what you receive
   d. too difficult for most people

5. The eco-tour emphasizes the _____.
   a. purity of water in the region
   b. ceremonial dances of the Pemón Indians
   c. indigenous people and their culture
   d. difficult hike that is required to get there

6. According to the passage, tourists can enjoy _____.
   a. the local food and drink   b. ceremonial dances of the Pemón
   c. learning about indigenous flowers and plants
   d. all of the above

7. The writer describes _____ as evidence of Canaima's spiritual energy.
   a. ceremonial dances and carnivorous plants
   b. strange rock formations and pink sandstone
   c. medicinal plants and herbs   d. energy lines and UFO sightings

8. The writer thinks that this eco-tour is not for everyone as it involves _____.
   a. living in natural settings without many amenities
   b. hiking for long periods through rough terrain
   c. a considerable expense   d. all of the above

(B) Check your answers with a partner. Count how many you got correct—be honest! Then, fill in the Reading Comprehension Chart on page 234.

Vocabulary Comprehension: Odd Word Out

(A) For each group, circle the word that does not belong. The words in *italics* are vocabulary items from the reading.

1. plunged	ascended	descended	*plummeted*
2. *awe-inspiring*	magnificent	astounding	unimpressive
3. unbelievable	*incredulous*	inconceivable	intentional
4. considerate	surly	courteous	*gracious*
5. *decked out*	dressed up	costumed	unadorned
6. encouragement	*inhibition*	restraint	reservation
7. uncanny	spooky	soothing	*eerie*
8. native	indigenous	*endemic*	foreign
9. *lucid*	incoherent	clear	explicit
10. invigorating	depressing	stimulating	*exhilarating*

B Now complete the sentences below using the words in *italics* from A. Be sure to use the correct form of each word.

1. If you are trying to learn another language, you can't allow your _____ to control your progress. You must be confident and willing to make mistakes.

2. Nigel tells some quite _____ stories sometimes. I never know when to believe him.

3. When traveling to certain tropical countries, find out what diseases are _____ to the region and take the necessary medications.

4. When Olivia, whose grandparents are from Spain, visited the country for the first time, she had an _____ feeling that she had been there before.

5. Although traveling can be exhausting, I always feel _____ when I arrive in a new country.

6. After spending several days hiking across the mountains with little food and water, Chen's speech was slurred and he did not appear _____.

7. Every New Year's Eve, James loves to get _____ in his party hat and clothes.

8. There are many amazing places to see in Egypt, but the Temple of Karnac, in Luxor, is certainly one of the most _____ sights I have ever seen.

9. We planned to have a barbecue last night, but the temperature _____ in the afternoon so we ended up eating indoors with the heat turned on.

10. I've found that in most countries the local people are quite _____; they want visitors to leave with wonderful impressions of their country.

Vocabulary Skill: The Root Word *ject*

In this chapter, you read the noun 'trajectory,' meaning 'the path of something moving through space.' The root word 'ject' comes from the Latin word 'jacere,' which means 'to throw.' It is combined with prefixes and suffixes to form many words in English.

A For each word, study the different parts. Using your knowledge of prefixes and suffixes, write the part of speech and a simple definition for each word. Working with a partner, use your dictionary to check your answers.

Vocabulary	Part of Speech	Definition
1. eject	verb	to throw out forcefully; expel
2. projector		
3. injection		
4. reject	verb/noun	
5. dejected		
6. interject		
7. project	verb/noun	
8. objection		

B Complete each sentence using the words from the chart. Be sure to use the correct form of each word.

1. Every time Jae-woo suggests a new idea, his boss _____ it. As a result, his motivation has plummeted.

2. Carla closed her eyes and braced herself for the painful _____ the doctor was about to give her.

3. The CEO reported today that total earnings are expected to exceed _____ figures in the coming months.

4. The journalist who shouted at the president as he made his speech was _____ from the press conference by security guards.

5. It's customary for students in the United States to _____ while other classmates, or even the lecturers, are speaking.

6. After his girlfriend told him she didn't want to date him anymore, Carl felt totally _____.

7. Stefan's computer crashed the night before his 9 A.M. presentation. Luckily, the _____ was set up so he copied his notes onto transparencies.

8. Mrs. Fahid made her _____ to the nuclear power station quite clear at the meeting.

C Can you think of any other words in English that include the root *ject*?

What Do You Think?

Discuss the following questions with a partner.

1. *Would you like to go on the eco-tour described in the reading? Why or why not?*

2. *Are there any monuments or natural sites in your country that are being damaged by mass tourism? What kind of damage is being inflicted on these places? What is being done to protect them? Do you think this action is enough?*

3. *The year 2002 was designated as the International Year of Eco-tourism by the United Nations. Do you know of any special events or promotions for eco-tourism that were held in your country?*

4. *Do you think it is possible for mass tourism to coexist with environmental conservation? If so, how is it possible? If not, what can be done to change this situation?*

Real Life Skill

Choosing a Travel Guidebook

When you travel, the more information you have before you set out on your trip, the more you'll get from it. That's why there are dozens of different series of travel guidebooks, covering thousands of destinations worldwide. Each series caters to a different type of traveler, so it's important to know what kind of approach you take to travel in order to choose the guidebook that's right for you, and your trip.

(A) Match these types of travelers with the definitions below.

> **a.** make frequent short trips, and may have little free time to see the sights. They require efficiency and comfort.
>
> **b.** travel together with their spouse and children, and look for safe destinations and activities that all ages can enjoy together.
>
> **c.** want 'only the best'—the most elegant hotels, the most succulent meals, the most exclusive shops. Expense is not a concern.
>
> **d.** enjoy reading about travel as a hobby. Many never actually use the guidebook to take a trip.
>
> **e.** are looking for unusual experiences and undiscovered destinations, and do not mind discomfort or even some degree of danger.
>
> **f.** want to travel as much as possible for the lowest price possible. The cost of everything is very important.

1. Budget travelers _____   **4.** Business travelers _____

2. Luxury travelers _____   **5.** Adventure travelers _____

3. Armchair travelers _____   **6.** Family travelers _____

(B) Read the following descriptions from the back covers of travel guidebooks. Which type of traveler are they intended for?

1. The world's most beautiful guidebooks—full-color photography on every page, plus poetry and art from the indigenous people.

_____

2. Double rooms for only $20, three-course meals for just $5—who says travel has to be pricey? We'll help you get top value for your vacation dollar, every time!

_____

3. Outdoor fun, kid-friendly museums, lots of rainy-day sights to see—even hotels that offer baby-sitting. You'll find it all here!

_____

4. All the essential facts you need for a productive stay, with suggestions to help you make the most of your leisure hours.

_____

5. Don't follow the crowd—follow us, to pristine rain forests, wild rivers, and remote mountain villages where life hasn't changed in centuries.

_____

6. For those who appreciate the finer things in life. We share inside tips, hot new discoveries, and the very best localities for everything you're looking for.

_____

(C) Work with a partner. Go back to the travel survey in Getting Ready on page 29. Look at your partner's answers to the survey and decide what type of traveler they are. Which of these guidebooks would you recommend for them? Explain your answer.

Haunted by the Past

Getting Ready

Discuss the following questions with a partner.

1. *Do you know of any well-known ghost stories or tales of hauntings? What happened?*

2. *Do you believe in ghosts? If not, how do you think these stories come to exist?*

3. *Do you ever read books or watch movies about ghosts or hauntings? Can you name some famous book or movie titles?*

4. *What feelings do you experience when you read ghost stories or watch scary movies?*

Before You Read:
Ghosts and Ghouls

Discuss the following questions with a partner.

1. Have you seen the movie entitled (in English) *The Blair Witch Project*? If so, what did you think of it? If not, what do you know about the story that inspired this movie?

2. What is one thing that many ghost stories have in common?

3. Some people claim that ghost stories are simply tricks or practical jokes, played by others, to scare people. What do you think? Are there logical explanations for what some people claim to be ghost stories?

4. The following words can all be found in the reading:

   tormented   nerve-racking   taunting

   indifferent   displeased

   Do you think they are positive or negative? How do you think they relate to the topic of ghost stories? Use your knowledge of prefixes, suffixes, and word roots, as well as your dictionary, to help you determine the meaning of each of these words.

Reading Skill:
Skimming for Content

> Skimming for content is a useful skill that can help you read, and comprehend, faster. You can get a good idea of the content of a passage without reading every word or sentence. By skimming quickly over the text you can pick up on the main points of the passage, as well as the main idea of what the reading is about.

(A) Do you know anything about the story of the Bell Witch? Read the following statements and see how many you can complete by circling the correct word or statement. If you do not know anything about the subject, just read the statements to get an idea of what the reading is about.

1. The story of the Bell Witch took place in the early (1800s / 1900s).
2. A (large / small) community in America was affected by the ghost.
3. The Bell Witch story is considered to be (true / fictional).
4. Many believed the Bell Witch was the ghost of a person named (Kate Batts / John Bell).
5. The Bell Witch frightened people by (talking to them / stealing from them).
6. The Bell Witch haunting continued for (a few months / a few years).
7. The ghost's ultimate act was to (poison someone / kill the family cat).
8. One explanation for the haunting is that it was the work of a young girl's (boyfriend / schoolteacher).

(B) Now, spend ONE minute skimming over the passage to get a basic grasp of the content. Do NOT try to read every word. Do not hesitate or stop when you see words you do not know, or read the footnotes; just let your eyes skim quickly back and forth over the text.

(C) Now go back to the statements above and see how many of them you can confidently complete. Change any answers that you now think are incorrect. Read through the passage to confirm your answers.

The Bell Witch

The following reading is adapted from *The Bell Witch*. Written by Stephen Wagner, About.com Guide to Paranormal Phenomena. Reprinted with permisssion of the author © 1999.

In 1817 one of the most well-known hauntings in American history took place in the small town of Adams, Tennessee.[1] In fact it was so well known that the story caught the attention of a future president of the United States.

Known as the Bell Witch, the strange activity that caused fear in the small farming community has remained unexplained for nearly 200 years. It is the inspiration for many fictional ghost stories, including the film *The Blair Witch Project*. Although they both attracted a great deal of public interest, the facts of the Bell Witch story share little in common with those created for *The Blair Witch Project*. Because it really happened, the Bell Witch story is perhaps much more frightening.

Like many stories, certain details of who or what the Bell Witch was vary from version to version. The prevailing account is that it was the ghost of a woman named Kate Batts, a mean old neighbor of John Bell. Batts believed Bell cheated her in a land purchase and on her deathbed[2] she swore[3] that she would haunt John Bell and his family. This version appears in a Tennessee guidebook published in 1933:

"Sure enough, tradition says, the Bells were tormented for years by the malicious spirit of Old Kate Batts. John Bell and his favorite daughter Betsy were the principal targets. Toward the other members of the family the witch was either indifferent or, as in the case of Mrs. Bell, friendly. No one ever saw her, but every visitor to the Bell home heard her all too well. Her voice, according to one person who heard it, 'spoke at a nerve-racking pitch[4] when displeased, while at other times it sang and spoke in low musical tones.' The spirit of Old Kate led John and Betsy Bell on a merry chase.[5] She threw furniture and dishes at them. She pulled their noses, yanked[6] their hair, poked[7] needles into them. She yelled all night to keep them from sleeping, and snatched food from their mouths at mealtimes."

News of the Bell Witch spread quickly. When word of the haunting reached Nashville,[8] one of its most famous citizens, General Andrew Jackson, decided to gather a group of friends and go to Adams to investigate. The future president wanted to come face to face with the phenomenon and either expose it as a hoax or send the spirit away. According to one account, Jackson and his men were traveling over a smooth section of road when suddenly the wagon stopped. The men pushed and pushed, but the wagon could not be moved. The wheels were even removed and inspected. Then came the sound of a voice from the bushes saying, "All right general, let the wagon move on. I will see you tonight." The astonished men could not find the source of the voice. The horses then unexpectedly started walking on their own and the wagon moved along again. Jackson indeed encountered the witch that night and left early the next morning, claiming he would rather fight the British than the Bell Witch!

The haunting of the Bell house continued for several years, ending with the ghost's ultimate act of vengeance. In October 1820 John Bell suffered a stroke.[9] In and out of bed for several weeks, his health never improved. The Tennessee State University in Nashville recounts this part of the story:

"On the morning of December 19, he failed to awake at his regular time. When the family noticed he was sleeping unnaturally, they attempted to rouse him. They discovered Bell was in a stupor[10] and couldn't be completely awakened. John Jr.[11] went to the medicine cupboard to get his father's medicine and noticed it was gone but a strange vial[12] was in its place. No one claimed to have replaced the medicine with the vial. A doctor was summoned to the house. The witch began taunting that she had placed the vial in the medicine cabinet and given Bell a dose of its contents while he slept. The substance was tested on a cat and discovered to be highly poisonous. John Bell died on December 20. 'Kate' was quiet until after the funeral. However, after the grave was filled, the witch began singing loudly and joyously until all of John Bell's friends and family left his graveside."

A few explanations of the Bell Witch phenomena have been offered over the years. One is that the haunting was a hoax created by Richard Powell, the schoolteacher of Betsy Bell and Joshua Gardner, the boy with whom Betsy was in love. It seems Powell was deeply in love with Betsy and would do anything to destroy her relationship with Gardner. Through a variety of tricks, and with the help of several friends, it is believed that Powell created all of the ghostly effects to scare Gardner away. In fact, Gardner eventually did break up with Betsy and left the area. It has never been satisfactorily explained, however, how Powell achieved all the effects. But Powell did come out the winner. In the end, he married Betsy Bell.

---

[1] **Tennessee** a state in the southeast of the United States
[2] **deathbed** the bed a person dies on; the last hours before death
[3] **swore** promised
[4] **pitch** a level or frequency of sound
[5] **a merry chase** idiomatic expression meaning 'a pursuit'
[6] **yanked** pulled sharply
[7] **poked** to jab or press with a finger or stick
[8] **Nashville** the capital city of Tennessee
[9] **(a) stroke** a blocked or broken blood vessel in the brain that causes a lack of muscle control, difficulty speaking, and sometimes death
[10] **stupor** a state of mental and/or physical inactivity
[11] **Jr.** junior; sons with the same name as their fathers often have 'junior' put after the first name
[12] **vial** a small container often holding medicinal liquid

The following questions are all about the reading. Answer each one using the information you have read. Try not to look back at the reading for the answers.

1. Where did the Bell Witch story take place?
2. What was the name of the ghost in the Bell Witch story?
3. Who did the ghost haunt?
4. Why did the ghost haunt these people?
5. Did the ghost make any noises? Describe the kind of noises it made.
6. What kind of experience did Andrew Jackson have with the ghost?
7. How did the haunting finally end?
8. What was one explanation for the haunting given in the reading?

Ⓐ The words in *italics* are vocabulary items from the reading. Read each question or statement and choose the correct answer. Compare your answers with a partner.

1. Something that is an *inspiration* makes someone want to _____.
   a. do it
   b. ignore it

2. If you are *tormented* by something it causes you to feel _____.
   a. pain and anguish
   b. confused

3. A *prevailing* view is one that is _____.
   a. unaccepted
   b. generally accepted

4. Which person is *indifferent*?
   a. someone who doesn't care about anything
   b. someone who worries about most things

5. Something *nerve-racking* is _____.
   a. stressful and frightening
   b. extremely relaxing

6. If you *encountered* someone on the street, you _____ him or her.
   a. avoided
   b. met

7. An act of *vengeance* is one of _____.
   a. kindness
   b. revenge

8. If you were trying to *rouse* someone, you would be _____.
   a. trying to get him/her to sleep
   b. trying to awaken him/her

9. If a crime is committed, who is *summoned* to the crime scene?
   a. the police
   b. criminals

10. If someone is *taunting* you, it means he or she is _____.
    a. teasing you
    b. yelling at you

B Now think of other examples using the vocabulary in A. Share your ideas with a partner.

1. When was the last time you had a feeling of *inspiration*? What were you inspired to do?
2. Have you ever been *tormented* by something?
3. What is the *prevailing* view of politicians in your country?
4. Name something you feel *indifferent* about.
5. What kinds of situations do you find *nerve-racking*?
6. Have you ever *encountered* someone for the first time, but felt that you had met him or her before?
7. Why would someone want to perform an act of *vengeance*?
8. Are you easy or difficult to *rouse* in the morning?
9. Have you ever *summoned* the police or firefighters to your home?
10. When you were at elementary school, was *taunting* common on the playground?

Vocabulary Skill:
The Root Word
pos/pon

In this chapter, you read the word 'expose,' which contains the root 'pos,' meaning 'put,' 'place,' or 'stand,' and the prefix 'ex-' which means 'to show.' Thus, 'expose' means 'to put on show' or 'to reveal.' The root 'pos,' or 'pon,' is used with a variety of prefixes and suffixes to form many different words in English.

A For each word, study the different parts. Then, write the part of speech and a simple definition. Use the list of prefixes and suffixes below, as well as your dictionary, to help you. Share your ideas with a partner.

Prefixes	
com-	with, together
dis-	not, apart
de-	remove, down, away
post-	after
op-	against
pro-	for
trans-	across, change

Suffixes
-tion (with nouns) the state of something
-able (with adjectives) able to

Vocabulary	Part of Speech	Definition
1. deposition	noun	a sworn statement used in court when the witness is absent
2. compose		
3. component		
4. disposable		
5. postpone		
6. oppose		
7. propose		
8. position		
9. transpose		
10. deposit		

B Now complete the sentences using the words from the chart. Be sure to use the correct form of each word.

1. Albert was saving his money, so he _____ his entire paycheck in the bank.

2. Even two months after her car crash, Sheena was too ill to attend the court trial of the other driver. Instead her lawyer took a _____.

3. I'm trying this alternative cold remedy. It's _____ of different plant roots and herbs, and tastes very strange.

4. Because of the pouring rain, we decided to _____ the picnic.

5. When our accountant _____ the figures he made a mistake. We ended up thinking we had made $10,000,000, not $100,000!

6. After years of working in a junior _____, Trina was promoted to management.

7. The problem with using so many _____ products is that it increases the volume of trash we produce.

8. The student union _____ that recycling bins be placed around the campus.

9. Good organization is one of the most important _____ of a well-written essay.

10. Though many people agree with the president, there are some who clearly _____ his views.

Think About It — Discuss the following questions with a partner.

1. *Do you believe that the ghost of Kate Batts was real? Why or why not?*

2. *The concluding paragraph of the reading offers an alternative explanation for the alleged haunting. What other possible explanations are there?*

3. *How would you have reacted to the ghost of Kate Batts if you had been a resident of the Bell household?*

4. *What do you think General Andrew Jackson meant when he said he would rather fight the British than the Bell Witch?*

Before You Read:
Spooky Strangers

Discuss the following questions with a partner.

1. What do you think the differences are between a ghost, a phantom, and a poltergeist? Use your dictionary to help you understand the meaning of each word.

2. Do you know of anyone, or of any stories, where living people have come into close contact with ghosts? What happened?

3. Do you believe ghostly tales of people seeing vanishing figures? Why or why not?

4. Where do you think such stories come from?

Reading Skill:
Developing
Reading
Fluency

Remember, you do not need to read every word of a passage to be able to understand what it is about. Focus on comprehending main ideas, keep reading steadily, and don't let unknown vocabulary stop you from reading to the end of the passage.

Time yourself as you read through the passage. Try to read as fluently as you can. Record your time in the Reading Rate Chart on page 234.

Vanishing Hitchhikers _____

The following reading is adapted from *Phantom Hitchhikers*. Written by Stephen Wagner, About.com Guide to Paranormal Phenomena. Reprinted with permission of the author © 1999.

One of the most entertaining types of ghost stories is that of the phantom, or vanishing, hitchhiker.[1] It's also one of the most chilling because, if true, they bring ghosts in very close contact with mortals.[2] Perhaps more disconcerting still, the stories describe the ghosts as looking, acting, and sounding like living
5 people—even physically interacting with the unsuspecting drivers who pick them up.

The basic story usually goes something like this: a tired driver traveling at night picks up a strange hitchhiker, drops him or her off at some destination, and then somehow later finds out that the hitchhiker had in fact died months
10 or years earlier—often on that very same date. Like most ghost stories, tales of

phantom hitchhikers are impossible to verify, and are most often considered to be urban legends.[3] There are many such stories, and it's up to you to determine whether or not you believe any of them. Here are just a few:

The Basketball Player

A woman, driving to her sister's house on a winter evening, sees a boy of about eleven or twelve years of age hitchhiking on the side of the road. She stops for him, he gets into the front seat next to her, and they chat as they drive down the highway. The boy says he's a basketball player for a local school, and she sees that, indeed, he has the height and build of an athlete. She also notices that he is not wearing a jacket of any kind, despite the fact that it's winter. The boy seems to have no particular destination in mind as he points to the side of the road and asks to be let out there. The woman is puzzled because she can see no houses or lights anywhere. Before she can pull over to the side of the road, however, the youth simply vanishes. She immediately stops the car, gets out, and looks around, but the boy is nowhere to be seen. She later learns that the same vanishing hitchhiker was first picked up at the same spot twenty-nine years earlier!

The Girl on the Side of the Road

A doctor, while driving home from a country club dance, picks up a young girl in a white dress. She climbs into the back seat of his car because the front seat is crowded with golf clubs, and tells him an address to take her to. As he arrives at the address, he turns to speak to her but she is gone. The curious doctor rings the doorbell of the address given to him by the mysterious girl. A gray-haired man answers the door and reveals that the girl was his daughter. She had died in a car accident exactly two years earlier.

Resurrection[4] Mary

The story of Resurrection Mary begins on a winter night when a young girl named Mary is killed in a car accident while on her way home from a dance. Five years later, a taxi driver picks up a young girl in a white dress on the same street. She sits in the front seat and instructs him to drive north. After driving a short distance, she suddenly tells him to stop, and then simply vanishes from the taxi. The taxi is stopped in front of Resurrection Cemetery,[5] where the girl is buried. According to an account many years later, a woman witnessed Mary locked inside the iron fence of the cemetery. Reportedly, the metal bars of the fence bore the imprints[6] of her hands.

The Smoking Ghost

On a dark winter night, a man stops for a stranger hitchhiking on the side of the road. The stranger is dressed in a military uniform and, after he gets into the car, asks if he can have a cigarette. The man gives him one, and a lighter with which to light it. With his peripheral vision,[7] the driver sees the flash of the lighter, but then, on turning his head, is astonished to see that his passenger has vanished into thin air.[8] Only the cigarette lighter remains on the seat.

The Grandmother

55 Two businessmen stop for a little old lady in a lavender[9] dress walking along the side of the road in the middle of the night. She tells them she is going to see her daughter and granddaughter, and they offer to drive her to the next town. On the way, she proudly tells them all about her children and grandchildren, such as their names and where they live. After a while, the men 60 become engrossed in their own business conversation, and when they reach their destination, the old woman is no longer in the back seat. Fearing the worst, the men retrace their route, but do not find the woman anywhere. Finally, recalling the daughter's name, they go to her house to report what they fear might have been a horrible accident. The men identify her from 65 photos in the daughter's house. It turned out that the old woman was buried exactly three years ago that day.

---

[1] **hitchhiker** a person who travels free by getting vehicles to stop at the roadside and pick them up
[2] **mortals** beings who will eventually die
[3] **urban legend** an invented story that is believed to be true
[4] **resurrection** the act of coming back to life from the dead
[5] **cemetery** a place where the dead are buried
[6] **imprints** marks made on a surface in the shape of something
[7] **peripheral vision** the outermost edge of the entire area that a person can see
[8] **vanish into thin air** idiomatic expression meaning 'disappear into nowhere'
[9] **lavender** pale or light purple color

Reading Comprehension: How Much Do You Remember?

Ⓐ Decide if the following statements about the reading are true (*T*) or false (*F*). If you check (✔) false, correct the statement to make it true.

	T	F
1. A common phantom in many ghost stories is a vanishing taxi driver.		
2. Some ghost stories, such as tales of phantom hitchhikers, can be easily proven.		
3. Many ghost stories are considered to be urban legends.		
4. The woman who picked up the boy in *The Basketball Player* was confused as he didn't look like an athlete.		
5. In *The Girl on the Side of the Road*, the doctor learned that his phantom passenger had directed him to her father's house.		
6. In the story of *Resurrection Mary*, Mary died because she was locked inside the cemetery.		
7. In the story of *The Smoking Ghost*, the ghost vanishes with the man's cigarettes and lighter.		
8. In the story of *The Grandmother*, the old lady was killed in a horrible accident.		

Ⓑ Check your answers with a partner. Count how many you got correct—be honest! Then, fill in the Reading Comprehension Chart on page 234.

Vocabulary Comprehension:
Word Definitions

A Look at the list of words and phrases from the reading. Match each one with a definition on the right.

1. vanishing _____
2. chilling _____
3. disconcerting _____
4. verify _____
5. despite the fact _____
6. puzzled _____
7. reveals _____
8. account _____
9. engrossed _____
10. fearing the worst _____

a. to have one's attention completely occupied
b. to prove; make certain of the accuracy of something
c. confused or baffled
d. in spite of something; even though
e. feeling that the worst possible thing has happened
f. a spoken or written description of an event
g. upsetting; making one feel worried or uncertain
h. makes known or shows
i. disappearing
j. frightening

B Now complete the sentences below using the vocabulary from A. Be sure to use the correct form of each word.

1. The way Seow Lin gives an _____ of her flying lessons is hilarious.
2. This crossword has had me _____ for hours.
3. Did you know that the rings inside a tree trunk _____ its age?
4. Don't try calling Rachel on Monday evenings; she gets so _____ in TV soap operas that she doesn't respond to anything.
5. _____ that Alan cut back on his spending, he still didn't have enough money to pay all his bills.
6. So-ra wanted to _____ that her interviewee was a good worker, so she called his former boss for a reference.
7. The most _____ story I heard wasn't a ghost story; it was a true story about a burglar who murdered all six people who lived in the house.
8. When I met Melissa's boyfriend he kept telling me he'd met me somewhere before and asked me lots of really personal questions. It was quite _____.
9. As quickly as she made the cookies, they _____ from the plate.
10. When Fred didn't come home from his fishing trip his wife immediately _____. She called the coastguard to ask for help.

Vocabulary Skill:
The Root
Word *mort*

In this chapter, you read the word 'mortal.' This word is formed from the root 'mort,' also written 'mor' or 'mur,' which means 'to die' or 'death.' There are many words in English that use this root and they are used in a variety of contexts.

Ⓐ Study the words in the chart. What do you think they mean? Use your knowledge of prefixes, suffixes, and the root *mort* to match each word with a definition.

Noun	Verb	Adjective
mortuary	amortize	immortal
mortgage*	mortify	moribund
murder*		morbid
morgue		
mortality		
post-mortem**		

* can also be a verb
** can also be an adjective

1. lasting or living forever   _____

2. obsessed with disturbing subjects like death   _____

3. a place where bodies of people found dead are kept for examination or identification   _____

4. to cause one to feel extreme shame or embarrassment   _____

5. the crime of intentionally killing a person   _____

6. an agreement that allows one to borrow money to finance a purchase, usually of property   _____

7. medical examination of a dead body to determine the cause of death   _____

8. to reduce a debt or expenditure by making installment payments over time   _____

9. a place, especially a funeral home, where dead bodies are kept before a funeral   _____

10. the quality or state of not living forever   _____

11. at, or near, the point of death; on the verge of becoming obsolete   _____

B Use the words from A to complete the paragraphs below. Which words are left over? Check your answers with a partner.

News in Brief

Six Feet Under Reaches 6 Million Viewers

All of us, at one point or another, face death and our own _____.
Perhaps this is what the creator of the television show *Six Feet Under* was
thinking when he conceived of the program to which 6 million people—the
highest viewing figures so far—tuned in last night. Despite the fact that some
consider the theme quite _____, it's obviously a popular topic. The
show takes place in a funeral home. The characters frequently have to go to
the _____ to retrieve bodies of the deceased, many of whom were
_____ or accident victims. The bodies are then placed in the
_____ until the funeral takes place. The show examines many
issues related to death, and reminds us that though our loved ones may pass
away, our thoughts will keep them _____.

American Dream Alive and Well

Who says the American Dream is _____? Today the dream of
owning a home is prevalent in many young people's minds. But with today's
house prices how can young people afford to buy their first home? When
you apply for a _____ for your home, the bank will use a table to
calculate how best to _____ the payment schedule. If you have a
steady income, your dream could quickly become a reality. The Learning
Bank is now making simplified versions of these tables available to potential
house-buyers to help them better understand the mortgage minefield.

What Do You Think?

Discuss the following questions with a partner.

1. *Do you believe that any of the stories recounted in this chapter's reading are true?*
2. *What other logical explanations are there for these stories?*
3. *Why do you think sightings such as these usually take place at night?*
4. *How many of your class members believe in ghosts? How many are skeptics? What reasons do they give to support their beliefs? Take a class poll to find out.*

Real Life Skill

Types of Stories

The same story, or set of events, can be narrated in many different ways, for different purposes. They might be told in a humorous way for entertainment, in a factual way as a news report, or in a certain order using specific phrases and language for educational purposes. Knowing how and why events are being told in a certain way can help you to understand the purpose of the information being provided.

Ⓐ Read these different types of stories and their definitions. Where would you most likely read each one? Match each story type to a type of reading material. Some of them can be used more than once. Can you add any other examples?

children's book	joke book	newspaper
magazine	corporate document	police report
self-help book	historical information	advice column

1. **tale**—an old story that has been told many times _____

2. **report**—a detailed and objective presentation of facts _____

3. **anecdote**—a short story about a real event, used to illustrate an idea _____

4. **account**—an explanation from one person's point of view _____

5. **chronicle**—a long narrative of events over time _____

6. **yarn**—an entertaining story that is loosely based on truth _____

7. **proverb**—a short sentence that expresses a moral lesson, e.g., 'When the cat's away, the mice will play.' _____

8. **statement**—a short summary of facts _____

9. **fable**—a short piece of fiction (often about animals) that teaches a moral lesson _____

10. **gossip**—a rumor about someone that is possibly untrue _____

Ⓑ Now complete the sentences below using one of the story types from A. Be prepared to give reasons for your choice.

1. My grandfather loves to tell _____ about his adventures when he was a boy.

2. The Ministry of Environmental Protection recently published its _____ on changes in air quality over the past ten years.

3. I don't believe that Carl is getting married. I think it's just idle _____.

4. That article has some interesting _____ about women who have started their own businesses.

5. 'Look before you leap' is my favorite _____.

6. At the meeting, Dr. Kim gave an _____ of his research trip to the Arctic.

7. In my country, we have a lot of _____ about giants and monsters.

8. The government issued a _____ about the president's health.

Business Matters

Getting Ready

Discuss the following questions with a partner.

1. *What are some of the leading companies in your country? What products do they sell?*

2. *Do you know who owns these companies? Are they owned by the same person or people who started them?*

3. *What do you think the main differences are between a large corporation and a small business?*

4. *An 'entrepreneur' can be defined as a person who starts a business, develops it, and assumes responsibility for the risks involved in making it profitable. Can you name any famous entrepreneurs in your country? What kind of business did they start?*

Unit 5

Chapter 1: Find Your Niche—and Stick to It

Before You Read:
Business Principles

Discuss the following questions with a partner.

1. What would you consider to be a small business?
2. What kind of small businesses are there in your neighborhood?
3. What challenges do you think many businesses face today?
4. What do you think is the most important thing to remember when running a business, large or small?

Reading Skill:
Identifying Meaning from Context

You can guess the meaning of important but unfamiliar words in a reading passage by using the following strategy: **1.** Think about how the new word is related to the topic of what you are reading about. **2.** Identify which part of speech the new word is by looking at how it fits with the other words in its sentence. **3.** Look at how the word relates to the rest of the information in the paragraph surrounding it. **4.** Use your knowledge of prefixes, suffixes, and word roots to identify the basic meaning of the word.

(A) The following is an extract from the reading passage. As you read through it, think about the topic of the reading, and what you already know about this topic. Pay attention to the underlined words and think about how they fit with the topic.

> How does a small-business owner (1) <u>define</u> his or her niche, (2) <u>target</u> the right clients, and have the courage to decline business from the 'wrong' people? In the conversation below, Leslie Godwin, a career and life- (3) <u>transition</u> coach, offers her advice to the small-business entrepreneur.

(B) Decide which part of speech each underlined word is, and write them below.

(1) _____ (2) _____ (3) _____

How do you know this? Circle the words in the sentence that work with or affect the underlined words, and tell you the part of speech. Look at how the word relates to the rest of the paragraph. Are there any other words or phrases that give you clues to the meaning of each word? If so, circle them.

(C) Now look at the parts of the words. Does each one have a recognizable prefix, root, or suffix? Use your knowledge of these word parts to try and identify the meaning of each word. Replace each one with a word or phrase, or write a definition.

(1) _____ (2) _____ (3) _____

(D) Use your dictionary to check whether you have interpreted the meaning of the words correctly. Share your answers with a partner.

(E) Look at the words in the chart below. Using the line references, locate each word in the passage and underline it.

Vocabulary	Part of Speech	Definition
1. multitasking (line 13)		
2. consultants (line 14)		
3. upholds (line 39)		
4. investors (line 44)		
5. digesting (line 56)		
6. sidetracked (line 60)		

F Using the same strategies you practiced above, identify the part of speech of each word. Look at how each one fits into the sentences or paragraph around it. Look at the parts of each word and try to work out the meaning. Replace them with words or phrases you know that have the same meaning, or write a definition. Share your answers with a partner, and use your dictionary to check your interpretations and definitions.

G Now read through the passage again, and complete the comprehension exercise that follows.

Find Your Niche—and Stick to It _____

The following reading is adapted from *Find Your Niche—and Stick to It* by Karen E. Klein. First published in *Business Week* March 22, 2002. Reprinted with permission of Business Week © 2002.

One of the fundamental beliefs of starting a small business is 'find a niche and stick to it.' Yet that advice is not always taken seriously enough by entrepreneurs, who often think selling to the widest possible market is a likelier path to success.

How does a small-business owner define his or her niche, target the right   5
clients, and have the courage to decline business from the 'wrong' people? In the conversation below, Leslie Godwin, a career and life-transition coach,[1] offers her advice to the small-business entrepreneur.

Q: Why do so many small-business owners seem to have so much trouble finding a niche?   10
A: They're afraid. If they pick one specialty area and commit to it, they'll have to turn away potential clients and that's scary, especially when they're getting started. The other thing is that people see multitasking as an asset: If they're business consultants, for example, they might be able to help clients do everything from ordering stationery to writing a business plan to helping with   15
a corporate merger.[2] But they can't market themselves that way. They can't focus in on target clients that way. I tell my clients that when they try to be all things to all people,[3] they're really not being very helpful to anybody.

Q: Does every business need its own niche?
A: The vast majority of successful businesses stick with a very narrow niche.   20
The principle applies to large corporations as well as small, by the way. They can lose their focus, just like the sole proprietor who is so excited that the phone is ringing that he'll do anything just to make a sale.

Q: How does an entrepreneur avoid falling into that trap?
A: Smart entrepreneurs will, from the very beginning, define what they're   25
about. They'll get better clients with a more narrow focus, and they'll get their ideal clients without having to compete on price because the clients will see that the company understands their concerns. It will take much less of a sales job to convince their customers they know how to serve them. That business consultant, for instance: If she narrows her focus to working strictly with sole   30
proprietors, she'll immediately define herself, she'll cut the competition in half since very few consultants focus on sole proprietors, and clients will be really

excited to find her because she'll know everything there is to know about their business and their problems.

35 **Q: How does an entrepreneur find the right niche?**
A: If they have a mission statement, this is the time to see what it says about the focus of the business. I ask my clients to write their mission statement based on what problem they most care about solving, who benefits from this solution, and how they will solve the problem in a way that upholds their
40 values, standards, and ethics.

Q: What about those businesses that seem to be successful and yet don't have just one niche area?
A: Companies can be incredibly lucky to start out because of positioning, good contacts, great investors, or because they become trendy. But being a
45 generalist is not a plan that will sustain long-term business growth, because they never create an identity that can sustain them.

Q: Many businesspeople seem to realize all this, but few act on it. Why?
A: They think they already have an identity. In their minds they know perfectly well what they're doing, and they don't realize their customers aren't
50 picking up on it.[4]

Q: How should they remedy that?
A: I'd recommend that they survey their current customers. Ask what they think of when they think of your company. Ask why they chose your company over others. Ask what they tell people when they refer your company. A well-
55 designed survey can illuminate a lot of disconnects between what the owner thinks he's conveying, and what the clients are digesting about the business. I also tell clients to talk to their customers on a regular basis. Ask about their needs, get to know them, do some careful listening. You can't meet all your client's needs, but you should at least know what they are. One caveat: Focus
60 on your ideal clients and their needs. Don't get sidetracked by what every client wants and needs because, again, you can't be all things to all people. Use your best efforts on your biggest, best, most loyal, longtime customers.

Q: How does the typical overworked, undercapitalized[5] entrepreneur find time to do all this?
65 **A:** They have to make time. Planning seems to take time away from running your business, but if you spend at least two hours a month, you'll save lots of hours and thousands of dollars every quarter[6] because you'll be focusing your time and your money on your ideal clients. People put off planning because they're responding to problems, and they don't think they have time to
70 strategize. But they need to guide their business where they want it to go, instead of letting it get out of control and then trying to catch up to it.

¹ **life-transition coach** person who helps people make, or cope with, major life changes
² **merger** the combining of two companies to form one larger company
³ **be all things to all people** help everyone to do everything they want
⁴ **picking up on it** noticing something and paying attention to it
⁵ **undercapitalized** underfunded; lacking in capital or spare money
⁶ **quarter** financial period lasting three months or a quarter of a year

Reading Comprehension: What Do You Remember?

The following statements are all about the reading. Complete each one using information you have read.

1. Finding a niche and sticking to it is a _____ principle for small businesses.

2. Finding a niche is a challenge for most entrepreneurs who think they will have more success selling to the _____ _____ _____. (three words)

3. Most successful businesses have a very _____ niche.

4. Most businesses get better _____ with a more narrow focus.

5. The narrow focus of your business should be included in your _____ _____. (two words)

6. Businesses that are too general do not create an _____ to sustain their growth.

7. Businesses should connect with their customers better by regularly _____ to them.

8. Taking time each month to _____ the future of your business is important for sustained success.

Vocabulary Comprehension: Odd Word Out

Ⓐ For each group, circle the word that does not belong. The words in *italics* are vocabulary items from the reading.

1. basic	*fundamental*	elementary	underlying
2. *niche*	position	consequence	corner
3. relinquish	*commit*	abandon	renounce
4. advantage	liability	*asset*	plus
5. center on	concentrate on	distract	*focus in on*
6. *proprietor*	customer	owner	possessor
7. dissuade	talk into	*convince*	persuade
8. clarify	shed light on	confuse	*illuminate*
9. transmitting	*conveying*	imparting	retracting
10. *caveat*	warning	permission	caution

(B) Now complete the sentences below using the words in *italics* from A. Be sure to use the correct form of the word.

1. Many job counselors and employers agree that being multilingual is certainly an _____ in today's business climate.

2. When attending an interview, it's so important that you dress appropriately. If you don't, you may end up _____ a message you hadn't intended to.

3. When you're preparing your résumé or job application letter, it's important to _____ exactly what the employer is looking for.

4. We will find out if our investors will _____ to this business venture on Monday. Until then, we have to wait.

5. No matter what, when making business decisions every _____ should stick to their gut feelings and work ethic. It's the only way to succeed.

6. Chantira said she enjoyed the benefits of working overseas for a large corporation, but still hasn't found her _____.

7. Alec thinks that looking through the job section in the newspaper will _____ some possibilities that he hadn't previously considered.

8. Buying a business is an exciting venture, but with one _____: take your time and do not rush into anything.

9. A _____ principle of any successful relationship or friendship is honest communication.

10. After years of my refusing, our accountant has finally _____ me to buy some shares as a form of investment for when I retire.

Vocabulary Skill:
The Root Word
fer

In this chapter, you read the words 'offer' and 'refer.' These are formed by combining prefixes with the root 'fer,' which comes from the Latin 'ferre,' meaning 'to carry.' 'Offer' combines the prefix 'ob-,' meaning 'to,' with 'fer' to mean 'to carry to,' or 'to present.' The prefix 're-,' meaning 'back,' is combined with 'fer' to form 'refer,' meaning 'to carry back,' or 'to go back to.'

(A) For each word, study the different parts. Then write its part of speech and a simple definition. Use your dictionary to help you. Share your ideas with a partner.

Vocabulary	Part of Speech	Definition
1. transferable	_____	_____
2. differently	_____	_____
3. cross-reference	_____	_____
4. confer	_____	_____
5. conference	_____	_____
6. circumference	_____	_____
7. defer	_____	_____
8. infer	_____	_____
9. preferably	_____	_____
10. insufferable	_____	_____

B Now complete each sentence using the words from the chart. Be sure to use the correct form of the word.

1. Jin Soo is looking for a new job again, _____ one that doesn't involve so much travel.

2. In order to fully appreciate the extensive gardens surrounding the estate, you have to walk the _____ of it.

3. Our new boss thinks very _____ in terms of how things get done, the result being we have made a lot of progress with our projects in a short space of time.

4. Because the company was experiencing financial difficulties, they made arrangements to _____ some of the payments they owed.

5. Before going into business, Ahmed attended a _____ which held workshops on how to start a business, and manage it successfully.

6. Janine loves running her clothing business but often admits to finding some people in the fashion industry _____.

7. We can only _____ that the reason Albert was asked to take early retirement was to save the company money.

8. William tried to use his wife's store card but discovered it was non-_____.

9. This new online information system makes it so easy to _____ one publication with another.

10. Every time our company has to make a big decision, we get together with the key shareholders and _____ on the relative issues.

C Can you think of any other words in English that include the root *fer*?

Think About It   Discuss the following questions with a partner.

1. *What do you think are the advantages and disadvantages of running your own business?*

2. *What business and non-business skills do you think you would need to run a company successfully?*

3. *What personal qualities do you think most successful business people have in common? How do you think these qualities contribute to their success?*

4. *How can success in running your own business be defined? Give some examples.*

Before You Read:

Real-Life Entrepreneurs

Discuss the following questions with a partner.

1. Look at the photos above. Can you name these two entrepreneurs? Can you name the world-famous businesses that each one started?

2. Can you name any other famous entrepreneurs? What line of business are they in? Which country are they from?

3. What do you think it takes to be a successful entrepreneur in today's business climate?

4. Look at the title of the reading. The following words and phrases can all be found in the passage.

venture   *legacy*   *innovators*   *tenacity*   *a handful of*

How do you think they relate to the topic of the reading? Use your knowledge of prefixes, suffixes, and word roots, as well as your dictionary, to help you determine the meaning of each of these words and phrases.

Reading Skill:

Developing Reading Fluency

> *Reading fluently means getting the main idea of the reading without slowing down to look up words in your dictionary. Remember to incorporate the skill of identifying meaning from context into your reading to help you read fluently.*

Time yourself as you read through the passage. Try to read as fluently as you can. Record your time in the Reading Rate Chart on page 234.

The Idol Life: Entrepreneurial Geniuses____

The following reading is adapted from *The Idol Life* by Aliza Pilar Sherman. Reprinted with permission from *Entrepreneur* Magazine © January 2002; http://www.Entrepreneur.com/article/0,4621,295495,00.html

When you think of the word 'entrepreneur,' who comes to mind? Whether you look at historical innovators such as Henry Ford[1] or Nelson Rockefeller[2] or at today's headlines, there are just a handful of entrepreneurs who stand out in each generation. We recently talked to two of today's entrepreneurial icons—people
5 whose names are synonymous with success, risk-taking, and independent thinking. How have they changed from their early days in business through today's volatile market, ever-changing technology, and crowded business landscape? And how has their entrepreneurial spirit endured? Let's find out.

Michael Dell

As a college student, Michael Dell declared that he wanted to beat IBM. In 1983, [10] he began conducting business out of his dorm room at the University of Texas in Austin, selling custom-made PCs and components. A year later, with $1,000 in start-up capital,[3] Dell officially set up his business and left school. "Being an entrepreneur wasn't on my mind," insists Dell. "What was on my mind was the opportunity I saw ahead, which was so compelling." [15]

He had no idea how big that opportunity really was. Dell Computer Corporation is now a $31.9 billion company. Though Dell himself had "no idea the Internet would come along," his company now runs one of the world's largest Windows-based e-commerce web sites. These days, Dell spends most of his time planning company strategy. "Strategy is the biggest point of impact I can have as the [20] company is much, much larger—it has 40,000 employees," he says. "So my ability to make an impact on anything else is pretty small."

Dell says he feels as entrepreneurial now as when he started. "There are plenty of markets to discover," he says, "and each new venture requires tenacity and a willingness to take risks." Dell shares his thoughts on what being an entrepreneur is [25] about below.

Q: How do you define 'entrepreneur'?
A: Somebody who has a new idea, or different idea, and takes a risk, and works hard to make it work.

Q: How do you keep your entrepreneurial spirit alive? [30]
A: There's always a new challenge, whether it's a new product line, a new customer, a new service, or some new milestone.[4]

Q: What was your dream when you started out?
A: My plan was to sell built-to-order computer systems directly to end-users.[5] I recognized there was a big opportunity there because of the inefficiencies of the [35] indirect system.[6]

Q: What would you hope to be your legacy?
A: Well, I don't plan to be remembered anytime soon. I'm 36 years old. But I hope they would think, this is a guy who built a company that created tremendous value for its customers, its employees, and its shareholders.[7] And perhaps, this is a guy [40] who helped people realize the power of computing and the Internet. And then the last piece, which is something only a few people would know, that this is a guy who was a great dad and a great husband.

Anita Roddick

As a young girl, starting a business was the last thing on Anita Roddick's mind. "I [45] wanted to be an actress," she says. Even when she began to pursue what would become The Body Shop, her environmentalism-minded skin- and hair-care company with more than 1,800 stores around the world, Roddick's goal was not to be an icon.

Roddick opened her first shop in 1976 with twenty-five hand-mixed products, [50] eventually franchising[8] The Body Shop, and then going public[9] in 1984. The Body

Shop now offers more than 1,000 items and reached sales of more than $1 billion in 2001/2002.

Though she no longer sits on The Body Shop's executive committee, Roddick still serves as co-chair,[10] finds new products, and keeps the company active in human rights, environmental, and animal-protection issues.

In 1997, Roddick helped launch a master's degree program in conjunction with Bath University in England, with the aim of making business education more socially responsible. More recently, she established The Body Shop's Human Rights Award, which recognizes individuals and organizations that focus on social, economic, and cultural rights.

The biggest challenge has been people's cynicism. "People feel there has to be an ulterior motive to The Body Shop's activism, as though our principles are a marketing ploy," Roddick says. Have the challenges affected Roddick's feelings about entrepreneurship? Not even slightly. "I don't think being an entrepreneur is something you question," says Roddick. "It's just something you are."

Q: How do you define 'entrepreneur'?
A: Entrepreneurs are obsessive visionaries, pathological[11] optimists, passionate storytellers, and outsiders[12] by nature.

Q: How do you keep your entrepreneurial spirit alive?
A: By being experimental. Success is twin-edged:[13] Managing success seems to kill the entrepreneurial spirit. So to maintain it, you must keep on experimenting.

Q: What was your dream when you started out?
A: My business was a response to the extravagance and waste of the cosmetics industry. I felt there were plenty of people like me hungry for an alternative.

Q: What would you hope to be your legacy?
A: The future is being shaped by the forces of global business, so I would hope that I've helped change the vocabulary and practice of business, and contributed to the awareness that it can, and must, be a force for positive social change.

---

[1] **Henry Ford** developer of the gasoline-powered motor car and founder of the Ford Motor Company

[2] **Nelson Rockefeller** member of the wealthy Rockefeller family; governor of New York (1959–1973) and Vice President of the United States (1974–1977)

[3] **start-up capital** money used to start a new company

[4] **milestone** important event or achievement

[5] **end-users** customers; people at the end of the supply chain who use the product

[6] **indirect system** process of manufacturer selling to another company or store that a customer buys from

[7] **shareholders** people who own shares in a company or business

[8] **franchising** legally agreeing for an individual or company to sell another company's goods or products

[9] **going public** offering shares to the public in a company or business

[10] **co-chair** joint chairperson

[11] **pathological** a state of disease or illness; used non-literally here to mean 'obsessive'

[12] **outsiders** not members of a group; very independent people

[13] **twin-edged** having two sides—usually one positive, one negative

Reading Comprehension: How Much Do You Remember?

Ⓐ Decide if the following statements about the reading are true (*T*) or false (*F*). If you check (✔) false, correct the statement to make it true.

	T	F
1. Michael Dell first began doing business while attending the University of Texas at Austin.		
2. Dell started his business officially, with $1,000 in start-up capital, two years later.		
3. Dell's dream when he started out was to build faster computers.		
4. Dell would like to be remembered mainly for being a great husband.		
5. Anita Roddick wanted to be an actress when she was younger.		
6. Roddick now serves as CEO of The Body Shop.		
7. The biggest challenge for The Body Shop has been convincing people that it is genuinely concerned with human rights and environmental issues.		
8. Roddick believes that managing success is essential to maintaining an entrepreneurial spirit.		

Ⓑ Check your answers with a partner. Count how many you got correct—be honest! Then, fill in the Reading Comprehension Chart on page 234.

Vocabulary Comprehension: Word Definitions

Ⓐ Look at the list of words and phrases from the reading. Match each one with a definition on the right.

1. a handful of _____
2. volatile _____
3. compelling _____
4. venture _____
5. tenacity _____
6. legacy _____
7. in conjunction with _____
8. cynicism _____
9. ulterior motive _____
10. ploy _____

a. hidden or secret reason for doing something
b. likely to change suddenly or unexpectedly
c. something said or done in order to trick someone or gain advantage over them
d. an attitude of jaded or scornful negativity
e. forceful and persuasive
f. something that is passed on from one generation to the next
g. a plan, often in business, that involves uncertainty or risk
h. persistence
i. a small number or quantity
j. together (with)

Ⓑ Complete the sentences below using the vocabulary from A. Be sure to use the correct form of the word.

1. Most people will tell you that the key to entrepreneurial success is

_____.

2. Other people's _____ is something that most entrepreneurs continually have to fight against.

3. Working on new business _____ is what keeps many entrepreneurs enthusiastic about their work.

4. Though many people try to become billionaires through entrepreneurship, only _____ them succeed.

5. Everyone assumed that the businessman who was running for Congress had an _____ when he donated a large percentage of his earnings to charity.

6. Eliza refuses to vote as she thinks most politicians tell lies as a _____ to get people to vote for them.

7. If Derek's new business venture takes off he will end up working _____ some of the biggest names in the computer industry.

8. My grandfather would like his _____ to be that of best golfer his country club has ever known.

9. Most business people will tell you that they are driven by some sort of _____ notion that their ideas will work.

10. Many people think it is very risky to invest while the stock markets are so _____. However, when share prices are low it's the best time to buy.

Vocabulary Skill:
The Root Word
ten/tain

In this chapter, you read the words 'maintain' and 'tenacity.' Both are formed using the root word 'ten' or 'tain,' which comes from the Latin word 'tenere' meaning 'hold on' or 'persist.' 'Ten' or 'tain' can be combined with prefixes, suffixes, and other root words to form many words in English.

Ⓐ The words below can all be completed by adding the root *ten* or *tain*. Decide which form each word uses and write it in the space provided. Then write which part of speech each word is and, using your knowledge of prefixes and suffixes, write a definition.

Vocabulary	Part of Speech	Definition
1. abs_____	_____	_____
2. un_____able	_____	_____
3. de_____	_____	_____
4. at_____	_____	_____
5. re_____	_____	_____
6. con_____er	_____	_____
7. sus_____able	_____	_____
8. _____ant	_____	_____
9. _____ure	_____	_____
10. main_____	_____	_____
11. ob_____	_____	_____
12. _____acious	_____	_____

(B) Use your dictionary to make sure you have the correct meaning for each word. Then, complete the following sentences using the correct words from A. Be sure to use the correct form of each word.

1. Jan's business grew so fast due to the _____ attitude of her employees.

2. As all the evidence in the murder case supported the defendant's guilt, his lawyer found himself in an _____ position.

3. Julio _____ the highest grade in his class this year.

4. Martin wants to sell his house and buy a property overseas but his _____ refuses to move out until the _____ on the property ends in two years.

5. Anna wants to go and work in Thailand but is having trouble _____ a work permit at the moment.

(C) Now write four more sentences using any of the remaining words from the list in A. Share your ideas with a partner.

1. _____

2. _____

3. _____

4. _____

What Do You Think?

Discuss the following questions with a partner.

1. *If you were to start your own company, what kind of business would you go into? Why?*

2. *What difficulties and competition would you face if you were to start the business you talked about in question one? How would you make sure you found your niche and didn't get sidetracked?*

3. *How do you feel about entrepreneurs like Michael Dell and Anita Roddick? Do you admire their tenacity and entrepreneurial spirit? Why or why not?*

4. *What would you like your legacy to be? Why?*

Real Life Skill

Reading Business News

News about corporations and other business enterprises can be found in the business pages of daily newspapers. A lot of special terminology and abbreviations are used on these pages, mainly to save space. It is useful to learn some of these abbreviations and terms in order to be able to understand the business news better.

Ⓐ Look at the list of terms, abbreviations, and meanings in the box below.

year-to-date	CFO	Limited	FTSE	IPO	YTD
A corporation	NYSE	Headquarters	New York	Stock Exchange	

The first time people can buy stock in a company
The most senior executive in a company
Chief Executive Officer
A measure of the U.K. stock market
The senior executive in charge of planning and financial records
National Association of Securities Dealers Automated Quotation

Ⓑ Complete the following chart using the information from the box in A.

Abbreviation	Term	Meaning
	Initial Public Offering	
CEO		
		The main place to buy and sell stocks in the United States
Ltd		
HQ		The head office of a business
	Chief Financial Officer	
	Financial Times Stock Exchange index	
NASDAQ		A computerized stock exchange in the United States
		Figures for this year, until today

Ⓒ Now complete this business news item using abbreviations from the chart above.

New York—Hyden Corporation's _____ James Parker announced the appointment of Sandra Lewis as the company's new _____. Lewis will oversee financial details of the company's planned expansion into Asia. Since Hyden first sold shares in their _____ of last January, the price of their stock on the _____ and the _____ in London has risen sharply. Ms. Lewis was formerly a financial analyst at the company's _____ in New York City.

Ⓓ Have you come across any other business-related terms not mentioned in the chart? What are they and what do they mean? List them below.

Sporting Achievements

Getting Ready

Discuss the following questions with a partner.

1. *How many of the well-known sports people in the photos above can you name? What are they famous for?*

2. *What do you know about their career achievements? What challenges or difficulties, if any, have they faced throughout their careers?*

3. *Which sports player do you most admire? Why?*

4. *What are two major things in life you would like to achieve? When and how do you think you will achieve them? How difficult do you think they will be to achieve?*

Before You Read:

A Soccer Hero

Discuss the following questions with a partner.

1. Look at the title of this chapter. What do you think a soccer player would have to do to be labeled the 'golden boy' of soccer?

2. Can you name any soccer player in your country, or in the world, who you think could successfully carry this label right now?

3. Is soccer a popular sport in your country? Who are the leading soccer players in your country?

4. Who do you think are the 'golden boys' or 'golden girls' of other sports in your country?

5. Which of the following adjectives can be used to describe a person?

precocious   outlandish   devastating

goofy   celebrated   relaxed

Are these words positive or negative? Use your knowledge of prefixes, suffixes, and word roots, as well as your dictionary, to help you determine the meaning of each of these words.

Reading Skill:

Skimming for the Main Idea

Skimming is one way to look for the main idea in a reading. When we skim, we read over parts of the text very quickly. We don't read every word, or stop to look up words we don't understand; we skim quickly just to get the gist of what something is about.

Ⓐ Skim the passage quickly. Read only the *title*, the *first* and *last paragraphs*, and the *first sentence of each other paragraph*. Don't worry about words you do not know. Then, complete the sentence below.

This reading is mainly about _____.

1. how Ronaldo helped Brazil to overcome their previous loss in the World Cup to France, and win in 2002.

2. how Ronaldo's depression and stress prevented Brazil from winning the World Cup.

3. how Ronaldo overcame personal failure to help Brazil win the World Cup in 2002.

Ⓑ Now read the passage and answer the comprehension questions that follow.

The Golden Boy of Soccer _____

The following reading is adapted from *Profile: Ronaldo—After a Career of Fits and Starts, the Golden Boy Is Back* by James Lawton. First published in *The Independent* 29 June 2002. Reprinted with permission of The Independent © 2002.

The man stares intently into the camera and says, "My name is Ronaldo Luiz Nazario de Lima. I am twenty-five years old and I want you all to know there is no doubt that, on the thirtieth of June, Brazil will win the World Cup." This was not bragging.[1] It was a statement of hope from an individual who represented the spirit of a nation. The declaration was filmed just before Brazil won the 2002 World Cup, at a time when Brazil—and even less Ronaldo—was given no serious chance of victory. Ronaldo was the mere husk[2] of a once great player, struggling to overcome injuries and the memory of a devastating setback in the previous World Cup.

In 1998, Brazil was the overwhelming favorite to beat France in the final. But suddenly, a shining career went horribly and, it seemed, irreparably wrong. Ronaldo suffered a fit[3] as the big game approached. He was rushed to a Paris hospital where he underwent a full body scan,[4] then arrived at the stadium just an hour before kick-off. Throughout the match, Ronaldo was a shadow of[5] the player who had dominated the game up to this point, and France coasted to an unexpected victory.

"What happened in Paris was terrible," said Ronaldo. "It was an unimaginable nightmare. When the doctor said she couldn't find anything wrong with me, I said I had no choice, I must play. It was my duty, what I was born to do. I knew I wasn't right, but sometimes in life you feel you are trapped and you just don't have any options."

Friends say the entrapment felt by the soccer prodigy ran deeper than the overwhelming circumstances that brought about his fit, now widely believed to have been a combination of stress, and a possible reaction to the high dosage of painkiller that had gotten him through the semi-final. Another part of his problem, say friends, was that he was unhappy with his personal life. Many suspected that his then girlfriend, the high society[6] Rio model Suzana Werner, was happy to ride the wave of publicity that came with her relationship with the world's most celebrated soccer player, but the game, and the pressures it brought to Ronaldo, meant little to her.

It seems that these events are now long behind him. Indeed, he is conspicuously happy with his personal life after marriage to Milene, who not only knows about soccer, but plays it with some accomplishment. With Suzana, Ronaldo's goofy, gap-toothed grin seemed to mask a certain uneasiness, but with Milene he is relaxed and always eager to tell stories from home, especially when they involve his son Ronald.

Just before Brazil's 2002 victory, he explained his new haircut, by far the most outlandish around. "Why did I have my crazy haircut?" asked Ronaldo. "I called home, and Milene said that Ronald had rushed to the TV and kissed it, shouting, 'It's Daddy, Daddy.' But it wasn't me. It was Roberto Carlos! Can you imagine? I said to Milene that it cannot happen again; I have to do something." Such stories are vital ingredients in the re-making of a great soccer player, and in creating a comeback unprecedented in the fabled[7] history of a nation that invests so much passion, and spirituality, in the game.

When Ronaldo was in the depths of his depression, and plagued by fears that he would never again play at the top of his game, Pele visited him. "Pele, the greatest of all soccer players, gave me back some belief," says Ronaldo. "He heard that I was finished, and he told me that people had said the same of him when he was forced out of the 1966 World Cup. But he refused to believe it was over. And now the whole world knows what he did in 1970, in the World Cup final against Italy."

Named after the doctor who assisted at his birth in the poor suburbs of Rio de Janeiro, Ronaldo's is the classic rags-to-riches story of a poor boy made good. As a 16-year-old he invaded the Brazilian second division, scoring 36 goals in 54 games for Sao Cristovao.[8] The following year he scored 58 times for Cruzeiro,[9] and that same season he received his first international cap[10] against Argentina, where he showed the precocity of all the great players before him. In his next game for Brazil he scored in a 3-0 win over Iceland. He was on his way to following in the footsteps of Pele, Jairzhino,[11] and his personal favorite, Romario.

Just days before Brazil's 2002 World Cup victory, Ronaldo confided, "A Brazilian soccer player always knows there will be shadows from time to time. It is impossible not to expect them when you know that so much importance is attached to what you do. But if you have been given talent, with a little luck there is always the dream. This dream is that you will conquer your fears, and when it matters most you will find power you never had before. I feel that is within my grasp now, and I'm living for that."

[1] **bragging**   boasting; to talk proudly of one's own achievements
[2] **husk**   outer layer or shell that is worthless; dry outer casing of some crops, e.g., corn
[3] **(a) fit**   a sudden attack causing bodily spasms or convulsions
[4] **body scan**   analysis of images of internal body organs to check for disease; usually known as an MRI (magnetic resonance imaging)
[5] **a shadow of**   idiomatic expression meaning a lesser or weaker version of someone or something than before
[6] **high society**   social group of wealthy, privileged, usually famous people
[7] **fabled**   legendary
[8] **Sao Cristovao** /saʊn krɪstəvaʊ/
[9] **Cruzeiro** /kruzɛiroʊ/
[10] **cap**   mark of recognition awarded to soccer players for each international game played for their country
[11] **Jairzhino** /dʒarzɪnioʊ/

Reading Comprehension: What Do You Remember?

Decide if the following statements about the reading are true (*T*) or false (*F*). If you check (✔) false, correct the statement to make it true.

	T	F
1. Ronaldo's statement about Brazil winning the World Cup reflected the feelings of many people in Brazil.		
2. Many people thought Brazil had a good chance of winning the 2002 World Cup.		
3. When Ronaldo fell ill before the 1998 World Cup final, doctors knew exactly what was wrong with him.		
4. Throughout the 1998 World Cup final Ronaldo dominated the match, but France still won.		
5. Ronaldo's relationship with model Suzana Werner may have led to his unhappiness.		
6. Ronaldo's happy family life has helped him to rebuild his career.		
7. The story of Ronaldo's success is an example of a rags-to-riches story.		
8. During his depression, Ronaldo spoke to his favorite footballer, who used his own experience to help Ronaldo believe in himself again.		

Vocabulary Comprehension: Odd Word Out

Ⓐ For each group, circle the word that does not belong. The words in *italics* are vocabulary items from the reading.

1. *intently*	purposely	earnestly	casually
2. beleaguered	tormented	*plagued*	cured
3. destroying	*devastating*	ruinous	flourishing
4. *irreparably*	incurably	aspiringly	hopelessly
5. sailed	slid	belabored	*coasted*
6. *following in the footsteps*	succeeding	preceding	replacing
7. *conspicuously*	secretly	obviously	noticeably
8. *outlandish*	eccentric	bizarre	common
9. predictable	*unprecedented*	surprising	unexpected
10. laziness	progressiveness	*precocity*	talent

Ⓑ **Complete the sentences using the words in *italics* from A. Be sure to use the correct form of the word.**

1. Angelo ran as fast as he could during the first leg of the race so he _____ to the finish line ahead of the others.

2. Some sports players have become more renowned for their _____ habits and lifestyle than they have for their skill at their game.

3. When the corporate merger took place, Juliana spent the entire week _____ by the thought that she may lose her job.

4. If you visit the beaches of Rio, you will see many _____ athletic children; they're naturally so adept at playing soccer.

5. That was an _____ win for the team. Considering last season's record, nobody expected them to win.

6. John felt his company had suffered a _____ loss when his sales director resigned.

7. Sebastian has decided to _____ of his father and grandfather, and work for the family law firm. Naturally, his parents are overjoyed.

8. The victim stared _____ at the faces of the suspects in an attempt to identify the person who stole her handbag.

9. After only three months of marriage Dean and Charlene have separated. They say the breakdown of their relationship is _____.

10. The teachers all agree that there is a higher degree of _____ among the pupils who entered the school this year.

Vocabulary Skill:
Word Families

When you learn a new word in English, it is helpful to also learn words that are related to it. Learning the different parts of speech that form the word family can help you to expand your vocabulary.

Ⓐ **Complete the chart with the noun, verb, adjective, and adverb forms of words from this chapter. Be careful—not every word will have all four forms. Look again at the reading to find related words, or use your dictionary to help you.**

Noun	Verb	Adjective	Adverb
_____	_____	devastating	_____
_____	_____	_____	intently
precocity	_____	_____	_____
_____	_____	_____	conspicuously
_____	_____	_____	irreparably
depression	_____	_____	_____
_____	_____	outlandish	_____
uneasiness	_____	_____	_____
_____	_____	overwhelming	_____
accomplishment	_____	_____	_____

B Now complete the paragraphs below using the correct words from the chart. Remember to look for context clues to help you decide which word form to use.

The Value of Sports in Kids' Lives

What would my life be like if my children didn't play sports? Well, it may be more relaxed on one hand. However, like other parents, I can see the immense benefits sports provide our children—and us grown-ups!

Organized sports offer children of all ages—_____ or not—the chance to exercise, be part of a team, and to form relationships they may not otherwise have. Working out not only helps to alleviate _____, it also helps teenagers overcome the _____ they may feel at times as they develop and change. It's important, however, that young people are not forced to play sports if they don't want to. It is thought that this can result in _____ psychological damage. They should not feel _____ being on a sports team; they should be on teams because they want to be. Being on a team can be helpful and stabilizing at a time when so many things in their lives seem _____. There's nothing like seeing a group of uniform-clad youngsters, heads together, _____ on winning, shouting as a group in a pre-game cheer. In addition, being part of a team, and sharing in both its _____ and failures, is a wonderful experience. Furthermore, though our presence on the sidelines may sometimes create embarrassment (we try not to behave too _____), our kids appreciate having us there. We remind them that no loss is ever too _____, and that in the end, we are all winners.

C Compare your answers with a partner. Do you agree with this view of the value of sports in young people's lives? Why or why not? Can you think of any other ways that playing sports can benefit our lives?

Think About It   Discuss the following questions with a partner.

1. *Have you ever found yourself in a situation comparable to Ronaldo's, where you have had to attempt to achieve something after failing to achieve it the first time? What happened?*
2. *How do you think sporting achievements mirror or reflect our achievements in life?*
3. *What lessons, if any, do you think we can learn about life from sports and sports players?*
4. *Do you think society places too much emphasis on sports players as our icons for success? Explain your answer.*

Before You Read:
Reaching the Summit

Discuss the following questions with a partner.

1. The two people in the photo above are famous mountain climbers. In 1953, they became the first people to reach the top of a well-known mountain. Can you name the mountain? Can you name these climbers?

2. Do you think some achievements in life can be compared to climbing a mountain? How and why?

3. The following words can all be found in the reading passage:

 summit   **expedition**   **conquer**   **crawling**

How do you think they relate to the topic of mountain climbing?

Reading Skill:
Developing Reading Fluency

When reading fluently, focus on what you CAN comprehend and not on what you can't. This will help you to read faster, and increase your overall comprehension ability.

Time yourself as you read through the passage. Try to read as fluently as you can. Record your time in the Reading Rate Chart on page 234.

Like Father, Like Son _____

The following reading is adapted from *Like Father, Like Son* by James M. Clash. Reprinted by permission of *Forbes Magazine* © 2002 Forbes Inc.

Jamling Tenzing Norgay grew up in the shadow of[1] his late father, Tenzing, who in 1953 made history by climbing Mount Everest with Sir Edmund Hillary. Jamling himself reached the summit as part of the 1996 expedition that filmed *Everest*, the blockbuster IMAX[2] movie. While at the top, Jamling
5 felt the strong presence of his father. It's no surprise, then, that his recent book is titled *Touching My Father's Soul*.

Did your father encourage you to climb Everest?

Jamling Tenzing: No. I even asked him to pull some strings so that I could climb with an Indian expedition, and he flatly said no. He climbed so that we wouldn't have to. Because he didn't have an education, he felt he needed to give us one. But the most surprising thing was that after my Everest climb, my uncles told me that Tenzing had always said I would climb that mountain, that I would follow in his footsteps. He knew it all along but never encouraged me. He wanted me to do it for myself, and by myself.

Did you climb any mountains with him when you were a kid?

Jamling Tenzing: B.C. Roy [a training peak] was one.

What did he say at the top?

Jamling Tenzing: He didn't talk much. But there was something about his smile. You can see a lot by a smile, and I could see that he was proud.

The Sherpa[3] view of climbing is different from the Western view.

Jamling Tenzing: We believe that mountains are places where the gods live, especially Mount Everest. Before we climb, we perform religious ceremonies to ask God for permission and safe passage. Sherpas don't have any interest in climbing mountains. Mostly they climb as a necessity, to make money. But the Western world looks at Everest as another rock and says, "Wow, this is the highest mountain. Let's go conquer it." You don't conquer Everest. You go on Everest just as if you are crawling into your mother's lap.[4]

Let's talk about the day you reached the summit of Mount Everest.

Jamling Tenzing: My desire to climb Everest grew even more after my father died in 1986. I wanted to climb to understand him. Throughout the whole climb, I thought about him. And, at a lot of places, I imagined what those guys had been thinking, where they might have slept. On the final day, halfway up from the South Col camp, I felt really strong. I felt my father was in front pulling me or behind pushing me, because I didn't know where this energy came from. When I finally got to the top, I took my goggles[5] and mask off and cried . . . I could see my dad there, right in front of me, with a big smile.

Was this the smile you saw on B.C. Roy?

Jamling Tenzing: Yes, exactly. And he was telling me, "You know, you didn't have to come this far." And then I realized I really didn't have to climb the mountain to understand him. The irony was that I had to climb the mountain to find out that I didn't have to climb the mountain. It's the experience that matters, not getting up there.

Who do you think got to the top of Everest first, your dad or Hillary?

Jamling Tenzing: Hillary says in his book that he stepped up there first. My father also went on to say that Hillary stepped first. My father climbed the mountain because it was something he had wanted to do all his life. He didn't want things to boil down to who climbed first because it was not important to him. I think the reason he said that Hillary climbed first was just to get rid of

50 the media and people asking him questions because he felt it shouldn't be brought down to that level. Fine, yeah, okay, Hillary climbed first.

Did you ever talk to him about it?
Jamling Tenzing: I did ask him before I came to the United States, and he said, "You know, it's not important, Jamling. We climbed as a team." I leave it
55 to the world to judge. My father had tried six times to climb this mountain. On the seventh attempt they were able to make it. He had been up the route before, so he had a lot of high-altitude experience. For Hillary, this was his first time on the mountain. I don't know how high Hillary had climbed before, but I don't think it was more than 6,700 meters. It is for people to
60 make up their own mind instead of me telling them, because I don't know. The Sherpas, Indians, Nepalese think that my father climbed first.

In your heart, was it your dad or Hillary who first stepped on top?
Jamling Tenzing: Well, as far as I'm concerned, it was my father. First, because he was my father. Second, he had more experience on the mountain.
65 But again, I'm no one to judge. He never told me that. My gut feeling says that maybe he was the one up there first. Those days, they were roped to each other. So the difference was what, only about a meter?

---

¹ **in the shadow of** under the dominating presence or influence of something or someone
² **IMAX** specially designed large-screen movie theaters that give the viewer the impression of being within the environment they can see on the screen
³ **Sherpa** Tibetan people who live in northern Nepal noted for their ability in mountain climbing; often employed by climbers as guides or assistants
⁴ **lap** front part of a person sitting from the body to the knees; usually a place of comfort and nurture
⁵ **goggles** tinted eyeglasses with side pieces to shield eyes worn usually for protection under water or against harsh weather conditions

---

Reading Comprehension: How Much Do You Remember?

(A) The following questions are all about the reading. Answer each one using information you have read. Try not to look back at the reading for the answers.

1. What inspired Jamling to title his book *Touching My Father's Soul*?
2. Why didn't Jamling's father encourage him to climb?
3. When Jamling and his father climbed B.C. Roy, what was his father's reaction?
4. How does the Sherpa view of climbing Mount Everest differ from the Western view?
5. Why do most Sherpas climb Everest?
6. Why did Jamling want to climb Everest?
7. What did Jamling learn from climbing Everest?
8. Why does Jamling think that his father, and not Hillary, may have stepped onto the summit of Everest first?

(B) Check your answers with a partner. Count how many you got correct—be honest! Then, fill in the Reading Comprehension Chart on page 234.

Vocabulary Comprehension: Word Definitions

A Look at the list of words and phrases from the reading. Match each one with a definition on the right.

1. summit _____
2. expedition _____
3. presence _____
4. pull some strings _____
5. flatly _____
6. permission _____
7. crawling _____
8. irony _____
9. boil down to _____
10. gut feeling _____

a. an often unexplainable emotional perception
b. firmly; completely and definitely
c. to exert control or influence for some kind of gain
d. supernatural feeling that something or someone is close
e. having the opposite meaning or outcome to what was expected
f. to reduce something to its basic point
g. moving slowly and closely to the ground
h. the highest point; the top
i. a journey taken for a specific purpose
j. consent; allowing something to happen

B Complete the sentences below using the vocabulary items from A. Be sure to use the correct form of each word.

1. My father drives me mad! Every time I ask him for _____ to use his car, he _____ refuses to give me the keys.

2. Although my grandmother passed away ten years ago, I still feel her _____ whenever the family gets together.

3. Life, as my grandfather always says, _____ one important ingredient: family.

4. You know, I had a _____ that Amanda's boyfriend was no good. It turned out he's married, and in trouble with the law.

5. Celine's research _____ to Antarctica was so successful she may go back again next year.

6. It's quite _____ that after Simon stormed out of the meeting and resigned, Alan announced he was selling the company.

7. We didn't think we'd be able to get concert tickets at all but Jefri's uncle _____ and we ended up with backstage passes!

8. While on holiday in Tokyo, we decided to climb Mount Fuji. It made me realize how unfit I am—we literally had to _____ up to the _____!

Vocabulary Skill: Idioms with Body Parts

In this unit, you read the idiom 'follow in (one's) footsteps;' in this chapter, the idiom 'gut feeling' appeared. An idiom is a fixed group of words that has a special, usually non-literal, meaning. There are many idioms that use the names of different body parts. Sometimes it is impossible to know what the idiom means by looking at the individual words, but it can be helpful to look at how the idiom is used in context in order to understand its meaning.

(A) Read the sentences below. The idiom in each one is in *italics*. Use the context of the idiom in the sentence to help you match each one with a definition underneath. Compare your answers with a partner.

1. Lena tried to remain calm, but in the end she just *lost her head*. _____
2. Paulo has to *face the music* after he was caught stealing his sister's pocket money. _____
3. Carmen looked all over the house for her keys only to find them *right under her nose*. _____
4. My definition of a good friend is 'someone who would *stick their neck out* for you.' _____
5. Mariko was so sweet to me when I first joined the office, but now she keeps *giving me the cold shoulder*. _____
6. Dennis wants everyone to meet in his office later. He looked quite annoyed earlier so I think there are a few things he wants to *get off his chest*. _____
7. Tim always seems very nice and friendly to everyone, but he has this terrible habit of *talking behind people's backs*. _____
8. When Alicia found out that both her children had lied to her she was *up in arms* over it, and grounded them for a month. _____
9. When I moved into my new apartment all my friends came over and *lent a hand*. The following week I threw a big dinner party to thank them all. _____
10. There's something very familiar about that man we just met. Right now, though, I can't quite *put my finger on* what it is. _____
11. Kou is such a prankster! He loves to *pull people's legs*. _____
12. The sofa in that shop would look great in my living room, but it *costs an arm and a leg*. _____

a. to be in plain view
b. to joke or tease
c. to let go of one's poise or self-control
d. to identify or remember something
e. to help out; offer assistance
f. to accept the unpleasant consequences, especially of one's own actions
g. to take a chance or risk on another's behalf
h. to be very expensive
i. to be extremely upset or angry about something
j. to ignore a person or treat them with neglect
k. to secretly gossip about someone
l. to discuss issues that are bothering one

B Now use some of the idioms from A to complete the paragraphs below. Be sure to use the correct verb form and pronoun in each idiom. Compare your answers with a partner.

New Adventures in Summer Camp

Tired of the same old camp every summer? Have you ever heard of practical joke camp? *Camp Joke-A-Lot* may seem like any other camp but, in fact, this camp, which offers no summer discounts (in fact it _____), is full of kids who want to be jokers. Here campers learn to keep their cool and not _____. There's always a friendly atmosphere—kids and counselors always _____ for each other. And, whenever someone needs it, they're ready to _____. Does this sound like the perfect place to spend your summer? Of course it does!

After a week at this camp you might think it's the best place on earth. However, let me warn you, something will happen midway through *Camp Joke-A-Lot* which you may not be able to _____. You will realize your decision to join this camp may not have been so wise after all! Suddenly, after they've been your friends, you'll notice that people will start _____. In addition, though they've been nice to your face until now, they might _____ about you _____ to everyone else. You might get _____ about it. You also might want to talk to people and _____. If they start to laugh at you, don't worry! Just remember, we're only _____!

C Do you have similar expressions for any of these idioms in your language? Do the expressions in your language use the same body parts? Think of some body idioms or expressions used in your language, and discuss with a partner how similar or different they are to expressions you have heard in English.

What Do You Think?

Discuss the following questions with a partner.

1. *Some people believe that in life, as in sport, the experience of taking part is more important than winning. Do you agree? Explain your answer.*

2. *How often do you get 'gut feelings' about things? Do you tend to trust your instincts?*

3. *Have you ever felt compelled to do something in order to be able to understand why someone else did it? If so, what was it? If not, do you think you would ever do something for this reason?*

4. *In this unit smiling is mentioned twice as a way of seeing what a person is feeling; in Ronaldo's case it was uneasiness, with Tenzing Norgay it was pride. What else can a smile hide or reveal about how a person is feeling?*

Real Life Skill

Reading the Sports News

Sports reports in the newspaper contain a lot of specialized terms, and writers try to make their reports lively by using words in unusual ways. To understand the sports news you need to know the specific terms that are used to describe the sport, and understand how they are used in context.

(A) Scan through the sports news below. Decide which sport each news item is reporting on and write the heading in the correct space above each report. You will not use all of the sports. Circle the words in each news item that tell you which sport is being reported.

tennis	basketball	car racing	boxing	baseball	cycling

1. _____

Chris Stewart beat the rest of the field yesterday at Indianapolis with a record qualifying lap at 182.9 miles per hour in his Ford, breaking his earlier record of 181.2 miles per hour. High temperatures made the 2.5 mile track hazardous.

2. _____

Suns pitchers struck out 17 Legends, and the Suns blazed out five home runs in the eighth inning on the way to their 7-3 victory last night at Winfield Park Stadium. But the Suns were not in top form, committing three errors in the third inning alone.

3. _____

Yoshiko Mori remains undefeated in the Lexington Classic, keeping her winning streak alive with a 6-3, 7-6 defeat of Justine Redmond last night. Mori hit several dazzling shots that kept Redmond dashing to the net.

4. _____

Jose Luis Diaz retained his middleweight title with a unanimous points victory over Marcus White in a 12-round fight in New York. Diaz has had 60 fights with 49 wins, 30 of them by knockout.

(B) Who won? Read the following sports headlines and check (✔) the name of the winning team. Use your dictionary if necessary.

1. The Royals mopped up the Dragons.   ____ Royals   ____ Dragons
2. The Cosmos tumbled to the Wildcats.   ____ Cosmos   ____ Wildcats
3. The Hurricanes gave in to the Blazers.   ____ Hurricanes   ____ Blazers
4. Centerville trounced Mapleton.   ____ Centerville ____ Mapleton
5. The Tigers dominated the Bulldogs.   ____ Tigers   ____ Bulldogs
6. Capital City was shut out by Metro.   ____ Capital City ____ Metro
7. The Titans walked over the Warriors.   ____ Titans   ____ Warriors

Home Sweet Home

Getting Ready

Discuss the following questions with a partner.

1. *What kind of home do most people in your country live in?*
2. *What kind of home do you live in? Describe it.*
3. *What other types of buildings do people in your country live in?*
4. *Do people tend to commute long distances to school or work where you live, or do they live close to their school or workplace?*

Before You Read:
Ideal Homes

Discuss the following questions with a partner.

1. What are houses in your country usually made of? What materials are commonly used to decorate the interior of homes in your country?

2. Are there a lot of differences between the construction of old houses and modern homes in your country? If so, what are the main differences?

3. How long do houses in your country usually last? Do you know when the oldest building in your country or city was constructed? What is it made of?

4. Look at the title of the reading. What do you think a house designed to save the earth would be constructed from?

5. Which of the following words and phrases do you think will be in the passage? Why?

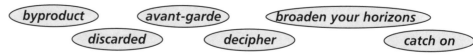

byproduct   avant-garde   broaden your horizons
        discarded   decipher   catch on

Reading Skill:
Identifying Meaning from Context

You can guess the meaning of important but unfamiliar words in a reading passage by using the following strategy:
1. Think about how the new word is related to the topic of what you are reading about. **2.** Identify which part of speech the new word is by looking at how it fits with the other words in its sentence.
3. Look at how the word relates to the rest of the information in the paragraph surrounding it.
4. Use your knowledge of prefixes, suffixes, and word roots to identify the basic meaning of the word.

(A) The following is an extract from the reading passage. As you read through it, think about the topic of the reading, and what you already know about this topic. Pay attention to the underlined words and think about how they fit with the topic.

> The average wood-framed house, after all, uses an astonishing 11,000 board feet (38.3 cubic meters) of lumber—enough, (1) <u>stacked</u> end to end, to top three Empire State Buildings. But the number of large-diameter trees used to supply this wood has steadily declined, and in addition to the environmental consequences, the (2) <u>diminishing</u> supply has led to a significant rise in the average price of lumber.

(B) Decide which part of speech each underlined word is, and write them below.

(1) _____   (2) _____

How do you know this? Circle the words in the sentence that work with or affect the underlined words, and tell you the part of speech. Look at how the word relates to the rest of the paragraph. Are there any other words or phrases that give you clues for the meaning of each word? If so, circle them.

(C) Now look at the parts of the words. Does each one have a recognizable prefix, root, or suffix? Use your knowledge of these word parts to try and identify the meaning of each word. Replace each one with a word or phrase, or write a definition.

(1) _____   (2) _____

(D) Use your dictionary to check you have interpreted the meaning of the words correctly. Share your answers with a partner.

Ⓔ Look at the words in the chart below. Using the line references, locate each word in the passage and underline it.

Vocabulary	Part of Speech	Definition
1. byproduct (line 6)	_____	_____
2. discarded (line 39)	_____	_____
3. identical (line 42)	_____	_____
4. brutal (line 44)	_____	_____
5. flawlessly (line 45)	_____	_____
6. substitute (line 52)	_____	_____

Ⓕ Using the same strategies you practiced above, identify the part of speech of each word. Look at how each one fits into the sentences or paragraph around it. Look at the parts of each word and try to work out the meaning. Replace them with words or phrases you know that have the same meaning, or write a definition. Share your answers with a partner, and use your dictionary to check your interpretations and definitions.

Ⓖ Now read through the passage again, and complete the comprehension exercise that follows.

A House to Save the Earth _____

The following reading is adapted from *Houses to Save the Earth* by Seth Shulman. Reprinted with permission from PARADE, copyright © 1996.

"You are walking on the casings of used fluorescent bulbs,"[1] says Steven Loken, pointing to the ceramic floor tiles in his bathroom. The rich blue tiles around the bathtub were made from recycled car windshield glass. It's the kind of detail Loken loves to volunteer about the dream house he built on the outskirts of Missoula, Montana.[2] In the kitchen, the sink looks like it is made of stone, but Loken explains   5
that it was molded from granite[3] dust—a byproduct left when granite is extracted from the earth. The carpets upstairs were once plastic milk containers. From the foundation to the roof tiles, the house is made almost entirely of recycled materials.

Despite the sound of it, the house doesn't look strange or avant-garde. In fact, without Loken's descriptions, a visitor would never guess the origins of the   10
materials—a feature he says was important when he set out to build his recycled house. "I wanted to show that you could use recycled building materials without making any compromises on the type of house most Americans want," says Loken. "This meant that the place had to look like any other house if the ideas behind it were going to catch on."   15

Since his house was completed, Loken's efforts have caught on in ways he never imagined, contributing to one of the country's hottest trends in house construction. In fact, over the past few years, Loken has become something of a guru[4] to an alternative-materials movement among builders. He travels the country regularly giving lectures about his building techniques. So far, 12,000 people, including   20
architects and builders from around the world, have visited his home.

Why make houses from recycled materials? To Loken it is a question of using the earth's resources efficiently. The average wood-framed house, after all, uses an astonishing 11,000 board feet (38.3 cubic meters) of lumber—enough, stacked end
25 to end, to top three Empire State Buildings. But the number of large-diameter trees used to supply this wood has steadily declined, and in addition to the environmental consequences, the diminishing supply has led to a significant rise in the average price of lumber.

But, as Loken puts it, builders are conservative when choosing materials, preferring
30 reliable alternatives. He realized that if he was going to change attitudes he would have to do something about it himself. "I realized I was part of the problem every time I blindly followed building practices that were inherently wasteful," he says.

The result was Loken's own house, in which he used recycled materials in virtually every part of construction. The house's insulation,[5] for instance, is made from a
35 byproduct of shredded[6] newspaper. Instead of using cement in the concrete for the foundation, he used a waste product from power stations. Loken used one-sixth of the wood required to frame a conventional house of the same size. The wood he did use was either salvaged[7] or 'composite' lumber made from the chips of slender trees, which are normally discarded.

40 For Loken, an important part of the project has been to live in the house with his family, testing the products over time. He says he has learned some lessons the hard way: The recycled sawdust[8] and cement tiles he used on his roof look identical to rock and came with a 50-year guarantee. But they are beginning to come off after five years of Montana's brutal climate. So far, however, most of the products Loken
45 used have worked flawlessly. And though it has a furnace,[9] the house is so energy-efficient that it can stay comfortable in winter with just ambient heat (from cooking, body heat, and other existing sources) and solar heat (enhanced by the home's southern exposure).

As an outgrowth of his building efforts, Loken founded an organization called the
50 Center for Resourceful Building Technology. The center serves as a clearinghouse[10] for new ideas about building materials, complete with samples of everything from strawboard (a plywood[11] substitute made from straw), to a wood-like material made from soybeans.

In the past several years, a half-dozen demonstration homes like Loken's have
55 followed his initial effort. All have offered builders a look at the new materials and have proved that competitively priced homes—which look and feel as solid, safe, and appealing as any other on the market—can be built today from recycled materials.

Loken is focusing more on affordability in his latest project—building a new, low-cost, resource-efficient house. Like his own home, this one uses considerably less
60 wood than the average home and incorporates many recycled products. This time the goal is also to meet or beat the cost of a comparable home that uses conventional materials.

Loken notes proudly that he has prospective clients from all over the United States.

He says he is happy to see many recycled building materials being used but views some of them as only temporary solutions. "I'm interested in cutting down on waste altogether and making more intelligent use of our resources," he says. The key is in turning one industry's waste into another's raw materials.

65

---

¹ **fluorescent bulbs** tubular light bulbs that emit bright light as a result of radiation absorption and emission
² **Missoula, Montana** city and state in the northern United States
³ **granite** a hard, grainy, light-colored rock often used for buildings and monuments
⁴ **guru** a spiritual leader or teacher; a leader or expert in a particular area
⁵ **insulation** material used to protect against loss of heat or cold
⁶ **shredded** cut or torn into small pieces
⁷ **salvaged** saved from being destroyed
⁸ **sawdust** small wood particles left over after wood is cut
⁹ **furnace** a heavy container for burning fuel, especially for heat
¹⁰ **clearinghouse** an office where checks, information, or accounts are processed
¹¹ **plywood** material made of thin layers of wood glued firmly together for strength

---

Reading Comprehension: What Do You Remember?

The following statements are all about the reading. Complete each one using information you have read.

1. Although Mr. Loken's house is made primarily of recycled materials, it doesn't look _____ or unusual compared to other homes in the United States.

2. Mr. Loken's ideas are leading an _____ movement among builders.

3. Loken built his home to show how building contractors can use the earth's _____ more efficiently.

4. Home builders usually choose _____ alternatives when selecting materials.

5. Loken realized that in order to change _____ he needed to set an example through his own house.

6. Loken _____ in the house with his family in order to _____ the recycled materials.

7. Loken founded an organization to share new ideas, and _____ of building materials.

8. The next step for Mr. Loken is to focus on the _____ of building his houses to show that these houses can be as affordable as conventional homes.

Vocabulary Comprehension: Odd Word Out

(A) For each group, circle the word that does not belong. The words in *italics* are vocabulary items from the reading.

1. *molded*	shaped	undone	fashioned
2. novel	old-fashioned	original	*avant-garde*
3. misunderstandings	*compromises*	concessions	agreements

4. *catch on*	popularize	take hold	fade
5. orthodox	traditional	*conservative*	outlandish
6. intrinsically	*inherently*	naturally	temporarily
7. *slender*	slim	thin	large
8. surrounding	separating	atmospheric	*ambient*
9. spinoff	*outgrowth*	development	division
10. much	by far	severely	*considerably*

Ⓑ Complete the sentences using the words in *italics* from A. Be sure to use the correct form of each word.

1. What I love most about this house is the _____ dining room. It reminds me of a room in a haunted castle.

2. My mother always told me that a good marriage is like any partnership; in order for it to work, both parties must make _____.

3. Even though the school holidays began yesterday, there doesn't seem to be _____ less traffic on the roads.

4. Nobody ever thought that a take-away steakhouse would _____ in this neighborhood, but the place is packed every lunchtime.

5. As an _____ of her design company, Stella has launched a style consultancy that is managed by her sister.

6. Paul loves traditional literature, but his taste in poetry is more _____.

7. Many people who don't have children believe that you can _____ a child to become anything you want. However, once you're a parent you realize how children have their own _____ personalities.

8. When you see him out at the weekend in his ripped jeans and leather jacket, it's hard to believe that on weekdays Shun dresses in such _____ clothes.

9. You can use these _____ vases to hold just one or two roses to decorate the table.

Vocabulary Skill:
Synonyms

A synonym is a word or phrase that has the same meaning as another word or phrase. One way of increasing your vocabulary is by learning synonyms.

Ⓐ Look at the words in the chart below. Write a short definition for each one. For those words you are not sure about, use your knowledge of prefixes, suffixes, and root words to try and figure out the meaning. Use your dictionary to check your answers.

Vocabulary	Definition	Synonym
1. unusual	_____	_____
2. endeavors	_____	_____
3. selecting	_____	_____
4. dependable	_____	_____
5. reside	_____	_____

Vocabulary	Definition	Synonym
6. intensified	_____	_____
7. enticing	_____	_____
8. concentrating	_____	_____
9. short-term	_____	_____
10. converting	_____	_____

B Now scan through the reading and find words or phrases that are synonymous with the words in the chart. Write them in the Synonyms column.

C Complete the paragraph below using the words from the Vocabulary column in A. Be sure to use the correct form of each word.

Local news A new trend in house building is emerging. A company called Eco-builders is designing and constructing new 'Reco' homes by _____ waste products from industry into building materials. These Reco (which stands for recycled-ecological) homes are becoming increasing popular thanks to the _____ of Eco-builders in promoting them. Last week the company _____ its sales campaign by running full-page advertisements in all the local newspapers, and _____ numerous households for a follow-up survey on their views of the homes. They hope to _____ more people who currently _____ in this area to take a look at their Reco homes. Eco-builders are _____ their advertising efforts on people who are open-minded to the concept of living in a house made primarily of recycled materials. Although the houses have proven to be safe and _____ (the company CEO lives in one), many people think they are too _____ and will not consider buying one. Eco-builders still hopes to persuade some of these people into changing their point of view, although they say that this ad campaign is, for the time being, _____ only.

Think About It   Discuss the following questions with a partner.

1. *In which country or city in the world would you most like to live? Why?*

2. *Describe your dream home. Where is it located and how many rooms does it have? Who lives there?*

3. *Would you like to live in the house described in the reading? Why or why not?*

4. *What do you think are the advantages and disadvantages of using recycled products to construct homes? Do you think the construction techniques described in the reading will ever catch on in your country? Why or why not?*

Before You Read:
Domestic Bliss!

Discuss the following questions with a partner.

1. Who do you live with at the moment? Are you comfortable with your living arrangement or would you like to change it?

2. Have you ever lived in a house or apartment on your own? What, in your view, are the advantages and disadvantages of having your own place?

3. Did you have a bedroom to yourself when you were a child or did you share a room with siblings? What were the advantages and disadvantages to this?

4. Look at the title of the reading. The following words and phrases can all be found in the passage:

sink or swim   butting in   undeniable   bearable   domesticated

How do you think they relate to the topic of the reading? Use your knowledge of prefixes, suffixes, and word roots, as well as your dictionary, to help you determine the meaning of each of these words and phrases.

Reading Skill:
Developing
Reading
Fluency

Remember to put the reading skills you learn and practice with the chapter one readings to good use with each chapter two reading. When you come across new words in this reading, use the strategies to identify meaning from context outlined in chapter one.

Time yourself as you read through the passage. Try to read as fluently as you can. Record your time in the Reading Rate Chart on page 234.

A Room of My Own _____

The following reading is adapted from *A Room of My Own* by Kathryn O'Halloran. Reprinted with permission of *Digs Magazine* © February 4, 2002; http://www.digsmagazine.com/lounge/lounge_aroomofmyown.htm

I was six years old the first time I felt the freedom of my own home. On a dull rainy day, with the help of some old bedspreads and a few towels, I built my own little house under the kitchen table. I furnished it with sofa cushions and filled it with books and supplies. I added a big door and put up a sign to say

5 that visitors were by invitation only. I didn't want anyone butting in and disturbing my peace. It was heaven to me since I had never even had a bedroom of my own. Sadly my little house had to be dismantled[1] far too soon —the table was needed for dinner—but for many years to come I dreamed about a place of my own.

It was a long time until I actually got a whole apartment to myself though. I suffered through years of living at home with argumentative sisters, then roommates both good and bad. Finally, I took control of my life and moved into a place by myself. It was scary, exhilarating, and very grown up: I would now sink or swim on my own.

This was it—pure freedom. I could decorate it with all the things I loved without ever having to accommodate someone else's collection of cat ornaments or knick knacks.[2] I could crank up[3] the stereo and sing at the top of my lungs. I could spend as long as I liked in the shower, or take a bath in the middle of the night. I could do what I wanted, when I wanted.

But when the euphoria died down I had to face some cold, hard facts. It's an undeniable truth that it costs a lot more to live alone than to share. Unlike that first little house under the table, this apartment came with a big, ugly rent bill. The apartment might have been all mine, but so was the rent, and the utility bills. There were other problems too. Not being very domesticated I easily let things slip. It was so easy to think that I didn't need to cook meals or bother too much with housework; after all, nobody would notice but me. But the danger of being able to do whatever you want is, actually, doing whatever you want, even when it's ill-advised. Spending a huge chunk of the budget on takeout meals. Flirting with malnutrition[4] when you decide to survive on canned soup, for example. Not to mention huge piles of dirty dishes and laundry.

So it took me some time to learn how to keep things running smoothly in this apartment of mine. I decided to use some common sense rules to keep the bills down. I got into the habit of turning off the computer, television, and radio the minute I was finished with them. I learned to put on extra clothing instead of running the heater unnecessarily. In the summer I would much rather cool off out in the shade than be stuck inside with electric fans or air conditioning.

I learned to cook efficiently for one. Half the battle, I discovered, was in the planning. If the cupboards were filled with all the essentials and the fridge with lots of yummy vegetables, then making a quick and simple dinner wasn't such a chore. As long as I shop sensibly and keep the kitchen stocked, I can throw together a stir-fry or pasta in minutes. The other half of the battle was purely mental: convincing myself that I'm worth cooking for. Cooking, I learned, doesn't have to be tied to entertaining. I still love making a meal that's going to win me admiration, but I can make a good meal for myself and sometimes even set up the table nicely with fresh flowers, instead of eating in front of the TV.

As for housework, that's been a whole other ball game.[5] Living on your own might mean less work to do, but it also means less people to pitch in. And

55

60

nothing could ever make doing the housework bearable. Unfortunately, it's one of those things that you can do frequently with minimal effort, or infrequently with a whole lot of work. And if you put off doing it until the mess has reached monstrous proportions, you're asking for trouble. So as much as I loathe it, I've fallen into the routine of spending Saturday mornings doing housework, then I'm free for the rest of the weekend. Once the dishes are done, the laundry is hung out, and the floors are swept clean, my apartment instantly feels like a better place to be. Which was the whole point of moving out on my own in the first place: creating a little somewhere nice for me to live.

65

Nothing beats sitting down with a good book, the house sparkling clean, the phone off the hook, and nobody in the world to disturb you. Despite all the hassles, I love living on my own. It may lack the charm of that little house under the table from long ago, but it's all mine and I'm not sharing.

¹ **dismantled** taken apart
² **knick knacks** small decorative ornaments usually of little monetary value
³ **crank up** colloquial expression meaning 'turn up the volume'
⁴ **malnutrition** condition in which the body is poorly nourished usually as a result of being severely underfed
⁵ **a whole other ball game** an entirely different subject or issue

Ⓐ The following questions are all about the reading. Answer each one using the information you have read. Try not to look back at the reading for the answers.

1. Where did the author 'build' her first house?
2. Why did she find this 'house' so pleasant?
3. What is one disadvantage the author gives for living with other people?
4. What is one disadvantage the author gives for living alone?
5. What is one way the author mentions of keeping her household expenses low?
6. The author mentions putting on extra clothing. Why did she do this?
7. The author learned to cook more efficiently. What was the key to her success in doing this?
8. How does the author successfully tackle the housework?

Ⓑ Check your answers with a partner. Count how many you got correct—be honest! Then, fill in the Reading Comprehension Chart on page 234.

Ⓐ The words in *italics* are vocabulary items from the reading. Read each question or statement and choose the correct answer. Compare your answers with a partner.

1. Which is an example of *butting in*?
   a. leaving people alone
   b. interfering in other people's business

2. Which expression shares the same meaning as *sink or swim*?
   a. Do or die!
   b. Keep trying!

3. If someone has a feeling of *euphoria*, which emotion would he or she be feeling?
   a. extreme sadness
   b. extreme happiness

4. A synonym for *undeniable* is _____.
   a. indisputable
   b. inaccurate

5. Someone who enjoys *flirting* with danger would most likely enjoy _____.
   a. extreme sports
   b. hiking

6. An example of *common sense* is _____.
   a. predicting the future
   b. not walking in front of moving traffic

7. If someone tells you to *pitch in*, they want you to _____.
   a. help out with something
   b. join a baseball game

8. Which is more *bearable*?
   a. relaxing on a tropical beach
   b. vacuuming on an extremely hot day

9. If you *loathe* something, you _____.
   a. adore it
   b. abhor it

10. Which job would probably give someone more *hassles*?
    a. police officer
    b. dishwasher

(B) **Now think of other examples using the vocabulary from A. Discuss your ideas with a partner.**

1. Is *butting in* on someone else's business ever necessary? Give examples.

2. Have you ever been in a *sink or swim* situation? What happened? If not, think of an example of a *sink or swim* situation.

3. Have you ever felt a sense of *euphoria*? When and why?

4. What are some *undeniable* truths about your hometown or country?

5. What do you think *flirting* with disaster means? Give an example.

6. Name one situation when *common sense* is very important.

7. What kinds of things do people in your community do to *pitch in* and help others?

8. What is something that you *loathe* doing?

9. How can you make doing the thing you loathe more *bearable*?

10. What are some study-related *hassles* that you have experienced? How did you get around them?

Vocabulary Skill: Idioms with *House* and *Home*

> *In this chapter, you read the idiom 'sink or swim.' An idiom is a fixed group of words that has a special meaning. Many idioms can be grouped by the particular words that they use. For example, there are many idioms that use the word 'house' or 'home.' Sometimes it's possible to know what the idiom means by looking at the individual words, but not always. Looking at how the idiom is used in the context of the sentence can also help you to understand its meaning.*

(A) **Each sentence below contains an idiom, highlighted in *italics*. Read each one and, using the context, write a short definition of the idiom. Share your answers with a partner.**

1. The play last night was OK, but really nothing to *write home about*.

    _____

2. This has been a huge project but we're *in the home stretch* with it now. It should be complete in the next few weeks.

    _____

3. Our trip to the countryside was wonderful! The cottage we stayed in was so comfortable—a real *home away from home*.

    _____

4. I don't mind having Jamie's friends over on the weekend, as long as I know they're coming in advance. They *eat us out of house and home* so I always have to stock up the refrigerator.

    _____

5. We were going to pay a design company to make our corporate brochure, but our own editors came up with such great ideas we've decided to do it *in-house* instead.

    _____

6. I met my new boss yesterday and we *got on like a house on fire*. We had so much to talk about that our lunch meeting lasted three hours.

    _____

7. Joe's act at the comedy club is great, and the audience loves him. He always manages to *bring the house down*.

    _____

8. Julius has to pass one more exam before he's *home free* and able to graduate from medical school.

    _____

9. Sam and Melinda are getting married. When she crashed her car it really *brought it home* to him how much he loves her. He proposed in the emergency room!

   _____

10. Ben seems to think he can tell everyone in the office what to do. He needs to learn a few *home truths* about his behavior.

    _____

Ⓑ Complete the following dialogs using some of the idioms from A. Share your ideas with a partner.

1. **A:** How did you get along with Steve last night?
   B: _____. He's a great guy.

2. **A:** How was your weekend at the beach?
   B: Great. The place we stayed at was _____.

3. **A:** How's the new house coming along?
   B: It's almost finished. We're _____.

4. **A:** Satoshi has such a huge appetite!
   B: I know. Every time he comes over he _____.

Ⓒ Answer the questions below, then discuss your answers with a partner.

1. Have you done anything recently that you thought was worth writing home about?
2. Have you ever stayed in holiday accommodation that was a real home away from home?
3. Name one person you get on with like a house on fire.
4. Do you know anyone who needs to be told a few home truths about something? Why?

What Do You Think?

Discuss the following questions with a partner.

1. *Do you think the author of the reading in this chapter makes the idea of having your own apartment sound appealing? Why?*
2. *How old do you think the author is? If she were living in your country, would her living arrangement be the same or different?*
3. *At what age do most people in your country move away from home and get their own place? Initially, do they usually rent or buy a place?*
4. *Who usually does the household chores and takes care of household issues in your home? How much do you help out?*

Real Life Skill

Reading Real Estate Ads

Many people who want to buy a house begin by reading the real estate advertisements in newspapers. These ads generally use a lot of abbreviations since they must describe all the details of the house in a limited space. Being familiar with these abbreviations is useful when looking for a house or an apartment in an English-speaking country.

(A) Read the following ad for a home for rent, and try to figure out the meaning of the abbreviations.

> Hartland Hills—Lovely new townhouse avail now. 3 BR, 2BA, fully furn, eat-in kit w/all appliances, A/C, 2-car gar + sm yard. No pets. $950/mo + deposit. Call 555-9876.

avail _____   w/ _____

BR _____   A/C _____

BA _____   gar _____

furn _____   sm _____

kit _____   mo _____

(B) Would this be a good place for you to live? Tell your partner why or why not.

(C) Now read this ad for a house for sale.

> **500 Woodfield Rd.**
> Beautifully decorated, great loc, and only three yo. 2-story home w/bsmt, 4 BR, 3 BA. Hardwood flrs in LR, DR, hall. Lrg kit w/door to yard. Home ofc + BA in bsmt. Approx. 2,548 sq ft. Call June Johnson Realtors, 555-8282.

(D) Using the information you have read, answer the questions below. Write the words or abbreviations from the ad that gave you the answer.

1. How old is the house? _____

2. How many floors or levels does it have? _____

3. How many bedrooms are there? _____

4. How many bathrooms are in the house? _____

5. In which rooms or areas of the house are the floors wooden?

   _____

6. What is in the basement? _____

7. Is the kitchen big or small? _____

(E) Would you like to live in this house? Why or why not?

A Good Read

Getting Ready

Discuss the following questions with a partner.

1. *How many different genres of literature can you name? Which genre do you read the most?*

2. *On average, how much time do you spend reading each week? How much of this time is spent reading academic material? How much of this time is spent reading for pleasure?*

3. *How much of the material you read is written in your first language? How much is written in English?*

4. *What do you generally look for in a book when you are choosing something to read?*

Chapter 1: What Exactly IS a Short Story?

Before You Read:
The Art of Reading

Discuss the following questions with a partner.

1. Do you usually read one book at a time, or do you read several different books at a time?

2. What was the last book you finished? Who wrote it? What was it about? Briefly explain the story.

3. How often do you read short stories? What do you understand to be the main differences between a short story and a novel?

4. What do you think are the main differences between a short story and a poem?

5. The following words can all be found in the reading:

(facet (line 17))　(precision (line 20))　(unity (line 52))　(intensity (line 53))

Using the line references, locate each word in the passage. Using the meaning from context strategies outlined on page 58, identify what these words mean.

Reading Skill:
Recognizing Simile and Metaphor

Good writers choose their words very carefully. Often, the words that an author chooses describe an image that expresses their ideas, and can help the reader understand them better. These images can be expressed as 'similes' or 'metaphors.' Similes are figures of speech in which direct comparisons are made between two things, illustrated by the use of 'like,' or 'as,' for example, 'love is like a bed of roses.' Metaphors are figures of speech that suggest a comparison is being made between two things by describing how one thing resembles another, for example, 'love is a battlefield.'

Ⓐ Read through the following paragraph taken from the reading passage. Look at the underlined sections. Which is an example of a simile, and which is an example of a metaphor? Write your answer below. Which words tell you this?

In a recent class I was asked "What is a short story?" My first answer was that it was something that could be read in one sitting and brought (1) an illumination to the reader, sudden and golden (2) like sunlight cracking through heavy cloud. I went on to say that in my opinion a 'real' short story was closer to poetry than to the novel.

(1) _____   (2) _____

1. Which example compares reading a short story to experiencing the light of understanding?

2. Which example compares the light of understanding to sunlight appearing through the clouds?

Ⓑ Now go to paragraph three and find an example of simile OR metaphor. Circle the correct choice below, then write the words that tell you which it is.

Simile / Metaphor: _____

What two things does the writer compare in this example?

Ⓒ Now work with a partner to find other examples of simile or metaphor in the paragraphs numbered below. Write them in the space provided.

Paragraph 4
Simile / Metaphor: _____

What two things does the writer compare here?

Paragraph 6
Simile / Metaphor: _____

What two things does the writer compare here?

Paragraph 9
Simile / Metaphor: _____

What two things does the writer compare here?

Paragraph 10
Simile / Metaphor: _____

What two things does the writer compare here?

(E) Now read through the passage again and answer the comprehension questions that follow.

What Exactly IS a Short Story?_____

The following reading is adapted from *What IS a Short Story?* by Alex Keegan. Reprinted with permission of the author © 1999.

1   In a recent class I was asked "What is a short story?" My first answer was that it was something that could be read in one sitting and brought an illumination to the reader, sudden and golden like sunlight cracking through heavy cloud. I went on to say that in my opinion a 'real' short story was closer to poetry than to the novel.   5

2   Not all my students were convinced. Let's discuss word count: when is a short story too long to still be a short? Is there an official point where a short becomes a novella,[1] another where a novella becomes a novel? Is Hemingway's *The Old Man & the Sea* truly a novel? Let's set an arbitrary limit of words. For now let's agree that stories up to 10,000 words in length are short stories.   10

3   I'm not trying to be definitive here, so let's look at some definitions of the short story. My favorite is Benét's, "something that can be read in an hour and remembered for a lifetime." One writer said, "the theme of a novel will not fit into the framework of a short story; it's like trying to squeeze a mural[2] into the frame of a miniature.[3] And as in a miniature painting, the details need to be   15 sharp."

4   The short story is an example of one facet of human nature. Often a character undergoes some event and experiences something that offers him or her change. This is why it's said that short stories usually 'say something,' often a small something, but sometimes delivered with such precision that the effect is   20 exquisite, even a life-moment for some readers, something similar to a religious experience or to witnessing a never-to-be-repeated scene in nature.

5   The perfect short story is written with a poet's sensitivity for language, with a poet's precision. The shape and sounds and rhythms of the words are more commonly part of the effect than they usually are in the novel. Just as in a   25 poem, the bare words themselves are never the complete meaning. They interact with each other. Their sounds do things. How they are placed on the page matters. The poem tries to create a piece of truth, an insight into being human, and the form is so tight, so sparse that we can argue over exact meanings long into the night.   30

6   One reason for the confusion students often have over the definition of short

35 stories is that other word forms, anecdotes,[4] sketches, vignettes,[5] or slices of life often find their ways into them. These are often pretty and faintly moving, but somehow they leave us with a slightly unsatisfied feeling. The less words we use, below a certain point—let's imagine this point is 1,500 words—the harder it is to have something clearly happen to a character, and have that occurrence change him or her.

7   So, for now, under 10,000 words at the long end of short stories, but how short? Are we saying under 1,500 words is not a short story? Great writers can
40 do in 600 words what a solid writer might manage in 1,100. Maybe at 500 words, the confinement begins to create a new form, often very interesting, but more of an intellectual exercise; literary showing off rather than a natural giving of truth.

8   In the United Kingdom, there's an annual competition for 'stories,' complete in
45 exactly fifty words. Here is one: *Frank believed in his luck. Frank smoked too much but he knew he'd never die of a heart attack or lung-cancer. Frank smoked all the time. One day there was a gas leak in Frank's kitchen. Frank went to fix it. He didn't die of a heart attack or lung-cancer.*

9   It's fun and sort of complete, but it isn't likely to find a place in our hearts and
50 change our outlook on life. Technically it's a story, and short it definitely is, but 'short story,' I argue, it is not.

10 There is a degree of unity in a well thought out short story, one I tend to call its theme. This kind of intensity in a novel would indeed tire the reader. But in the one-sitting contract with the reader of a short story, it is presumed that he
55 or she will cope. Hence, when the story has quality, often the experience seems profound.

11 OK, so let's form a definition here: A short story is a narrative,[6] rarely over 10,000 words or below 500 words—more commonly 1,500–5,000 words—a single-sitting read, but with enough time and weight to move the reader. It is
60 narrow and focused to produce a singular effect through the story, most commonly through events affecting some change, or denial of change, in an individual. All aspects of a short story are closely integrated and cross-reinforcing;[7] language, point of view, tone and mood, the sounds as well as the meanings of the words, and their rhythm.

65 12 Writer Isabelle Allende once wrote: "Novels are, for me, adding up details, just work, work, work, then you're done. Short stories are more difficult—they have to be perfect, complete in themselves."

¹ **novella** a story that is longer than a short story but shorter than a novel
² **mural** a large work of art usually applied directly onto a wall
³ **miniature** a small painting containing a great amount of detail
⁴ **anecdotes** short, interesting or amusing stories
⁵ **vignettes** /vɪnyɛts/ short, descriptive scenes from a story
⁶ **narrative** the telling of a story
⁷ **cross-reinforcing** relating to each other and adding to each other's meaning

Reading Comprehension: What Do You Remember?

Use the information you have read to select the correct answer to each statement. Try not to look back at the reading for the answers.

1. We can infer from the opening paragraph that the author is a _____.
   a. teacher
   b. poet
   c. student
   d. painter

2. According to the author the ideal short story should be _____.
   a. at least 10,000 words in length
   b. below 500 words
   c. under 1,500 words
   d. around 1,500 to 5,000 words

3. The author suggests that in a short story the main character _____.
   a. experiences a change
   b. falls in love
   c. is confident and strong
   d. is intense

4. Well-written short stories have a sensitivity for _____.
   a. poetry
   b. unity
   c. language
   d. life

5. Included in a short story may be all the following *except* _____.
   a. anecdotes
   b. vignettes
   c. novellas
   d. sketches

6. The author considers the unifying concept of a short story to be its _____.
   a. word length
   b. theme
   c. religious experience
   d. satisfaction to the reader

7. By stating, "Great writers can do in 600 words what a solid writer might manage in 1,100," the author means that _____.
   a. great writers do not have a large vocabulary
   b. good writers have to practice making their stories shorter
   c. good writers are not following the rules for writing short stories
   d. great writers can say things better using fewer words

8. The title of this reading suggests that _____.
   a. defining the characteristics of a short story is not an easy task
   b. a short story is definitively similar to poetry
   c. writers intuitively know how to write short stories
   d. short stories are similar in definition to other forms of writing

Vocabulary Comprehension: Odd Word Out

Ⓐ For each group circle the word that does not belong. The words in *italics* are vocabulary items from the reading.

1. broadness	vagueness	obscurity	*precision*
2. *arbitrary*	subjective	discretionary	objective
3. perspective	*facet*	aspect	falsehood
4. horrific	elegant	*exquisite*	beautiful
5. dense	thin	scant	*sparse*
6. *showing off*	flaunting	disporting	inhibiting
7. limitation	freedom	*confinement*	restriction
8. association	separation	connection	*unity*
9. plenitude	depth	*intensity*	frailty
10. *profound*	indelible	superficial	intense

Ⓑ Complete the sentences using the words in *italics* from A. Be sure to use the correct form of the word.

1. Oh, how irritating! Here comes Margo _____ her brand new company car.

2. During his interview, Chris answered the questions with such _____ that the interviewers could not fail to be impressed.

3. This book is so true to my own life that reading it was a _____ emotional experience.

4. I really don't think Jun thought about these sales figures at all. I'm sure he must have picked some _____ numbers out of thin air.

5. Some people find it easy to work in this small office, others feel too restricted by the _____.

6. These days it seems that audiences prefer the _____ of action that fast-paced movies provide.

7. Just one _____ of our business is to provide online training for employees.

8. _____ of ideas is important, not only in stories, but for any written work to make sense.

9. Natasha has created a minimalist home. She's decorated as _____ as she can and, I must admit, the house has a certain elegance about it.

10. Everybody has different taste in home furnishings. What one person considers to be _____, another might think is horrendous.

A Study each word in the chart below. Using your knowledge of prefixes and suffixes, write the part of speech and a simple definition for each one. Use your dictionary to help you. Share your answers with a partner.

Vocabulary Skill:
The Root Word *scribe*

The root word 'scribe,' also written as 'scrip' or 'script,' comes from the Latin word 'scribere,' meaning 'to write.' Many words in English that are related to writing contain this root so it is a useful one to know.

Vocabulary	Part of Speech	Definition
1. subscribe	_____	_____
2. manuscript	_____	_____
3. postscript	_____	_____
4. scribble	_____	_____
5. prescription	_____	_____
6. describe	_____	_____
7. superscript	_____	_____
8. inscription	_____	_____
9. transcribe	_____	_____
10. conscript	_____	_____

B Now use some of the words from A to complete the sentences below. Be sure to use the correct form of the appropriate word.

1. Who _____ on my folder? It's covered in ink now!
2. Read the _____ on this stone. This building is over 500 years old!
3. In every letter or e-mail she sends, Emily adds a _____ and writes a joke.
4. Do you _____ to this magazine or did you buy it at the newsstand?
5. Most actors like to receive their _____ to read over before rehearsals begin.
6. From the way Steven _____ his girlfriend, you'd think she were a model.
7. I don't believe it. I only have a sore throat but this _____ is for three different medications!

C Now ask and answer the following questions with a partner.

1. Do you subscribe to any newspapers, magazines, or web sites? Which ones?
2. Do you ever add postscripts to letters or e-mails?
3. Describe a member of your family—his or her appearance and character.
4. When was the last time you had to get a prescription from the doctor?

Think About It Discuss the following questions with a partner.

1. *Look over the reading again. How many ways is a short story defined in the passage? Who makes these definitions?*
2. *Do you agree with the writer's definition? Why? What about Benét's, or Allende's?*
3. *Does reading this passage inspire you to read more short stories? Why or why not?*
4. *Do you think your view of short stories as a literary genre has changed as a result of reading this passage? If so, how and why has it changed?*

Before You Read:
A Writer's Story

Discuss the following questions with a partner.

1. Do you know who J.K. Rowling is? What is she famous for?

2. Have you read any of her books? If so, which ones, and which language did you read them in?

3. If you have read any of her books, did you like them? What did you like about them? If you haven't read any of her books, would you like to? Why or why not?

4. What reputation does she have in your country as a writer? Are there any writers from your native country whose work can be compared in any way with J.K. Rowling's?

5. Look at the title of the reading. The following words can all be found in the passage:

hero   exaggerated   settled on   draft   diagrams

How do you think they relate to the topic of the reading?

Reading Skill:
Developing
Reading
Fluency

Time yourself as you read through the passage. Try to read as fluently as you can. Record your time in the Reading Rate Chart on page 234.

An Interview with J.K. Rowling _____

The following reading is adapted from J.K. Rowling's *Interview with Amazon.co.uk*. Reprinted with permission of Amazon.co.uk. Amazon.co.uk is a trademark of Amazon.com, Inc. in the United States and/or other countries. © 2002 Amazon.com. All rights reserved.

Divorced, living on public assistance[1] in an Edinburgh apartment with her infant daughter, J.K. Rowling wrote *Harry Potter and the Philosopher's Stone* at a café table. Fortunately, Harry Potter rescued her! In this Amazon.co.uk interview, Rowling discusses the birth of our hero, the Manchester hotel where Quidditch[2] was born, and how she might have been a bit like Hermione[3] when she was 11 years old.

How old were you when you started to write, and what was your first book?
Rowling: I wrote my first finished story when I was about six. It was about a rabbit called Rabbit. Very imaginative. I've been writing ever since.

Why did you choose to be an author?
Rowling: If someone asked for my recipe for happiness, step one would be finding out what you love doing most in the world and step two would be finding someone to pay you to do it. I consider myself very lucky indeed to be able to support myself by writing.

Do you have any plans to write books for adults?
Rowling: My first two novels—which I never tried to get published—were for adults. I suppose I might write another one, but I never really imagine a target audience when I'm writing. The ideas come first, so it really depends on the idea that grabs me next.

Where did the ideas for the Harry Potter books come from?
Rowling: I've no idea where ideas come from and I hope I never find out, it would spoil the excitement for me if it turned out I just have a funny little wrinkle on the surface of my brain which makes me think about invisible train platforms.

How do you come up with the names of your characters?
Rowling: I invented some of the names in the Harry books, but I also collect strange names. I've gotten them from medieval[4] saints, maps, dictionaries, plants, war memorials, and people I've met!

Are your characters based on people you know?
Rowling: Some of them are, but I have to be extremely careful what I say about this. Mostly, real people inspire a character, but once they are inside your head they start turning into something quite different. Professor Snape and Gilderoy Lockhart both started as exaggerated versions of people I've met, but became rather different once I got them on the page. Hermione is a bit like me when I was 11, though much cleverer.

Are any of the stories based on your life, or on people you know?
Rowling: I haven't consciously based anything in the Harry books on my life, but of course that doesn't mean your own feelings don't creep in. When I reread chapter 12 of the first book, *The Mirror of Erised*, I saw that I had given Harry lots of my own feelings about my own mother's death, though I hadn't been aware of that as I had been writing.

Where did the idea for Quidditch come from?
Rowling: I invented Quidditch while spending the night in a very small room

in the Bournville Hotel in Didsbury, Manchester. I wanted a sport for wizards,
45 and I'd always wanted to see a game where there was more than one ball in
play at the same time. The idea just amused me. The Muggle[5] sport it most
resembles is basketball, which is probably the sport I enjoy watching most. I
had a lot of fun making up the rules and I've still got the notebook I did it in,
complete with diagrams, and all the names for the balls I tried before I settled
50 on Snitch, Bludgers, and Quaffle.

Where did the ideas for the wizard classes and magic spells come from?
Rowling: I decided on the school subjects very early on. Most of the spells are
invented, but some of them have a basis in what people used to believe
worked. We owe a lot of our scientific knowledge to the alchemists![6]

55 **What ingredients do you think all the Harry Potter books need?**
Rowling: I never really think in terms of ingredients, but I suppose if I had to
name some I'd say humor, strong characters, and a watertight plot.[7] These
things would add up to the kind of book I enjoy reading myself. Oh, I forgot
scariness—well, I never set out to make people scared, but it does seem to
60 creep in along the way.

Do you write longhand[8] or type onto a computer?
Rowling: I still like writing by hand. Normally I do a first draft using pen and
paper, and then do my first edit when I type it onto my computer. For some
reason, I much prefer writing with a black pen than a blue one, and in a
65 perfect world I'd always use narrow feint[9] writing paper. But I have been
known to write on all sorts of weird things when I didn't have a notepad with
me. The names of the Hogwart's Houses[10] were created on the back of an
airplane sick bag. Yes, it was empty.

---

1 **public assistance** government money to provide food, shelter, or medical care to unemployed people
2 **Quidditch** /kwɪdɪtʃ/ an imaginary sport played by wizards in the Harry Potter books
3 **Hermione** /hɜrmioʊni/ female character in the Harry Potter books
4 **medieval** related to the Middle Ages, a period of European history from about A.D. 476 to 1450
5 **Muggle** the term for non-wizard humans in the Harry Potter books
6 **alchemists** scientists from the Middle Ages who tried to change ordinary metals into gold
7 **plot** the main story line in a novel, story, play, or film
8 **longhand** writing by hand onto notepaper rather than typing onto a computer
9 **narrow feint** a particular type of lined writing paper
10 **Hogwart's Houses** four teams or groupings into which all students are divided at the wizard school in the Harry Potter books

Reading Comprehension: How Much Do You Remember?

(A) Decide if the following statements about the reading are true (*T*) or false (*F*). If you check (✔) false, correct the statement to make it true.

		T	F
1.	J.K. Rowling wrote her first book when she was 16 years old.		
2.	Rowling has already published two books for adults.		
3.	Rowling does not know exactly where the ideas for the Harry Potter books came from.		
4.	All the characters in the Harry Potter books are based on people Rowling knows well.		
5.	Rowling subconsciously gave Harry Potter many of the feelings that she experienced after the death of her mother.		
6.	Quidditch most resembles basketball, but with multiple balls in play at the same time.		
7.	Rowling thinks four things are necessary to make any book successful: humor, strong characters, a plot, and a scary setting.		
8.	Rowling writes first on paper then edits as she types the story into her computer.		

(B) Check your answers with a partner. Count how many you got correct—be honest! Then, fill in the Reading Comprehension Chart on page 234.

Vocabulary Comprehension: Word Definitions

(A) Look at the list of words and phrases from the reading. Match each one with a definition on the right.

1. infant ____
2. grabs me ____
3. wrinkle ____
4. exaggerated ____
5. consciously ____
6. creep in ____
7. diagrams ____
8. settled on ____
9. watertight ____
10. draft ____

a. perfectly designed; without flaws or loopholes

b. with awareness; deliberately

c. sketches or drawings to show how something works

d. overstated; presented as greater than in actuality

e. a line or crease in something

f. sneak in; enter surreptitiously

g. finally decided

h. a preliminary outline or version of a plan, document, or picture

i. a very young child

j. captures my attention

(B) Now complete the sentences below using the vocabulary from A. Be sure to use the correct form of each word.

1. Even though Mei-ling is usually a very optimistic person, she sometimes lets negative thoughts about her future career _____.

2. It wasn't until our daughter was born that we finally _____ a name for her.

3. Bill was half asleep, so he really wasn't _____ of what he was saying.

4. Even famous writers will go through multiple _____ of a work before coming up with the final manuscript.

5. Leonardo da Vinci produced some amazing _____ for inventions that were only made real hundreds of years after he died.

6. Some people may think that _____ are a sign of aging, but others believe they are a sign of living.

7. Much to everyone's disbelief, Christina's mother claims that she started singing and dancing as an _____.

8. The best storytellers know how to _____ just enough to make their tales more fascinating, but still believable.

9. This book really isn't that interesting. Unless something on the next page _____, I'm not going to finish it.

10. Police were stunned by the skills the bank robbers used. They believe the thieves masterminded a plan that was completely _____.

Vocabulary Skill: Idioms of Thinking

In this chapter you read the idiom 'come up with.' An idiom is a fixed group of words that has a special meaning. There are many idioms that relate to the subject of thinking. Sometimes it's possible to know what the idiom means by looking at the individual words, but it can also be helpful to look at the idiom in context in order to understand its meaning.

Ⓐ Each of the sentences below contains an idiom in *italics*. Read the idioms and look at how each one is used in the context of the sentence. Try to determine what they mean, and write a short definition for each one. Compare your ideas with a partner.

1. Juan thought about his study problem all night, but he just couldn't *come up with* a solution.

   _____

2. Alex could not *make up his mind* which shirt to wear to the party. In the end his girlfriend had to decide for him.

   _____

3. Sue hates doing housework and, rather than getting it done quickly, she always tries to *think up* some way of delaying it.

   _____

4. Although Satoshi's boss has made him an incredible offer of promotion, it will mean moving overseas. Rather than make an immediate decision he has decided to *think it over* for a day or two.

   _____

5. With unemployment as bad as it is, you really ought to *think twice* before you quit your job.

   _____

6. When Alan's position was made redundant he assumed he would get another job. The thought of going back to school never *crossed his mind* until his wife suggested it to him.

   _____

7. This course is way too difficult. That lecture went right *over my head*; I couldn't understand any of it.

   _____

8. Oh no! I meant to call that client back but it completely *slipped my mind*. I'll have to call tomorrow.

_____

9. Look at the price of that vase! Nobody *in their right mind* would pay that much money.

_____

10. I *racked my brain* trying to think of a great advertising gimmick, but I still haven't come up with anything. Do you have any ideas?

_____

Ⓑ Ask and answer the questions below with a partner. Share your answers with other students in the class.

1. Can you *come up with* a way to make learning English vocabulary easier?
2. Have you *made up your mind* about what kind of job you would like to do when you graduate?
3. *Think up* two ways you can get more practice reading in English.
4. What would you advise somebody to *think twice* about? Why?
5. Has it ever *crossed your mind* to quit school and go traveling for a year? Where would you like to go?
6. Do you have a good memory or do things tend to *slip your mind*?
7. If you had to write a story now, would you have to *rack your brain* to think of an idea, or would one come easily? Share your story idea if you have one.

What Do You Think?

Discuss the following questions with a partner.

1. *Do you have a favorite author? Who is this author and why do you like their work?*
2. *Do you ever read this author's works in any other languages besides the original language in which it was written? Do you think any meaning or originality is lost in the translation?*
3. *Do you tend to read books more than once? What would make you read a book again?*
4. *List three books you would encourage other people to read. Why would you recommend these books to others?*

Real Life Skill

Understanding Literary Terms

The analysis of literature uses a special set of terms and vocabulary. Knowing these terms will help you to talk about literature you read in your classes, and to understand book reviews and other writings about aspects of literature.

Ⓐ Read these common literary terms and their definitions below. Do you have any similar terms in your native language?

simile:	a direct comparison between two things Your smile is *like sunlight*.
metaphor:	an indirect comparison between two things *The journey of life* takes us down many strange roads.
alliteration:	a series of words with the same consonant sound repeated They *stopped* and *stood still*.
assonance:	a series of words with the same vowel sound repeated We *reached* the shore of the *deep sleeping sea*.
onomatopoeia:	a word that imitates a sound Behind the door, Ellen could hear the *murmur* of voices.

Ⓑ Read the following sentences and write the literary term that applies to each.

1. Lee's expression was as cold as ice. _____
2. In front of us, we saw a sad sight. _____
3. Thunder boomed, and the rain poured down. _____
4. Going back home was like waking up from a dream. _____
5. The black cloud of his anger hung over us all day. _____
6. The dog growled, but the cat purred happily. _____
7. When I was a child, I liked to ride my bicycle. _____
8. My love for you is a fire that will burn forever. _____

Ⓒ Read the following poem and identify the literary terms which are incorporated into it.

> *Inhale clean, crisp, country morning air,*
> *Watch sun rise and puffs of cloud,*
> *Drift across a clear blue sky,*
> *Underfoot a soft, thick carpet of snow,*
> *Freshly laid the night before,*
> *For special guests expected,*
> *Birds twitter in the trees,*
> *Robins singing seasonal song,*
> *And the joyful twenty-fifth begins.*

Ⓓ What do you think this poem is about? Which words tell you this? Share your thoughts and ideas about the poem with a partner.

A New Generation of Thinking

Getting Ready

Discuss the following questions with a partner.

1. *What do you understand by the word 'intelligence'?*
2. *Do you think intelligence can be measured? Explain your answer.*
3. *Do you think there are certain qualities or characteristics that all intelligent people display? If so, what are they?*
4. *Why do you think some people can excel in certain areas of study where others fail, and vice versa?*

Before You Read:
What's Your EQ?

Discuss the following questions with a partner.

1. Do you know what an IQ test is? What does it measure? How does it do this?
2. Have you ever taken an IQ test? If so, do you remember your score?
3. Are there other ways we can measure intelligence?
4. Do you know what emotional intelligence or EQ is? What do you think it measures?
5. The following words can all be found in the reading:

restraint   astute   malaise
empathy   regress   rattled

Is each word positive or negative? How do you think they relate to the topic of emotions? Use your knowledge of prefixes and suffixes, as well as your dictionary, to help you determine the meaning of each of these words.

Reading Skill:
Skimming for Content

> *Skimming for content is a useful skill that can help you read, and comprehend, faster. You can get a good idea of the content of a passage without reading every word or sentence. By skimming quickly over the text you can pick up on the main points of the passage, as well as the main idea of what the reading is about.*

Ⓐ How much do you know about the subject of emotional intelligence? Read the following statements and see how many you can complete by circling the correct word or statement. If you do not know anything about the subject, just read the statements to get an idea of what the reading is about.

1. *Emotional Intelligence* is a popular (TV show / book).

2. The writer of *Emotional Intelligence*, Daniel Goleman, states that emotional stability is (more / less) important than IQ in achieving success in life.

3. Goleman's findings are based on experiments conducted on (children / teenagers), who were tested again as (teenagers / adults).

4. The experiment highlights differences in (academic / social) competence between individuals.

5. Those individuals who did (better / worse) on the test as children were more organized, confident, and dependable later in life.

6. If more (positive / negative) emotions are stored in our brains as we grow up, we end up possessing a higher level of emotional intelligence.

7. More recent scientific studies have shown (an increase / a decline) in the overall emotional aptitude of children.

8. Goleman feels that his book may make people (more / less) aware of the role our emotions play in everyday life.

Ⓑ Now, spend ONE minute skimming over the passage to get a basic grasp of the content. Do NOT try to read every word. Do not hesitate or stop when you see words you do not know, or read the footnotes; just let your eyes skim quickly back and forth over the text.

Now go back to the statements on page 114 and see how many of them you can confidently complete. Change any answers that you now think are incorrect. Read through the passage to confirm your answers.

Emotional Intelligence

The following reading is adapted from *The Author Talks About Emotions—Success Depends on Self-Control, He Says* by Patricia Holt. Reprinted with permission from the *San Francisco Chronicle* © 1995.

Daniel Goleman is discussing his famous 'impulse[1] control' test at a San Francisco lecture and has the entire audience's attention. Goleman, a psychologist and science writer, is the author of the best-seller *Emotional Intelligence*, a fascinating book about recent discoveries in brain research that prove emotional stability is more important than IQ in determining an individual's success in life. One of the highlights of the book, that Goleman explains to his audience of foundation leaders, educators, and grants donors, is a test administered thirty years ago that Goleman calls 'The Marshmallow Challenge.'

In this experiment, four-year-old children were individually called into a room at Stanford University during the 1960s. There, a kind man gave a marshmallow to each of them and said they could eat the marshmallow right away, or wait for him to come back from an errand,[2] at which point they would get two marshmallows.

Goleman gets everyone laughing as he describes watching a film of the preschoolers while they waited for the nice man to come back. Some of them covered their eyes or rested their heads on their arms so they wouldn't have to look at the marshmallow, or played games or sang to keep their thoughts off the single marshmallow and waited for the promised double prize. Others—about a third of the group—simply watched the man leave and ate the marshmallow within seconds.

What is surprising about this test, claims Goleman, is its diagnostic power: A dozen years later the same children were tracked down as adolescents and tested again. "The emotional and social difference between the grab-the-marshmallow preschoolers and their gratification[3]-delaying peers was dramatic," Goleman says.

The ones who had resisted eating the marshmallow were clearly more socially competent than the others. "They were less likely to go to pieces, freeze or regress under stress, or become rattled and disorganized when pressured; they embraced challenges and pursued them instead of giving up, even in the face of difficulties; they were self-reliant[4] and confident, trustworthy and dependable."

The third or so who grabbed the marshmallow were "more likely to be seen as shying away from social contacts, to be stubborn and indecisive, to be easily upset by frustrations, to think of themselves as unworthy, to become immobilized[5] by stress, to be mistrustful or prone to jealousy, or to overreact to certain situations with a sharp temper."

And all because of a single marshmallow? In fact, Goleman explains, it's all because of a lone neuron[6] in the brain, only recently discovered, that bypasses[7] the

5

10

15

20

25

30

35 neocortex—the area of the brain where rational decisions are made—and goes straight to the amygdala, or emotional center of the brain. It is here that quicker, more primitive 'fight or flight'[8] responses occur, and are stored for future use. The more that emotional memories involving temper, frustration, anxiety, depression, impulse, and fear pile up in early adolescence, the more the amygdala can "hijack[9]

40 the rest of the brain," Goleman says, "by flooding it with strong and inappropriate emotions, causing us to wonder later, 'Why did I overreact?'"

But if the emotions stored in the brain are those of restraint, self-awareness, self-regulation,[10] self-motivation, empathy, hope, and optimism, then we become endowed with an 'emotional intelligence' that serves rather than enslaves us for the

45 rest of our lives.

The bad news, says Goleman, is that a widely praised but disturbing study from out of the University of Vermont has shown a "decline in emotional aptitude among children across the board." Rich or poor, East Coast or West Coast, inner city or suburb, children today are more vulnerable than ever to anger, depression, anxiety—

50 what he calls a massive 'emotional malaise.' The good news, however, involves another recent discovery—that the amygdala takes a long time to mature, around fifteen or sixteen years, which means to Goleman that "emotional intelligence can be taught, not only in the home but perhaps, more importantly, in school."

Goleman's own story is as intriguing as his book. The author or co-author of nearly

55 a dozen other books involving brain research and behavior, he experienced steady but modest sales until *Emotional Intelligence* hit the stores. Later came the cover of *Time* magazine and appearances on television, such as the Oprah Winfrey show.[11]

"But I think the book also points out the real strength in what has been a feminine preserve in this culture," claims Goleman. "Girls are raised to be emotionally astute

60 and perceptive, but sons learn little about emotions except how to control anger. Women are absolutely more empathic than men on average, but they've felt powerless to bring up the idea of emotions as a serious topic."

The irony, Goleman feels, is that if he had written a book about women and emotions, school reform, emotion-based leadership in business, or child psychology,

65 "the book wouldn't have gotten much attention. As it happens this is a book about all those things, but women and children and school reform are marginalized[12] in this society. So I come along with a lot of scientific data that says, 'Hey, this stuff is consequential'; and maybe some doors are opening in our society."

---

1 **impulse** a sudden urge to do something
2 **errand** a short trip taken to do a specific task, e.g. mailing letters
3 **gratification** sense of pleasure and satisfaction
4 **self-reliant** able to rely on one's own ability to do things
5 **immobilized** unable to progress; impeded
6 **neuron** a nerve cell
7 **bypasses** avoids something by taking an alternative route
8 **fight or flight** psychological and physiological reaction to stress causing one to react negatively

9 **hijack** take or seize control
10 **self-regulation** self-control
11 **Oprah Winfrey show** U.S. TV talk show hosted by female celebrity Oprah Winfrey
12 **marginalized** pushed to the outside of something as a result of being considered unimportant

Reading Comprehension: What Do You Remember?

The following questions are all about the reading. Answer each one using the information you have read. Try not to look back at the reading for the answers.

1. As well as being the author of *Emotional Intelligence*, what else does Daniel Goleman do for a living?

2. What is the 'marshmallow challenge'? Describe how the test worked.

3. List two differences that Goleman found between the children who ate the marshmallow and those who resisted it.

4. Where is the neocortex? What happens there?

5. What is the emotional center of the brain called?

6. Can emotional intelligence be taught? Why is this possible?

7. Is *Emotional Intelligence* Goleman's only published book?

8. What are the main differences that the book points out in terms of emotional intelligence between men and women?

Vocabulary Comprehension: Words in Context

Ⓐ The words in *italics* are vocabulary items from the reading. Read each question or statement and choose the correct answer. Compare your answers with a partner.

1. If you are worried about someone's *stability*, you are afraid that _____.
   a. they may become upset easily
   b. they may suddenly fall over

2. If you manage to *track down* a book you have been looking for, you _____.
   a. order it from a bookstore
   b. find it in a bookstore

3. Someone who is described as *prone to* fits of anger is someone who _____.
   a. has many temper tantrums
   b. has a calm, stable personality

4. Someone who shows *restraint* at an all-you-can-eat lunch would _____.
   a. eat until they are comfortably full
   b. eat as much as possible

5. Having *empathy* means _____.
   a. you get frequent headaches
   b. you can understand others' feelings

6. If someone is *endowed with* something, it means he/she has _____.
   a. a natural talent or ability
   b. a tendency to please other people

7. If your employer announces wage cuts that will "affect staff *across the board*," then _____ will have their salary cut.
   a. everyone in the company
   b. only senior members of staff

8. A *malaise* is something that makes people _____.
   a. behave positively
   b. behave negatively

9. Someone who has a *modest* income probably earns _____.

    a. thousands of dollars a week   **b.** hundreds of dollars a week

10. Being *astute* is an important quality for _____.

    a. dog walkers   **b.** politicians

Ⓑ Now think of other examples using the vocabulary from A. Discuss your ideas with a partner.

1. Give an example of one way a person could demonstrate that they have a high level of emotional *stability*.

2. How will you go about *tracking down* a good job when you graduate from university?

3. Are you *prone to* catching colds in winter? What do you usually do to prevent them?

4. Give an example of a time when you had to show *restraint*.

5. Can you name someone you know who is always *empathetic* towards others?

6. Do you know anyone who is *endowed with* a special talent? What can they do?

7. What are some things that students *across the board* on your campus would like to change or improve?

8. If one of your friends complained to you that he/she was suffering from general *malaise* and couldn't study, what advice would you give?

9. Ten years from now, do you think your income will be *modest* or generous? Explain your answer.

10. Do you agree with the statement in the reading that girls are raised to be more emotionally *astute* than boys? Give reasons and examples from your own upbringing.

Vocabulary Skill: The Root Word *tend*

In this chapter you read the word 'attention,' which contains the root 'tent.' This root word can also be written as 'tend' or 'tens,' and comes from the Latin word 'tendere,' meaning to 'stretch,' 'move,' or 'be pulled.' This root is combined with prefixes and suffixes to form many words in English.

Ⓐ Following the example below, divide the following list of words into their different parts. Using your knowledge of prefixes, suffixes, and the root *tend*, write a short definition for each word. You can also refer to the chart on page 48. Check your definitions using your dictionary and share your ideas with a partner.

intensify = in / tens / ify	prefix = in root = tens ending = ify	meaning: into meaning: stretch meaning: to become
Part of speech: verb	**Meaning:** to become more involved or extreme	

1. distend = dis / tend   prefix = _____ meaning: _____

                         root = _____ meaning: _____

    Part of speech: _____ **Meaning:** _____

2. tension   root = _____ meaning: _____

            ending = _____ meaning: _____

    Part of speech: _____ **Meaning:** _____

3. extended

prefix = _____ meaning: _____

root = _____ meaning: _____

ending = _____ meaning: _____

Part of speech: _____ Meaning: _____

4. extensive

prefix = _____ meaning: _____

root = _____ meaning: _____

ending = _____ meaning: _____

Part of speech: _____ Meaning: _____

5. contend

prefix = _____ meaning: _____

root = _____ meaning: _____

Part of speech: _____ Meaning: _____

6. tendency

root = _____ meaning: _____

ending = _____ meaning: _____

Part of speech: _____ Meaning: _____

(B) **Now complete the sentences below using the words from A. Be sure to use the correct form of each word.**

1. One major reason why many people don't like traveling in the winter is because they have to _____ with bad weather conditions.

2. Even though Laura has a _____ to put things off until the last minute, she always gets things done in the end.

3. After an _____ search for the lost girl that covered five neighborhoods, police finally found her at her school playground.

4. Due to the huge popularity of the band, their tour was _____ by an extra five dates.

5. As the two sides of the leading political party still cannot agree on the issue of welfare, _____ has increased within the government.

6. Children who are victims of famine usually have very _____ stomachs.

Think About It   Discuss the following questions with a partner.

1. *If you had been involved in the Stanford University experiment, do you think you would have resisted the marshmallow or eaten it? Give reasons for your answer.*

2. *The reading states that emotional intelligence is more important than IQ in determining an individual's success in life. How much do you agree with this? Give reasons for your answer.*

3. *If you were to take an emotional intelligence test now, do you think you would achieve a high score? Why?*

4. *The reading describes one way that emotional intelligence was tested and measured in children. How do you think emotional intelligence could be tested and measured in adults?*

Before You Read:
Brain Games

Discuss the following questions with a partner.

1. Do you enjoy playing games that test different mental skills? If so, what type of games do you like to play?

2. How often do you play board games? Which board games do you play the most?

3. What is the most challenging board game you've played? What made it challenging?

4. What is the most fun board game you've played? What made it fun?

5. The following words and phrases can all be found in the reading:

| conceived | dynamics | gifted | novelty |

How do you think they relate to the topic of board games? Use your knowledge of prefixes, suffixes, and word roots, as well as your dictionary, to help you determine the meaning of each of these words.

Reading Skill:
Developing Reading Fluency

> *Remember to use all the skills you have learned so far when you are reading: scanning, skimming, identifying main ideas, and identifying meaning from context. These will all help you to become a more fluent reader.*

Time yourself as you read through the passage. Try to read as fluently as you can. Record your time in the Reading Rate Chart on page 234.

Left Brains, Right Brains, and Board Games

The following reading is adapted from *Left Brains, Right Brains, and Board Games: Cranium Turns the Board Game Industry on Its Head* by Jennifer LeClaire © 1999. Reprinted with permission of the author.

It's not an easy task to do: You need to whistle[1] the song *Stayin' Alive* with enough skill for your teammate to identify the 1970s disco hit. On your next turn, your partner draws a clue with his eyes closed, and you have to guess what it is. You might also find yourself spelling words backward in order to
5 win a round. These odd challenges are part of the 'whole brain' board game that tries to satisfy the world's intellectual hunger, appropriately called Cranium®.

In November 1997, personal experience led Richard Tait to consider this new type of board game that, unlike popular uni-skill games, incorporates a variety of talents. On vacation with his wife and another couple, they found themselves stuck indoors one rainy afternoon and decided to pass the time with a board game. They first played Pictionary®[2] and Tait and his wife badly beat the other team. His competitors then sought revenge and quickly challenged Tait and his wife to a game of Scrabble®.[3] Tait admits his friends were the overwhelming victors in the popular word game.

"I felt terrible and wondered why there wasn't a game where everyone that plays can have a chance to shine—still a competitive, fun board game, but one where everyone can show what they are good at," explains Tait.

When Tait and his good friend Whit Alexander left their jobs at Microsoft®, they vowed to jump at any future opportunities to work together. So Tait approached Alexander to help him examine the possibilities of producing a new board game. In only nine short months, the two former Microsoft® employees conceived a unique game that is designed to include something for everyone, and took it to a market that's been craving something different.

Once they decided to take the proverbial[4] plunge, they began conducting research to further develop the concept of their 'whole brain' game. The two gathered as much knowledge as they could about the history of social games, comparing their findings against the criteria for Cranium.

Their conclusion was to develop a left brain/right brain game, but neither knew much about the hypothesis, so they began researching the field of intellectual psychology.[5] Tait and Alexander would soon discover a Harvard University researcher named Howard Gardner whose 'Theory of Multiple Intelligences' postulates that there are eight core competencies where people show intelligence, such as linguistic, mathematical, interpersonal, or spatial.[6] "We thought it was a really rich framework to try to base the game design on, so we built up from Gardner's work," explains Alexander.

The two inventors identified a number of occupations that people might pursue if they are gifted in one of Gardner's intelligences. They then broke down the findings into subject matters or areas of interest that those same people would be exceptionally strong in, ensuring each player their moment to shine.

After about three months of research, Alexander and Tait realized the novelty of their approach to the board-game market. In total, they had come up with fourteen different activities, each one innovative in its own right. One such example is 'sculpterades.' As the name suggests, this activity requires players to sculpt clues from clay while their teammates guess what they are sculpting, bringing out the child in the most mature adults. The duo's commitment to research and quality design took them through ten different Cranium Clay recipes and multiple scents before settling on a purple, citrus-smelling clay that

50 boasts a long shelf life. Tait says that customers often e-mail them for more of the stuff because they like it so much.

Next, they decided upon four unique groups of question cards, including 'Creative Cat,' which features sculpting and drawing activities; 'Data Head,' which focuses on trivia; 'Word Worm,' which includes vocabulary-based
55 questions; and 'Star Performer' featuring performance-based activities. It is the team with the best combination of these skills that eventually wins the game.

Cranium avoids play dynamics that allow one group to overwhelm another by limiting each team to one task before passing the turn to the next player. Tait says this is just one example of hundreds of game dynamics they fine-tuned
60 throughout the play tests. But, he adds, there was one constant throughout the testing period: People were having a good time.

"We originally started with a much broader vision than just a board game," explains Tait. He says they looked at the 1980s and how the heart was so heavily emphasized in conjunction with good health. He thinks that the brain
65 is going to be the organ of focus for the new millennium. "And we would like to be the company that's at the forefront of providing fun things to do with your brain to keep it happy and healthy." This strategy has made Cranium a standout among its competitors in the board-game industry, as there simply is no other game that offers such a large variety of activities.

70 Today, the pair's main challenge is building the Cranium brand name, and Tait alludes to a potential TV show as well as new Cranium products in the distant future.

---

1 **whistle** a high-pitched noise made by blowing air through the teeth or through pursed lips
2 **Pictionary** board game whereby one person draws pictures to enable their teammates to guess a word or phrase
3 **Scrabble** board game played by forming words from sets of randomly chosen letters
4 **proverbial** well known; widely referred to
5 **intellectual psychology** branch of psychology that deals with the intellect and mental capacity
6 **spatial** related to space and relationships with objects in it

A Decide if the following statements about the reading are true (*T*), false (*F*), or not mentioned (*NM*). If you check (✔) false, correct the statement to make it true.

	T	F	NM
1. Cranium is a very popular board game.			
2. The game was developed by two former software company employees.			
3. The game is based on the theory that there are eight core areas in which people show intelligence.			
4. The questions for the games were based on occupations for each area of intelligence.			
5. The game consists of four groups of questions that, collectively, contain fourteen activity types.			
6. One activity type involves players using a purple, scented clay to shape objects.			
7. The game allows one team to dominate the game and, in doing so, win.			
8. No future Cranium products will be developed.			

B Check your answers with a partner. Count how many you got correct—be honest! Then, fill in the Reading Comprehension Chart on page 234.

A Look at the list of words and phrases from the reading. Match each one with a definition on the right.

1. conceived _____
2. craving _____
3. take the plunge _____
4. criteria _____
5. hypothesis _____
6. postulate _____
7. novelty _____
8. dynamics _____
9. gifted _____
10. alludes to _____

a. refers to something or someone in an indirect way
b. interactions; relating to interpersonal relationships
c. being new and unusual or different
d. naturally, and exceptionally, talented
e. a strong or uncontrollable desire
f. a theory or idea based on facts but not yet proven
g. conditions or standard by which something can be measured or judged
h. to immerse oneself in a potentially risky situation
i. to claim something is true without proof
j. thought up

Ⓑ Now complete the questions below using the words from A. Be sure to use the correct form of each word. Then, answer the questions using your own information, and share your answers with a partner.

1. When you are looking for a romantic partner, are there any special _____ that you consider?

2. Have you ever _____ of a new game? If so, explain it. If not, what is your favorite game and how do you play it?

3. Does the media in your country ever _____ about the activities of movie stars or other famous people? Do you tend to believe these stories?

4. Have you ever _____ and done something daring or unusual? What did you do?

5. Can you think of a trend or fashion in your country for which the _____ has worn off recently?

6. Which of your personal qualities contributes the most to the key _____ in your friendships with others?

7. Do you ever have _____ for certain foods? What foods are they?

8. Do you think it is just a _____ that UFOs exist, or do you think that stories of sightings can be taken as fact?

9. Do you know anyone who is _____ at anything? What is it they can do well?

10. If you were discussing your favorite bands or musical artists with someone, what type of music would you be _____?

Vocabulary Skill:
The Root
Word *cap*

In this unit, you read the words 'conceive' and 'concept,' which are formed using the root word 'cap,' also written as 'cep,' 'cip,' or 'ceive.' This root comes from the Latin word 'capere,' meaning to 'take,' 'receive,' or 'seize.' It is combined with prefixes and suffixes to form many words in English.

Ⓐ For each word, study its different parts. Using your knowledge of prefixes, suffixes, and the root *cap*, write the part of speech and a simple definition. Use your dictionary to check your answers. Share your ideas with a partner.

Vocabulary	Part of Speech	Definition
1. accept	_____	_____
2. intercept	_____	_____
3. recipient	_____	_____
4. anticipate	_____	_____
5. captivate	_____	_____
6. receive	_____	_____
7. capacity	_____	_____
8. captor	_____	_____

B Now complete each sentence below using the words from the chart. Be sure to use the correct form of each word.

1. I think the maximum _____ in a taxi in this country is four people. As there are six of us, we'll have to take two.

2. Due to the global economic downturn I don't _____ that we will make our original sales goal.

3. Shelly is a great designer, but sometimes her ideas are so avant-garde that they are not always _____ by her colleagues or clients.

4. Customs officials managed to _____ the goods being smuggled into the country at the airport.

5. Anthony's debut stage performance _____ the audience.

6. Did we _____ any mail this morning? I'm waiting on a letter from the bank.

7. The president's daughter has been kidnapped! Her _____ are demanding a six million dollar ransom.

8. Those employees who were not _____ of prize money in the annual charity draw will receive restaurant vouchers from the CEO.

What Do You Think?

Discuss the following questions with a partner.

1. *What activities do you find mentally stimulating? How often do you do these activities?*

2. *Do you notice differences in the ways your friends or family members approach certain learning tasks? Explain some of these differences. After studying this chapter, do you understand better why these differences exist?*

3. *What skill (for example, verbal, musical, logical/mathematical, visual/spatial, interpersonal, intrapersonal) do you think best demonstrates your own intelligence? Give examples to explain your answer.*

4. *What other ways can people demonstrate their intelligence?*

Real Life Skill

Understanding Academic Titles

Teachers and researchers at universities have many different academic titles. These differ from one country to another, and even among universities within the same country, but every university has a ranking system for its faculty members. If you ever apply to, or attend, a university in the United States, it will be helpful to you to know some of these titles.

(A) Read the following paragraph and note the academic titles in bold.

An American university is organized into many departments, such as English and Chemistry. Among the professors in each department, one is chosen to be **department chair**. The head of the entire university is called the **president**. Many people who want to have a university career begin teaching even before they have earned their Ph.D. As **teaching assistants**, they may teach low-level courses while completing their own studies. Their goal, of course, is to become a full **professor,** but this may take many years. After completing their Ph.D., many faculty members begin as **instructors**, teaching on a yearly contract, while some are fortunate enough to obtain a position as an **assistant professor.** This puts them on the 'tenure track'—the academic ladder that leads to a lifelong position. The next step, reached after several years, is **associate professor.** In order to receive tenure, and a permanent appointment as a professor, candidates must carry out significant research and publish scholarly papers.

(B) List the titles from the paragraph in order from the highest rank to the lowest.

1. _President_
2. _____
3. _____
4. _____
5. _____
6. _____
7. _____

(C) What academic titles do each of these people probably hold?

1. Janet is the head of twelve professors of mathematics.

_____

2. Jack is extremely busy teaching and studying at the same time.

_____

3. Harold has held his position for thirty-two years, and will retire next year.

_____

4. Sharon really enjoys teaching, and she hopes she will have this job again next year.

_____

5. Elaine hopes to become a full professor next year.

_____

It's Dinner Time!

Getting Ready

Discuss the following questions with a partner.

1. *What foods do you eat every day? At which meals do you eat these foods?*
2. *Do you consider yourself to be a healthy eater? Why or why not?*
3. *Do you think that in your country people, in general, have a healthy diet? Explain your answer.*
4. *What do you know about modern farming and food production methods? Do you think they are safe?*

Before You Read:
Food for Thought

Discuss the following questions with a partner.

1. How many meals or snacks have you eaten so far today? What foods did you eat?

2. Are you aware of how these foods were grown or manufactured? Describe how you think they were farmed or produced.

3. What do you understand by the term 'genetically modified (GM) foods'? Are you aware of how GM foods are different from other foods? Do you know if they are available in your local supermarket?

4. Do you think that the use of modern technology in food production methods is positive or negative? Give reasons for your answer.

5. Look at the title of the reading. The following words can all be found in the passage. How do you think they relate to the reading topic?

| fuss | alert | ambiguity | proponents |

Reading Skill:
Arguing For and Against a Topic

Many reading passages present two sides of an argument—one argues for, or in favor of, the topic; the other argues against it. Phrases such as 'advocates of,' 'proponents of,' and 'in favor of' signal that information that supports one side of the argument will be introduced. Phrases like 'advocates against,' 'critics of,' 'skeptics of,' or 'concerns about' signal that information against the topic is coming. Also, words and phrases like 'argues that,' 'questions,' 'however,' 'though,' 'in contrast,' and 'in spite of' signal that an opposite or different opinion is about to be introduced.

Ⓐ Scan the reading passage below and complete the chart with information from the passage.

Genetically Modified Food

Reasons For	Reasons Against
1. _____	1. _____
2. _____	2. _____
3. _____	3. _____
4. _____	4. _____
5. _____	

Ⓑ Compare your answers with a partner. Are there any other reasons you can add to your list?

Ⓒ Now read the passage again and complete the comprehension exercise that follows.

Genetically Modified Food _____

The following reading is adapted from *The Fuss Over Genetically Modified Food* by Leanne Hachey. Originally written for CBC News Online; http://cbc.ca/news/indepth/foodfight/hachey.html Reprinted with permission from CBC News Online © 2002.

"What's for dinner?" It used to be that the answer to that household question was an issue for debate among family members only. But not any more. Now scientists, advocacy groups,[1] economists, trade experts, geneticists,[2] and politicians are all discussing what should be served for dinner.

5 The food fuss revolves around one phrase: genetic modification.[3] There are two groups with strong views on both sides of that phrase. One side argues that genetic

modification of food enhances the quality and nutritional value of already-existing foods as well as generating new ways to produce that food. The other side questions the technology's safety and long-term effects, arguing that people simply don't know what they're putting in their mouths.

The term 'genetically modified' (GM) is an offspring of another term: biotechnology. A word that's been around for about thirty years, biotechnology was created in the shadow of new techniques that allowed scientists to modify the genetic material in living cells.[4] Basically, that means playing around with various biological processes to produce substances that, arguably, benefit things like agriculture, medicine, and the environment.

If you know how to cut-and-paste on a computer, you've figured out genetic modification. The Canadian Food Inspection Agency describes it like this: it all begins with a cell made up of chromosomes;[5] the chromosomes are made up of DNA[6] and are organized into sections called genes; genes determine the characteristics of an organism. These genes can be 'cut' from one organism and 'pasted' into another. Several foods that people eat every day are products of this process, such as tomatoes that ripen on the vine[7] and maintain their texture and tough skin for several weeks. A potato plant developed to resist an insect known to attack it is another example. In the latter case, the GM version eliminates the need for chemical pesticides.[8]

Proponents of GM foods argue using biotechnology in the production of food products has many benefits. It speeds up the process of breeding[9] plants and animals with desired characteristics, can be used to introduce new characteristics that a product wouldn't normally have, and can improve the nutritional value of products. And, say the supporters, all of this is done safely.

Groups who advocate against the use of GM foods don't see things quite the same way. They point to studies that argue GM foods could be harmful to people's health. To the groups on this side of the issue, that 'could' provides more than enough reason to go forward with extreme caution, something they say isn't currently being done. GM critics say enough time hasn't passed to study the long-term effects of the foods.

In Europe, hardly a week goes by without some headline about GM foods or, rather, 'Frankenfoods'[10] as they've been called by the European media. The Church of England has entered the debate, criticizing the production of GM crops. Ever responsive to consumer demands, the European Union has taken a strong position on this issue, going so far as to propose a moratorium[11] on approving GM foods. These responses are the outcome of a grassroots campaign.[12] Various scares, the best-known being mad cow disease,[13] have consumers in Europe cautious of food genetically altered to kill pests or resist herbicides.[14]

Two British food companies have even dropped GM ingredients from their products, something the North American branches of these companies haven't done. That's not all that surprising for one simple reason: there's an unmistakable

split in the policies toward GM foods between the two sides of the Atlantic that
50 some call the Atlantic Divide. Supporters argue North America's approach is more
progressive, while skeptics argue it's less safe.

Whatever the case, the Atlantic Divide can be attributed to two things. The first is
all about experience: the North American side of the Atlantic hasn't seen a scare
comparable to mad cow disease. The second is all about dollars: North Americans
55 expect their food to be cheap. And while the Atlantic may divide the approach to
GM foods, it doesn't stop the two sides from butting heads.[15]

The fuss over food extends to whether the manufacturing process is made known.
Canada has adopted both a mandatory and voluntary labeling policy. According to
the Canadian Food Inspection Agency, mandatory labeling applies to all foods that
60 have been changed nutritionally or compositionally, or to alert consumers of
possible allergens.[16] That doesn't mean, though, that *all* GM foods will be labeled. If
it can be shown through tests that the nutrition or composition of such foods
remains unchanged, no special label is required. Even though labels are not
required, they are allowed, but only when 'truthful and not misleading.' A good
65 example is the 'fat free' claim made on some products. Because of the ambiguity
surrounding voluntary labeling, it's been determined that clearer rules are needed.

The GM debate makes us consider the role technology has in our lives. What
makes this debate unique is that every meal we eat is at its very core. And that fact
means one thing: it's an issue that will be discussed not only around policy tables,
70 but dinner tables as well.

---

1 **advocacy groups** groups of people who support, or are in favor of, something
2 **geneticists** scientists or doctors who specialize in the field of genetics—the branch of biology that deals with heredity
3 **genetic modification** the intentional alteration of the genetic material of an organism, usually for a specific purpose
4 **cells** smallest units of an organism
5 **chromosomes** parts of a cell that contain DNA and are responsible for determining and passing on characteristics of the organism from parent to young
6 **DNA** abbreviation of Deoxyribonucleic Acid; bonded sequence of chemicals present in each cell chromosome that determines hereditary characteristics
7 **ripen on the vine** grow to maturity while still attached to the plant from which it comes
8 **pesticides** chemicals used to kill pests, usually insects that attack plants as they are growing
9 **breeding** producing young from parents
10 **Frankenfoods** word created by combining 'Frankenstein' with 'foods'; Frankenstein being the monster—created from body parts of different dead people and brought to life by a medical student named Frankenstein—that featured in the fictional novel of the same name written by Mary Shelley
11 **moratorium** a suspension of, or a ban on, something
12 **grassroots campaign** organized effort to draw attention to an issue, usually political, at a local level
13 **mad cow disease** cattle disease that causes deterioration of the brains of cows, a form of which can be passed to humans by ingesting infected meat
14 **herbicides** chemicals used to destroy or inhibit the growth of plants, usually weeds
15 **butting heads** arguing as a result of opposing views
16 **allergens** substances that cause allergies

• •

The following statements are all about the reading. Complete each one using information you have read.

1. The _____ _____ (two words) centers on one phrase: genetic modification.

2. Advocates of GM foods argue that it _____ the quality and nutritional value of foods; their opponents question the technology's _____ and _____ effects.

3. The characteristics of an organism are determined by _____, which form its _____.

4. The process of genetic modification works by _____ genes from one organism and _____ them into another.

5. The European media has nicknamed GM foods '_____.'

6. Some people have called the disagreement between the United States and Britain over the issue of GM foods the _____ Divide.

7. Two things have led to the divide between the United States and Britain: _____ and _____.

8. The GM debate makes us think about the role _____ plays in our lives.

• •

Ⓐ **For each group, circle the word that does not belong. The words in *italics* are vocabulary items from the reading.**

1. *fuss*	commotion	bother	calm
2. focuses on	centers on	turns on	*revolves around*
3. producing	resisting	*generating*	bringing about
4. finish	*texture*	aroma	appearance
5. supporters	opponents	advocates	*proponents*
6. *attributed to*	ascribed to	accredited to	spoken to
7. required	*mandatory*	voluntary	imperative
8. *compositionally*	structurally	morphologically	mortally
9. warn	caution	frighten	*alert*
10. incongruity	security	*ambiguity*	inconsistency

Ⓑ Complete the sentences below using the vocabulary in *italics* from A. Be sure to use the correct form of the word.

1. The new construction project in the center of town has _____ close to one hundred new jobs.

2. Sergio presented what seemed to be a clear argument, but on closer examination it was clearly full of _____.

3. Attendance at the first aid workshop is _____; all students must be there.

4. My parents don't understand what all the _____ is about computer viruses. I had to buy them some software and explain to them how and why it works.

5. Carl's a really nice guy, but his conversation usually _____ his fixation with motorbikes.

6. If you were to analyze this soup _____, you would find that it is a good source of essential vitamins and minerals the body needs.

7. Calvin loves the _____ of his dog's fur so much he often tries to sleep in the dog basket—with the dog!

8. _____ of stricter gun control laws have tried for years to gain more support throughout the country.

9. Jill's success can be _____ her tenacity and hard work in the office.

10. It was only after reading about food and allergies that Angelina was _____ to the possible cause of her son's illness.

Vocabulary Skill:
The Root Word
sist

In this chapter, you read the word 'resist,' which means 'to fight against,' and 'existing,' which means 'being,' or 'having life.' The root word 'sist,' also written as 'stat' and 'stit,' comes from the Latin word 'stare,' meaning 'to stand,' 'remain,' or 'to last.' This root is combined with prefixes and suffixes to form many words in English.

Ⓐ The words below can all be completed by adding the root *sist*, *stit*, or *stat*. Decide which form each word uses and write it in the space provided. Then, using your knowledge of prefixes and suffixes, write which part of speech each word is and a definition.

Vocabulary	Part of Speech	Definition
1. in_____	_____	_____
2. con_____ently	_____	_____
3. sub_____ute	_____	_____
4. per_____	_____	_____
5. _____ue	_____	_____
6. in_____ute	_____	_____
7. super_____ion	_____	_____
8. de_____	_____	_____
9. con_____ute	_____	_____

B Complete the sentences below using words from the chart. Be sure to use the correct form of each word.

1. It may seem like a silly _____, but I never walk under ladders.

2. I believe this _____ is a replica of a famous work by Rodin.

3. I really didn't want to go into the haunted house as I was too scared, but my friend _____.

4. After months of sleepless nights and constant arguing, the neighbors agreed to take action to _____ their dog from barking.

5. Although this margarine tastes fine, I think it's a very poor _____ for real butter.

6. The art _____ is having a fund-raising exhibition next week. It looks interesting; we should go along.

C Now write three more sentences using the remaining words from the list in A. Share your ideas with a partner.

1. _____
2. _____
3. _____

Think About It   Discuss the following questions with a partner.

1. *Based on the arguments presented in the reading, do you think GM foods are safe to eat? Give reasons for your answer.*
2. *Does anything you have read in this passage about GM foods worry you? If so, what concerns you and why?*
3. *Who does the grocery shopping in your household? Does this person ever read the labels on food before they buy things?*
4. *Do you think that all GM foods should be labeled, so that people can be informed about what exactly they are eating?*

Before You Read:
Food for Life

Discuss the following questions with a partner.

1. What foods are grown in large amounts in your country?
2. Are these foods a staple of the diet in your country?
3. What foods, if any, tend to be eaten in moderation in your country?
4. Are there foods commonly eaten in your country which you know are typically not part of the diet in other countries? What are they?
5. Look at the title of the reading. Do you know which countries of the world adhere to the principles of the Mediterranean diet? What foods do you think are eaten in abundance in these countries? Which foods do you think form the staple of the Mediterranean diet? Scan through the reading quickly to find the answers to the questions above.

Reading Skill:
Developing Reading Fluency

By reading fluently you will be able to read more material. Reading more material will enable you to encounter more new words. By encountering more new words you will be able to increase the size of your vocabulary.

Time yourself as you read through the passage. Try to read as fluently as you can. Record your time in the Reading Rate Chart on page 234.

Mediterranean Diet _____

The following reading is adapted from *Mediterranean Diet*. From *The Gale Encyclopedia of Alternative Medicine* by Douglas Dupler © The Gale Group, 2001. Reprinted by permission of The Gale Group.

The Mediterranean diet is based upon the eating patterns of traditional cultures in the Mediterranean region.[1] Several noted nutritionists and research projects have concluded that this diet is one of the most healthful in the world in terms of preventing such illnesses as heart disease and cancer, and increasing life
5   expectancy.[2]

The countries that have inspired the Mediterranean diet all surround the Mediterranean Sea. These cultures have eating habits that developed over thousands of years. In Europe, parts of Italy, Greece, Portugal, Spain, and southern France adhere to principles of the Mediterranean diet, as do Morocco and Tunisia in North Africa. Parts of the Balkan region[3] and Turkey follow the diet, as well as Middle Eastern countries like Lebanon and Syria. The Mediterranean region is warm and sunny, and produces large supplies of fresh fruits and vegetables almost year round that people eat many times per day. Wine, bread, olive oil, nuts, and legumes[4] are other staples of the region, and the Mediterranean Sea has historically yielded[5] abundant quantities of fish.

International interest in the therapeutic qualities of the Mediterranean diet began back in the late 1950s, when medical researchers started to link the occurrence of heart disease with diet. Dr. Ancel Keys performed an epidemiological analysis of diets around the world (epidemiology being the branch of public health that studies patterns of diseases and their potential causes among populations). Entitled the *Seven Countries Study*, it is considered one of the greatest studies of its kind ever performed. In it, Keys gathered data on heart disease and its potential causes from nearly 13,000 men in Greece, Italy, Croatia, Serbia, Japan, Finland, the Netherlands, and the United States. The study was conducted over a period of decades. It concluded that the Mediterranean people in the study enjoyed some significant health advantages. The Mediterranean groups had lower mortality rates in all age brackets and from all causes, particularly from heart disease. The study also showed that the Mediterranean diet is as high or higher in fat than other diets, obtaining up to 40 percent of all its calories from fat. It has, however, different patterns of fat intake. Mediterranean cooking uses smaller amounts of saturated fat and higher amounts of unsaturated fat, mostly in the form of olive oil. Saturated fats are fats that are found principally in meat and dairy products, although avocados, some nuts, and some vegetable oils also contain them. Saturated fats are used by the body to make cholesterol,[6] and high levels of cholesterol have since been directly related to heart disease.

Several other studies have validated Keys' findings regarding the good health of people in Mediterranean countries. The World Health Organization (WHO) showed in a 1990 analysis that four major Mediterranean countries (Spain, Greece, France, and Italy) have longer life expectancies and lower rates of heart disease and cancer than other European countries and America. The data are significant because the same Mediterraneans frequently smoke and don't have regular exercise programs like many Americans, which means that other variables may be responsible. Scientists have also ruled out genetic differences, because Mediterraneans who move to other countries tend to lose their health advantages. These findings suggest that diet and lifestyle are major factors.

The Mediterranean diet gained even more notice when Dr. Walter Willett, head of the nutrition department at Harvard University, began to recommend it. Although low-fat diets were recommended for sufferers of heart disease, groups of Mediterraneans in his studies had very high intakes of fat, mainly from olive oil. Willett and others proposed that the risk of heart disease can be reduced by increasing one type of dietary fat—monounsaturated[7] fat—the type found in

olive oil. Willett's proposal went against conventional nutritional
recommendations to reduce all fat in the diet. It has been shown that
55 unsaturated fats raise the level of HDL cholesterol, which is sometimes called
'good cholesterol' because of its protective effect against heart disease. Willett
has also performed studies correlating the intake of meat with heart disease and
cancer.

The Mediterranean diet has several general characteristics:
60 • The bulk of the diet comes from **plant sources,** including whole grains,
breads, pasta, polenta,[8] bulgur,[9] and couscous, rice, potatoes, fruits,
vegetables, legumes, seeds, and nuts.
• **Olive oil** is used generously, and is the main source of fat in the diet as well
as the principal cooking oil. The total fat intake accounts for up to 35
65 percent of calories. Saturated fats, however, make up only 8 percent of
calories or less, which restricts meat and dairy intake.
• **Fruits and vegetables** are eaten in large quantities. They are usually fresh,
unprocessed,[10] grown locally, and consumed in season.
• **Dairy products** are consumed in small amounts daily, mainly as cheese and
70 yogurt.
• **Eggs** are used sparingly, up to four eggs per week.
• **Fish and poultry** are consumed only one to three times per week, with fish
preferred over poultry.
• **Red meat** is consumed only a few times per month.
75 • **Honey** is the principle sweetener, and sweets are eaten only a few times per
week.
• **Wine** is consumed in moderate amounts with meals (1–2 glasses daily).

---

[1] **Mediterranean region** area surrounding the Mediterranean Sea incorporating Spain, southern
France, Italy, Greece, Portugal, Sardinia, Sicily, and countries along the
Northern African coast

[2] **life expectancy** the average age to which a person is expected to live

[3] **Balkan region** area of southeast Europe including Albania, Bulgaria, part of Greece, southeast
Romania, part of Turkey, and Yugoslavia

[4] **legumes** plants such as beans, peas, and seeds

[5] **yielded** produced

[6] **cholesterol** substance found in animal tissue and other foods that affects levels of fat stored in
the human body

[7] **monounsaturated** type of saturated fat that has only one bond in its carbon chain

[8] **polenta** thick porridge-type meal made of cornmeal boiled with water

[9] **bulgur** dried cracked wheat

[10] **unprocessed** not treated or altered in any way; in a natural state

---

Reading Comprehension: How Much Do You Remember?

Ⓐ Choose the best answer for each question or statement below. Compare
your answers with a partner.

1. The Mediterranean region produces large amounts of _____ all year round.

   a. red meat and wine   **c.** nuts and olive oil

   b. fruits and vegetables   **d.** fish and dairy products

2. International interest in the Mediterranean diet began _____.

   a. in the 1950s   **c.** in the 1970s

   b. in the 1990s   **d.** thousands of years ago

3. The Mediterranean diet has different patterns of fat intake as the cooking uses _____.

   a. more meat and less dairy products   **b.** more nuts and less olive oil

   c. less saturated fat and more unsaturated fat

   d. more avocados and less vegetable oil

4. A World Health Organization study showed that people from Spain, Greece, France, and Italy _____.

   a. smoke and exercise more than Americans

   b. experience health advantages by moving overseas

   c. live, on average, longer than Americans

   d. are genetically less prone to cancer and heart disease

5. Medical studies have linked the Mediterranean diet to _____.

   a. epidemiological analysis   **c.** patterns of heart disease in men

   b. cancer and smoking   **d.** lower levels of heart disease

6. Medical studies have shown that _____ affects the risk of heart disease and cancer.

   a. smoking and exercise   **c.** diet and lifestyle

   b. genetic differences   **d.** conventional nutrition

7. The majority of the Mediterranean diet comes from _____.

   a. fish and poultry   **c.** plants

   b. dairy products   **d.** meat

8. The main source of fat in the Mediterranean diet comes from _____.

   a. cooking oil   **c.** meat

   b. dairy products   **d.** olive oil

Ⓑ Check your answers with a partner. Count how many you got correct—be honest! Then, fill in the Reading Comprehension Chart on page 234.

Vocabulary Comprehension: Words in Context

Ⓐ Look at the following words. Using the line references, go back to the reading and locate them in the passage. Use the context to try and work out the meaning of each one.

adhere to (line 9)	staples (line 14)	abundant (line 15)
therapeutic (line 16)	analysis (line 19)	validated (line 37)
ruled out (line 44)	correlating (line 57)	accounts for (line 64)
restricts (line 66)		

Ⓑ Read the paragraph below and fill in the blanks using the vocabulary items from A. Be sure to use the correct form of each word.

Get in Shape; Walk It Off!

Do you _____ an exercise program or have you _____ working out? Lack of exercise _____ a large percentage of ill health. Did you know that incorporating a daily routine of walking into your schedule can help you stay in shape? There are many reasons to walk: First of all, it's _____. While you are walking, you can work on your mind, as well as your body. Doctors are consistently _____ healthy bodies with healthy minds, so clearing the mind and walking off your worries can have positive effects on your health. Furthermore, walking means you are not _____ to exercising in the confines of a gym—you can walk at any time. There is also no need for _____ exercise equipment, weights, or clothing. Many people have started 'walking clubs' at their workplace. During lunch, or for thirty minutes in the morning, a group may get together to walk a few blocks around the neighborhood they work in. This is a great way to _____ your exercise routine, and keep you motivated and on track. Finally, as well as using exercise to get in shape, give your diet a careful _____. What are your _____ foods? Start replacing those fattening mid-morning snacks with fruit—it's just as filling, but with half the calories and fat! So tomorrow when you wake up, strap on those sneakers, pick up some fruit, and start to walk it off—it's easy!

Ⓒ Now think of other examples using some of the vocabulary from A. Discuss your ideas with a partner.

1. What are some good eating habits that you try to *adhere to*?
2. What are the *staple* foods of your own diet?
3. If you could eat an *abundant* amount of any food, what would it be, and why?
4. Take a moment to *analyze* your lifestyle. Would you say it is healthy or unhealthy? What changes do you need to make, if any, to make it better?

Vocabulary Skill:

Numerical Root Words: *mono, dec, cent, mill*

Ⓐ Study the words in the chart below. What do you think they mean? Use your knowledge of prefixes, suffixes, and the roots *mono, dec, cent,* and *mill* to try to work out the meaning of each word.

Noun	Verb	Adjective
monologue	monopolize	monotonous
decathlon	decimate	centennial
decibel		millennial
percentage		
centenary		
centenarian		
millipede		

Complete the sentences below using the vocabulary from A. Be sure to use the correct form of each word.

In this chapter, you read the word 'monounsaturated' which contains the root 'mono,' meaning 'single' or 'one.' There are several roots in English that correlate to numbers. For example, 'dec' or 'deci' means 'ten,' 'cent' or 'centi' means 'one hundred,' and 'mill' or 'milli' means 'one thousand.'

News in Brief

Biologists have discovered a new breed of _____. The discovery was made when lettuce farmers reported that this years' crop had been _____ by an insect. A high _____ of the farms affected are in the southern United States.

A group of _____ attended a dinner party with the President last night. The dinner was held as part of the President's agenda to provide recognition for citizens who have lived through the last _____, and in doing so contributed to the country's economic growth and development. The President gave a _____ on this topic during the evening which was met with indifference from some of the older folks; a couple said they found his speech _____, while others complained that his talk was so long he ended up _____ the evening!

World class athlete Guy Simpson won gold in the _____ event at the World Games in Athens yesterday. As Simpson received his medal, the cheer from the crowd was so loud it reached new _____ levels, and drowned out the national anthem!

A leading politician has proposed a new sporting event to be held once every one hundred years. The _____ Games, as they would be known, would be held to honor athletes at the peak of their career at the time of the games. While some people have denounced the idea as ridiculous, others have taken it one step further and proposed that the games that fall on the thousand year anniversary of the start of the games be named the _____ Games! It seems, for some, the Olympics just aren't good enough.

What Do You Think?

Discuss the following questions with a partner.

1. *How is your diet similar to or different from the Mediterranean diet outlined in the reading? Which do you think is healthier?*

2. *Are you aware of the mortality rates in your country for heart disease and cancer? Do you think there is any aspect of diet and lifestyle that people in your country could change in order to reduce the number of deaths related to these diseases?*

3. *As you get older, do you think you will become more conscious of what you eat? Why?*

4. *There is a saying in English: 'You are what you eat.' What do you understand this saying to mean? Do you think this is true? Explain your answer. Is there a similar saying in your native language?*

Real Life Skill

Understanding Punctuation

Formal academic and business writing uses a number of specialized punctuation marks. Knowing the meanings of these marks, and how and why they are used, will enable you to understand the exact meaning of what you are reading, and how you should read it. They are also important to know when writing in English formally, or for academic purposes.

Ⓐ Match each punctuation mark with its function and description of how it works.

Punctuation mark	Function
1. [ ] square brackets _____	**a.** shows two alternatives
2. ( ) parentheses _____	**b.** separates ideas in a sentence or used before a list
3. . . . ellipsis _____	**c.** shows that words or letters were left out
4. – dash _____	**d.** shows separate information inside a sentence
5. - hyphen _____	**e.** connects two closely related sentences
6. / slash or virgule _____	**f.** refers to a note at the bottom of the page
7. & ampersand _____	**g.** shows a quotation inside another quotation
8. ' ' single quote marks _____	**h.** a symbol for *and*
9. : colon _____	**i.** adds information to explain the first clause of a sentence
10. ; semi-colon _____	**j.** combines two closely connected names or words
11. * asterisk _____	**k.** shows words that were not originally in the text but added later by the editor

Ⓑ Use all of the marks above to punctuate the sentences below.

1. The reporter stated that "The man accused of the crime stood up in court and shouted not guilty at the judge."

2. Many new forms of communication were introduced during the twentieth century fax, e-mail, and cell phones.

3. One of the leading companies in the pharmaceutical industry is Palmer Jackson.

4. She put on the dress, then looked at herself in a full length mirror.

5. We accept payment by credit card, also by check money order.

6. Good nutrition is important for athletes it's also vital for the rest of us.

7. Joyce yelled, "If you don't stop that right now, I'll   "

8. John gave all of his own money to Fred why I'll never know.

9. A police report recently released shows a disturbing increase in the incidence of violent crime in city centers. See note 1.

Ⓒ Now write three sentences of your own that use punctuation marks from A.

1. _____

2. _____

3. _____

Beyond Planet Earth

1. _____   4. _____   7. _____

2. _____   5. _____   8. _____

3. _____   6. _____   9. _____

Getting Ready

Discuss the following questions with a partner.

1. *Can you name all the planets in the solar system? Label the picture above.*
2. *What other objects or bodies exist in the solar system?*
3. *Do you believe that there are life forms, either basic or intelligent, on other planets?*
4. *Do you think that one day humans may inhabit other planets? Why or why not?*

Before You Read:
Avoiding Asteroids

Discuss the following questions with a partner.

1. Do you ever watch science fiction or adventure movies about space? Do you think any of the events portrayed in those films can happen? Why or why not?

2. What is an asteroid? What is a meteoroid? Do you think they pose a threat to the planet Earth? If so, how and why?

3. Do you think that if an asteroid was on a collision course with Earth, we would have the power to prevent the collision, and the devastation that would follow? Explain the reasons for your answer.

4. Look at the title of the reading. The following words can all be found in the passage:

spine-chilling   plunge   dreary

perilously   monstrous

Is each word positive or negative? How do you think they relate to the topic of the reading? Use your knowledge of prefixes, suffixes, and word roots, as well as your dictionary, to help you determine the meaning of each of these words.

Reading Skill:
Understanding Inference

Information in a reading passage can be found in two ways: by what is stated directly and written clearly on the page, or by what we can infer. When we infer, we use the information that is stated directly to draw conclusions about events, or the writer's opinion or purpose. Knowing how to infer can help you to better understand the writer's purpose and ideas. It is a useful skill to know when reading for pleasure, and can help you better understand reading passages in exams.

Ⓐ Read through each of the following statements carefully. Scan through the reading passage and decide if each statement is stated (*S*) or inferred (*I*). Check (✔) the correct column.

	S	I
1. If asteroid XF11 hit the earth, it would destroy much of the planet and its inhabitants.		
2. Brian Marsden was very embarrassed about his mistake.		
3. Asteroids vary widely in shape and size.		
4. Isaac Asimov is a writer of science fiction stories.		
5. If all the asteroids were joined together, there may be enough material to form a planet.		
6. Earth will most probably be hit by an NEO in the future.		
7. Earth is scattered with evidence of previous NEO impacts.		
8. Public concern about XF11 coincided with the release of two Hollywood disaster movies.		

Ⓑ Check your answers with a partner. Discuss the reasons for your answers by making reference to the relevant parts of the reading.

Ⓒ Now read the passage again and answer the questions that follow.

Near-Earth Objects: Monsters of Doom? __

The following reading is adapted from *Near-Earth Objects: Monsters of Doom?* by Martin Gardner. Reprinted with permission of the *Skeptical Enquirer* © July–August 1998.

In March of 1998 astronomer Brian Marsden at the Harvard-Smithsonian

Astrophysical Observatory issued a spine-chilling announcement. Based on eighty-eight days of observing asteroid 1977 XF11, he calculated that this massive rock would come perilously close to Earth in 2028. It could miss us by a mere 30,000 miles[1]—only about one-eighth our distance from the moon. Almost a mile[2] wide, if the rock struck Earth the devastation would be too awful to contemplate.

The next day, Marsden was humbly apologizing. NASA's Jet Propulsion Laboratory located a photo of XF11 that permitted a more precise calculation of its path. On its 2028 crossing of the Earth's orbit, it will miss us by 600,000 miles,[3] about two-and-a-half times the average distance between Earth and the moon.

Near-Earth Objects (NEOs) is a contemporary term for massive objects that periodically cross Earth's orbit, and in doing so come close to our planet. They include asteroids, meteoroids, and comets.[4] The word 'asteroid' is Greek for 'starlike,' so named because early telescopes[5] could see them only as points of light. Two large asteroids have since been photographed up close by space probes.[6] They resemble misshapen potatoes, their surfaces covered with craters[7] like the surface of our moon. Almost all asteroids are confined to the asteroid belt,[8] but many wander far beyond the orbit of Jupiter, and others plunge inward past the orbit of Venus. Larger asteroids are spherical, but smaller ones are extremely irregular. It is estimated that more than a thousand asteroids are at least a mile wide. Perhaps a dozen are three or more miles wide. There is no lower limit to asteroid size because they grade down to tiny rocks and particles of dust, but no asteroid is big enough to hold an atmosphere. It is these large NEOs that pose a monstrous threat to humanity if they come close to Earth or hit it.

What produced the asteroids? The writer Isaac Asimov posed the once popular science fiction idea that asteroids are remnants of a small planet whose inhabitants discovered nuclear energy and blew their world to smithereens.[9] But not even a nuclear explosion would be great enough to form the asteroid belt. The prevailing scientific view is that asteroids are material that failed to coagulate into a planet. There is no doubt that eventually Earth will be struck by a massive NEO because such events have occurred in the past. The most recent was the 1908 crash of a large NEO in the Tunguska River valley of central Siberia. It flattened trees for many miles around and killed a herd of reindeer. Earth is spotted with dozens of visible craters that testify to similar impacts, and there surely are thousands of craters that vanished long ago from erosion.[10] It is widely believed that the impact of a giant NEO caused a mass extinction of life that included the dinosaurs, 65 million years ago.

In 1937 the asteroid Hermes,[11] half a mile wide, missed us by about twice the distance between Earth and the moon. In 1989 an asteroid called Asclepius, also about half a mile across, came even closer. In 1991 a small asteroid about 30 feet[12] wide missed the earth by less than half the distance to the moon. The latest near miss was in 1996 when JA1, a third of a mile wide, set a record for large asteroids by missing us by a mere 280,000 miles,[13] only 40,000 miles[14] longer than the distance between Earth and the moon.

50 Disasters caused by NEOs striking Earth are common themes in early science fiction and some modern disaster movies. Sci-fi writer H. G. Wells pioneered the theme. His short story *The Star*, for example, is a vivid account of devastation caused by a mammoth NEO. In the story, an asteroid from the outskirts of the solar system is shifted from its orbit and collides with Neptune. The two coalesce to form a flaming 'star' that almost demolishes the 55 Earth before it plunges into the sun.

On the movie screen, New York City has twice been destroyed by NEOs. It was demolished in the dreary 1979 film, *Meteor*. In the 1951 film, *When Worlds Collide*, a wandering star called Ballus flattens the city with a gigantic tidal wave. The XF11 scare was also great publicity for two disaster movies 60 about NEO impacts: *Armageddon* and *Deep Impact*.

If some time in the future an asteroid is determined to be on a near collision course with Earth, what can be done to prevent disaster? One suggestion, not overlooked in science fiction, is to attach a nuclear bomb to the rock that will blow it into a harmless orbit. In fact, early science fiction envisioned using 65 cannonballs[15] to deflect comets. The danger of bombing an asteroid is that this could produce fragments that would hit the earth, causing even more damage than the intact rock. Better techniques for diverting an asteroid may be landing a rocket engine on it to nudge it away, or attaching a large solar sail to let the sun's radiation do the nudging.

70 Perhaps those sci-fi movies and Hollywood blockbusters aren't quite so far-fetched after all.

1 **30,000 miles** equal to approximately 48,280 kilometers
2 **a mile** equal to approximately 1.6 kilometers
3 **600,000 miles** equal to 965,606 kilometers
4 **comets** solid bodies with tails of gas, observable as bright streaks in the sky when their orbits are close to the sun
5 **telescopes** instruments used to view distant objects more closely
6 **space probes** spacecraft that carry various analytical instruments to explore and discover more about outer space
7 **craters** bowl-shaped hollows in a surface (usually land), caused by the impact of something else
8 **asteroid belt** a strip or band of asteroids, situated between Mars and Jupiter, that orbits the sun
9 **smithereens** tiny pieces or fragments
10 **erosion** the wearing away of a surface, usually rock, by the action of wind or water
11 **Hermes** /hɜrmiz/
12 **30 feet** equal to 9.1 meters
13 **280,000 miles** equal to 450,616 kilometers
14 **40,000 miles** equal to approximately 64,374 kilometers
15 **cannonballs** heavy metal balls fired from cannons (very large tube-shaped guns)

•••

The following questions are all about the reading. Answer each one using the information you have read. Try not to look back at the reading for the answer.

1. Where does Brian Marsden work?
2. What did NASA use to recalculate the path of XF11?
3. Where does the word 'asteroid' come from?
4. What does an asteroid look like?
5. What was Isaac Asimov's theory on how asteroids are formed?
6. What is the accepted scientific view of how they are formed?
7. Disasters caused by NEOs hitting the earth are common in what?
8. What suggestions does the passage give for preventing an asteroid from colliding with Earth?

•••

A Look at the list of words from the reading. Match each one with a definition on the right.

1. spine-chilling _____
2. perilously _____
3. contemplate _____
4. plunge _____
5. remnants _____
6. coagulate _____
7. testify _____
8. coalesce _____
9. dreary _____
10. nudge _____

a. to cause a liquid to transform into a solid or semi-solid mass
b. to move forward or downward suddenly or violently
c. to grow or bond together to form a whole
d. to provide or serve as evidence
e. extremely frightening; eerie
f. dangerously
g. dull; boring
h. to push gently
i. to think about or consider carefully
j. smaller pieces of something left over from a larger piece

B Complete the paragraph below using the vocabulary from A. Be sure to use the correct form of each word.

Meteorite Dream

Many years ago, my parents took me to the Museum of Natural History in New York City. That's where I saw my first meteorite—a meteorite that inspired a _____ dream!

In this dream I was walking alone, at night, in a large canyon. I could see a bright light in the sky that gradually approached the canyon. Suddenly, the light was right above me and a deafening sound filled the air. Numerous rocks _____ down from the sky and hit the floor of the canyon, _____ close to me. I leaped out of the way, and hid behind a boulder to avoid being hit by _____ from each one that flew through the air.

I was terrified; my whole body was frozen. As I crouched behind the boulder, I noticed spots of silver liquid that had landed on the ground. I watched in horror as the liquid began to _____ into a shape—it was forming some kind of spacecraft! I heard a noise and looked across the canyon to see the rocks move towards each other and _____ into larger shapes. Gradually, much to my shock, they began to resemble humans! I crouched lower behind the boulder and _____ what to do next. Would these 'humans' know I was there? How could I escape? My heart was pounding and I was sweating with fear; I made a run for it. As I raced across the canyon, dodging boulders and leaping over rocks, I felt a heavy hand on my left shoulder, and heard a loud voice calling my name.

I opened my eyes to see my mother standing over me, _____ me to wake up. "Come on, breakfast's ready," she said, as I stared up at her in surprise. "What on earth were you dreaming about?" Over breakfast I told her about my dream. "Well, you certainly don't have _____ dreams," was her only comment, as she laughed at my story. After breakfast, I picked up the paper to read that the previous day a woman had _____ to the FBI that she saw large rocks fall out of the sky and land in a canyon near her home. According to her report, a few minutes later, aliens emerged from the canyon and walked off into the distance.

Had my nightmare been just that—a bad dream—or was it real?

Vocabulary Skill:
The Prefix *mis-*

In this chapter, you read the word 'misshapen,' meaning 'badly shaped' or 'deformed.' This word uses the negative prefix 'mis-,' which means 'bad' or 'wrong,' with the word 'shapen.' 'Mis-' is combined with many roots to form other words in English.

(A) For each word below, study the different parts. Then, write the part of speech and a simple definition. Use your dictionary to help you. Share your ideas with a partner.

Vocabulary	Part of Speech	Definition
1. misconception	_____	_____
2. mistakably	_____	_____
3. misbehavior	_____	_____
4. miscommunication	_____	_____
5. misdemeanor	_____	_____
6. mismanage	_____	_____
7. mispronounce	_____	_____
8. misfit	_____	_____
9. misfortune	_____	_____
10. misrepresent	_____	_____

B Complete each sentence using the words from the chart. Be sure to use the correct form of each word.

1. As a result of so many years of being _____, the company went bankrupt.

2. I get so tired of people _____ my name. I always ask people how to say their name correctly.

3. Jean and I ended up not talking as a result of our _____. I said one thing, but she took it completely the wrong way.

4. I find that many people who have not traveled outside of their own countries have huge _____ about what goes on in other parts of the world.

5. Katrina was blamed for all the mistakes in the report, and _____ so; she wasn't the one who typed it.

6. The actor's real words were _____ in the press, and he was made to sound like a terrible person.

7. Although it was only for a _____, Alicia was still taken to the police station and cautioned.

8. Although Allison has warned her children many times about their _____, they don't seem to take much notice of her.

9. The teachers say that Paulo is very gifted and really too intelligent for other children his age. That's why he comes across as such a _____ in school.

10. It was a terrible _____ that Alexander broke both his legs on his skiing trip.

Think About It   **Discuss the following questions with a partner.**

1. *Have you seen any of the movies mentioned in the reading? If so, what did you think of them? Did you believe the events in the film were possible or purely fictitious?*

2. *Now that you have read the passage, is your answer to question 3 of Before You Read on page 142 still the same? If it is different, explain why your opinion has changed.*

3. *Do you think that government space agencies such as NASA already have procedures laid out to combat the effects of an NEO colliding with Earth? Give reasons for your answer.*

4. *If an asteroid were known to be on a collision course with Earth, and would hit in one week, what things would you want to do in that week?*

Before You Read:
Mars Amazes

Discuss the following questions with a partner.

1. What do you know about the planet Mars? Do you know if it contains any signs of life?

2. How much do you know about the exploration of Mars by humans so far?

3. Do you think that in the near future astronauts will be able to visit Mars? Why or why not?

4. Why do you think that space exploration has held so much interest among people over the years?

5. Look at the title of the reading. The following words can all be found in the passage:

venture onto · stunning · microscopic · hospitable · marvels

How do you think they relate to the topic of the reading? Use your knowledge of prefixes and suffixes, as well as your dictionary, to help you determine the meaning of each of these words.

Reading Skill:
Developing
Reading
Fluency

Improve your reading fluency by not stopping at every word you do not know. Focus on understanding the 'gist' or the general idea of what you are reading.

Time yourself as you read through the passage. Try to read as fluently as you can. Record your time in the Reading Rate Chart on page 234.

Wanted: Mars . . . Dead or Alive? _____

The following reading is taken from *Wanted: Mars . . . Dead or Alive?* by Geoffrey A. Landis. Adapted from ODYSSEY'S January 2001 issue: *2001: A Space Odyssey,* © 2001, Cobblestone Publishing Company, 30 Grove Street, Suite C, Peterborough, NH 03458. All rights reserved. Reproduced by permission of Carus Publishing Company.

When Mariner 4 flew past Mars in 1965, scientists on Earth got the first-ever close-up view of the Red Planet. What they saw came as a surprise and a disappointment. The Mars that Mariner's cameras revealed was a cratered desert with an atmosphere so thin that it was barely more than a vacuum.[1]

The planet was bitterly cold and dry, held no trace of life—not even microscopic plants—and appeared to have no water.

The news was shocking, for up until the Mariner pictures, scientists had thought that Mars was a planet a lot like Earth, only somewhat colder. The Red Planet has always fascinated astronomers. It is certainly the most earthlike of all the planets in the solar system—far more hospitable than the furnace of Venus or the hydrogen clouds of Jupiter and Saturn. But the Mariner spacecraft found that Mars was not so much like Earth after all.

As revealed by Mariner and its later cousins, Mars is a planet of stunning superlatives. Its great volcano, Olympus Mons, reaches up almost 25 kilometers above sea level (or the limit where sea level would be, if Mars had a sea). That's like three Mount Everests stacked on top of each other! Valles Marineris is a canyon so huge that if it were placed on Earth, it would stretch from New York to Los Angeles. Even the sky of the Red Planet is different—a pinkish yellow instead of a bright blue. For all these marvels, it's even more disappointing that Mars doesn't have any life. Or does it?

The robotic spacecraft that followed Mariner to Mars gave us a somewhat modified view of the planet. Mars is inhospitable now, but was it always cold and dry? Photographs taken in orbit show many features on the planet surface that look like dry riverbeds. Mars could not have dry riverbeds unless it once had rivers. Scientists think that long ago, Mars had liquid water, like the Earth. They also speculate that billions of years ago, Mars had a much thicker atmosphere, which made it warmer than it is now.

Further evidence supporting the theory that Mars once had water recently came from the Mars Global Surveyor. The craft has mapped the altitude of the Red Planet's surface, which shows that a large area in its northern hemisphere is very low compared to the rest of the planet. This low area is smooth—much smoother than the highlands and mountains in the planet's southern hemisphere. Some scientists think that the low area is the basin[2] of an ancient ocean that once existed on Mars. However, other scientists disagree, and think that there is not enough evidence to be certain.

But let's assume that the scientists are correct about the ocean. On Earth, in every habitat where liquid water can be found, there is some form of life. So, if Mars once had liquid water, it might once have supported life as well.

Could life still exist there? On Earth, living things are very tenacious. From the polar snows to the ocean depths, life has learned to survive no matter how extreme the environment. So, if life started on Mars when it was warm and wet, maybe as it slowly grew cooler and drier, life forms adapted to survive.

But those life forms would have had some serious adapting to do, since we know that the surface of Mars today is extremely harsh. Besides no water and

45 a very thin atmosphere with no oxygen, the planet's surface is flooded with ultraviolet light,[3] which kills bacteria.

Perhaps life on Mars is hidden deep underground in hydrothermal[4] springs. Perhaps the water on Mars is very salty. Since salt water freezes at a lower temperature than fresh water, it could still be liquid even at Mars'
50 temperatures. Recently, scientists found places on Mars where, according to their analysis, water had burst up from underground aquifers[5] and flowed across the planet's surface in geologically recent time.

If there is underground water on Mars, it is possible that there are forms of bacteria living in these springs. Such life would be very primitive, perhaps like
55 the extremophile[6] bacteria that live in underground springs on Earth. If we do find life on Mars, even simple bacteria, we will know that life is not unique to Earth, but exists on two planets—and perhaps is common across the galaxy.

You may wonder if we will ever find out for certain whether life exists on Mars. Although robot 'rovers' continue to help scientists discover more about
60 the Red Planet, some people think that question will only be answered for sure when human astronauts venture onto its surface. The astronauts would use microscopes to examine soil samples taken from many spots on the surface, and drill down into the aquifers. They would dig into dried lakebeds and look for frozen life in the polar caps. In fact, right now, some scientists are
65 proposing plans for an expedition to Mars in fifteen to twenty years time. This question might finally be answered in the first quarter of the twenty-first century.

---

[1] **vacuum** a completely empty, airless space
[2] **basin** a bowl-shaped area that is sunk lower than its surroundings
[3] **ultraviolet light** very bright light carried on the wavelength just beyond violet on the visible spectrum
[4] **hydrothermal** of, or relating to, hot water, or volcanic fluid containing water
[5] **aquifers** water-bearing rocks
[6] **extremophile** organism that exists at its best in extreme environments, e.g., extremes of temperature

Ⓐ Decide if the following statements about the reading are true (*T*) or false
(*F*). If you check (✔) false, correct the statement to make it true.

	T	F
1. Scientists got their first close-up view of Mars in 1964.		
2. Photographs from Mariner 4 confirmed scientists' beliefs about Mars.		
3. Before 1965, Mars was thought to be very similar to Earth.		
4. The sky of Mars is a bright blue color.		
5. Scientists think that billions of years ago, Mars was colder and wetter than it is now.		
6. It is believed that if life once existed on Mars, it could still exist there today.		
7. Scientists believe that life on Mars may be hidden deep underground.		
8. Astronauts have been to Mars to drill for water.		

Ⓑ Check your answers with a partner. Count how many you got correct—be
honest! Then, fill in the Reading Comprehension Chart on page 234.

Ⓐ For each group, circle the word that does not belong. The words in *italics*
are vocabulary items from the reading.

1. *bitterly*	pleasantly	bitingly	severely
2. indication	evidence	*trace*	confusion
3. indiscernible	*microscopic*	miniscule	full-fledged
4. *hospitable*	welcoming	hostile	comfortable
5. impressive	drab	amazing	*stunning*
6. wonders	*marvels*	mysteries	spectacles
7. *burst up*	erupted	spewed	popped
8. streamed	*flowed*	coursed	overflowed
9. step on	proceed onto	*venture onto*	look into
10. unearth	uncover	expose	*drill down*

Ⓑ Complete the sentences below using the words in *italics* from A. Be sure to
use the correct form of each word.

1. Before anyone _____ that stage, you had better make sure it's
secure.

2. Traveling to foreign countries is a real eye-opening experience; the world is
filled with amazing _____.

3. I had a wonderful time touring around Asia. The people were most
_____.

151

4. There were some _____ examples of students' work at the fashion show; this year's class contains a lot of talent.

5. We only realized our main water supply was leaking when water _____ through the flowerbeds in the garden.

6. Although the murderer tried not to leave a _____ of evidence at the crime scene, detectives found _____ spots of his own blood on the carpet.

7. In order to examine patterns of climate change, scientists often _____ into the earth to collect, and examine, soil samples.

8. Many people only imagine the _____ cold weather when they think of Alaska, but there's lots to see and do there.

9. Just seconds after the volcano erupted, lava could be seen _____ down the side of the mountain.

Vocabulary Skill: The Root Word *vac*

In this chapter, you read the word 'vacuum,' which means 'an empty airless space.' This word is formed from the Latin 'vacuus' or 'vacare,' meaning 'to be empty.' A variant of this root is 'void' or 'van,' which share the same meaning. These roots are combined with prefixes and suffixes to form many words in English that have a similar meaning.

(A) For each word, study the different parts. Then write the part of speech and a simple definition for each one. Use your knowledge of prefixes and suffixes and your dictionary to help you. Share your ideas with a partner.

Vocabulary	Part of Speech	Definition
1. void	_____	_____
2. devoid	_____	_____
3. evacuate	_____	_____
4. vacant	_____	_____
5. vanish	_____	_____
6. avoid	_____	_____
7. vacation	_____	_____
8. vacuous	_____	_____

(B) Now complete each sentence using the words from the chart. Be sure to use the correct form of each word.

1. As soon as the earthquake started, everyone was ordered to _____ the building.

2. I've just been told by my tutor that my essays can only be described as dull, boring, and _____.

3. Although he has many hobbies, the _____ that was left in my grandfather's life when my grandmother died has never been filled.

4. Troy is such a serious person, he comes across as being completely _____ of any sense of humor.

5. Thailand is an incredibly interesting country to travel to, but you must remember to _____ drinking the tap water or you'll become ill.

6. I have to finish this report by Friday as I'm leaving for a two-week
_____ to Barbados on Saturday afternoon.

7. This apartment will only be _____ from next month. Until then,
someone will be living here.

8. In scary movies, someone always _____; the plot is so predictable!

C Write two sentences of your own using any two words from the chart in A.

1. _____

2. _____

What Do You Think?

Discuss the following questions with a partner.

1. *Do you think that, from the information you have read, scientists will one day find life on Mars? Why or why not?*

2. *Do you think that governments can justify spending billions of dollars on space exploration, or should that money be put to better use on Earth? Explain your answer.*

3. *Which planet, if any, do you think should be explored next? Why?*

4. *Skeptics believe that man never landed on the moon, and it was all a hoax. What do you think?*

Real Life Skill

Parts of a Book

Many books have special sections at the beginning and the end that give more information about its content. Understanding what each of these sections mean, and the type of information they contain is very useful for getting the most out of your reading material.

A Read these definitions of book sections. Then match them with the examples from a book about fish.

1. Glossary—a list of topic-specific words used in the book, with their meanings _____

2. Bibliography—a list of books and articles that the author referred to while writing _____

3. Index—alphabetical list of the main topics in the book with page numbers _____

4. Table of contents—list of the chapters in a book, with titles and page references _____

5. Acknowledgments—a list of the people who helped the author in some way _____

6. Title page—page after the cover giving the book title, author's name, and publisher _____

a. 2. Eating 34
3. Swimming 49
4. Reproduction 62

b. I wish to thank Dr. Eleanor Clark of Central University, Dr. Peter Nguyen of the Institute for Oceanography, and Chris Peterson of InnerSpace Inc. for their assistance in the writing of this book.

c. Lindsey, B. 2002 *Marine Biology*. London: Ocean Publications
Lo, T. 1998 Communication between fishes. *Ecology* 52:267–280
Martinez, J. 2001 *Sharks of the Pacific*. Los Angeles: University Press

d. FISHES OF THE CORAL REEFS
Loretta Carson
Nautica Books, Miami, Florida

e. *diurnal*: active in daylight hours
dorsal fin: fin that extends along the back of the fish
ethology: the scientific study of animal behavior

f. fins, and swimming ability 51
fire coral 203
flounders 87–89

B Which of these parts would you usually find at the beginning of a book?

_____

C Which of these parts would you usually find at the end of a book?

_____

D Use the examples in A to answer the questions below. In which part of the book did you find the answers?

1. How do we refer to a fish that swims and eats during the day? _____

2. Who wrote the book that these pages are from? _____

3. Which chapter tells about how fish have their babies? _____

4. What page has information about fins? _____

Energy for Life

Getting Ready

Discuss the following questions with a partner.

1. *What is the main form of power used in your home?*

2. *How many different forms of power or energy have you made use of so far today? Which of these are you making use of right now?*

3. *Where does the fuel used to provide these forms of power come from? How does it get from its source to your home?*

4. *Do you think that energy in your town, city, or country is produced in a clean, safe, reliable way? Why or why not? What other methods of energy production do you know of?*

Chapter 1: Biomass: Let's Set the World on Fire

Before You Read:

Global Warming

Discuss the following questions with a partner.

1. What do you understand by the term 'global warming'?
2. What are considered to be the main causes of global warming?
3. How are scientists or government members in your country working to address the issue of global warming? Do you think they are doing enough?
4. What other action can, or should, be taken to further address this issue either globally or in your country?
5. What do you understand by the term 'alternative energies'? Name some types of alternative energies. How can the use of these energies help in addressing the issue of global warming?

Reading Skill:

Identifying Fact versus Opinion

A fact is something that can be checked and proven. An opinion is one person's personal belief or feeling about something. In writing, opinions are often expressed using words and phrases like 'in my opinion,' 'believe,' and 'should,' or speculative language such as 'could,' 'might,' and 'may.' Being able to distinguish between fact and opinion is an important reading skill as much of what we read can be a mixture of both. Using this skill can help you to better understand a reading, become a more critical reader, and put the information you have read to good use.

(A) Read each of the following statements. Circle *F* if you think the statement expresses a fact, or *O* if you think it expresses an opinion. Underline the words that helped you determine your answer.

1. Fossil fuels are getting harder to find.   F   O
2. Nuclear power has proved to be prohibitively expensive.   F   O
3. Solar panels require eight years of use to replace the conventional energy used to manufacture them.   F   O
4. In time, the fossil fuel waves may come to be seen as something of a historical blip.   F   O
5. Power generation produces twice as much heat as electricity.   F   O
6. Bioenergy power stations could be located near the settlements they would serve.   F   O
7. Farmers could transform themselves into energy heroes by changing their crop.   F   O
8. Ravaged rural economies would be boosted by the creation of tens of thousands of new jobs in forestry, transportation, and power plant operation.   F   O

(B) Compare your answers with a partner. Scan through the passage to find where the information in each statement above is mentioned, and check your answers.

(C) Now read through the passage and complete the comprehension exercise that follows. Underline any other facts and opinions you find as you are reading.

Biomass: Let's Set the World on Fire _____

If coal, oil, and gas are just the residues of plants that once lived above ground, then why not burn plants on the surface? With ready access to abundant sources of food in many countries of the world, there is a smaller need to devote vast territories of farmland to food production. In contrast, the
5 demand for energy has no limits.

The fossil fuels[1] on which we have come to depend are growing harder to find, and therefore more expensive. The latest findings on global warming suggest that the diversion of the Gulf Stream[2] and the melting of polar ice caps[3] may be among the least of the environmental problems ahead of us. Once methane[4] bubbles up from the sea and the forests catch fire, releasing yet more carbon instead of absorbing it, warming may increase to a level at which human life will become impossible, anywhere on the planet.

We know we must replace coal, oil, and gas with renewable sources of energy. But how? The answer used to be 'go nuclear,' but nuclear power has proved prohibitively expensive. Hydropower sounds clean, but you have to flood entire valleys for it to work. Much is heard of wind, wave, and solar power. Unfortunately, intermittent energy sources need to be backed up by conventional power, for the wind does not always blow, and the sun does not always shine. Even more problematic is the manufacture of the hardware that such sources of power require. This can use up almost as much energy as they generate. Put a solar panel[5] on your roof, and it will take the first eight years of its use to replace the conventional energy that was needed to make the panel.

The hard truth is that since humans first discovered fire, we have found no energy source that begins to measure up to nature's hydrocarbons.[6] Yet coal, oil, and gas are formed from the mineral residue of plants that once lived above ground. Suppose that, instead of extracting and burning fossil fuels, we burned plants growing on the surface. And suppose we constantly replanted the areas from which we harvested this living fuel, and then burned the replacement plants. Suddenly things would be very different. Scarcity would disappear, as fuel became endlessly renewable. So, too, would the threat to the climate. Carbon would be released when the first plants burned, but an equivalent amount of carbon would be reabsorbed by the replacement plants. In effect, the same carbon would go around and around, as we extracted the energy we need by burning it over and over again.

What a good idea! And it is the same good idea that humanity relied upon until quite recently. In time, the fossil fuel waves—first coal, then oil, and now gas—may come to be seen as something of a historical blip, just like so many other twentieth-century phenomena. But could we really meet our energy needs today by burning plants? We could.

A ton of straw,[7] when biologically converted from cellulose[8] to bioethanol,[9] will produce 300 liters of vehicle fuel. Two tons of dry wood will produce as much electricity as one ton of coal, oil, or gas. Not as good, you may think, but there is more to the story. Power generation produces twice as much heat as electricity. At present, however, electricity is produced in huge power stations sited for easy access to fossil fuel supplies. These stations cannot use the heat that they produce so it is simply wasted. Up to 20 percent of the electricity these stations produce is also wasted through overproduction to meet demand peaks, and friction during the long-distance journeys around grids.[10]

Plants, however, can grow anywhere, so bioenergy power stations could be located near the settlements they would serve. Biofuel could be fed into furnaces as demand required. Numerous small generating stations could capture the heat they gave off and pipe it to surrounding communities. Power
55 plants such as these can burn any kind of biomass. Wood produced from the short-rotation cutting back[11] of fast-growing trees works best, but long grasses will also do. All you need is the land to grow the plants. Where would that come from?

Before the era of mass fossil fuel use, Britain devoted about one-third of its
60 land surface to growing fuel. Recovery of that land, together with existing woodland, for biomass production could enable Britain to meet its entire electricity needs, and much of its heat energy besides. The fiscal[12] restructuring of its energy market would swiftly direct energy distributors toward the new fuel of choice.

65 Farmers could transform themselves into energy heroes merely by changing their crop. Conservationists would see tree cover in places like Britain, currently lower than almost anywhere else in Europe, return at last to respectable levels. The ravaged rural economies in many countries would be boosted by the creation of tens of thousands of new jobs in forestry,
70 transportation, and power plant operation.

Will it happen? Saving the world may not be a priority among nations, but it should be.

---

1 **fossil fuels** fuels that are derived from living matter embedded in the earth that is thousands or millions of years old
2 **Gulf Stream** a warm ocean current that flows from the Gulf of Mexico through the Straits of Florida then north and northeast to merge with the North Atlantic
3 **polar ice caps** the areas above the north and south poles of the earth that are permanently covered with ice
4 **methane** an odorless, colorless, flammable gas used as a fuel
5 **solar panel** flat board containing a group of connected cells that absorb sunlight to produce energy
6 **hydrocarbons** organic materials that contain only carbon and hydrogen, e.g., methane
7 **straw** grain stalks used as animal bedding and food or for weaving into mats and baskets
8 **cellulose** the main substance of the cell walls of most plants
9 **bioethanol** a type of liquid, which can be used as fuel, produced from biofuel (processed plants)
10 **grids** networks of cables and power stations used to transmit electricity
11 **short-rotation cutting back** process of harvesting plants that grow and mature quickly enough to be able to be harvested and replanted in a short space of time, usually a few years
12 **fiscal** of, or relating to, money and finances

••

The following statements are all about the reading. Complete each one using information you have read.

1. Humans now have ready access to _____ sources of food.

2. Fossil fuels are becoming _____ to find and, as a result, more _____.

3. In the future, _____ _____ (two words) may increase to a level at which human life will become impossible.

4. Coal, oil, and gas are formed from the (two words) _____ _____ of plants that once lived above ground.

5. The author believes that by harvesting, burning, and replanting plants growing on the earth's surface we will have an endlessly _____ source of fuel.

6. Up to 20 percent of electricity produced in power stations is wasted through _____ and _____.

7. At one time in the past, Britain devoted about _____ of its land surface to growing _____.

8. The author believes that biomass production could turn farmers into _____ _____ (two words) and boost rural _____.

••

Ⓐ Look at the following words. Using the line references, go back to the reading passage and locate them in the text. Use the meaning from context strategies outlined on pages 58 and 86 to try and work out the meaning of each one. If necessary, go back to those pages and revise this skill before you begin.

residues (line 1)	devote (line 4)	absorbing (line 11)
intermittent (line 17)	measure up to (line 25)	scarcity (line 30)
blip (line 38)	era (line 59)	swiftly (line 63)
ravaged (line 68)		

Ⓑ Read the paragraph below and fill in the blanks using the vocabulary items from A. Be sure to use the correct form of each word.

Building Environmental Awareness

We are living in an _____ when environmental issues such as global warming are of great concern. The burning of fossil fuels extracted from the earth has resulted in huge amounts of carbon being released into the atmosphere. At the same time, forests are being _____ by fires, meaning there are fewer trees available to _____ the carbon and recycle it into oxygen. In addition, our waterways are constantly being polluted by chemical _____ from industry, and household detergents. The future safety of our water supply is uncertain and some countries may soon be faced with a _____ of clean water.

Some people believe this is just a climatic _____ in the history of the Earth;

others believe that people around the world need to _____ more time and energy to environmental awareness. They believe that _____ solutions are not the answer and that governments need to act _____, and work continuously, to encourage people everywhere to take responsibility for the future of our planet. One obvious way to start cleaning up the planet would be to find alternative sources of fuel that _____ the reliability of the fossil fuels we have become so dependent on.

Ⓒ Now think of other examples using the vocabulary from A. Share your ideas with a partner.

1. When you study at home do you devote yourself to what you are doing for long periods of time, or do you work *intermittently*?

2. What topics, or types of information, do you have an easy time *absorbing*? What are some topics, or types of information, that you find difficult to absorb?

3. What do you think are some attitudes and trends that symbolize the *era* we are currently living in?

4. Does the area you live in ever get *ravaged* by storms? If so, how often does this happen?

5. When you walk, do you tend to move quite *swiftly*? What's your usual walking pace?

6. What do you think can be done to avoid any future *scarcity* of food or water in the world?

7. If coal, oil, and gas are the *residues* of ancient plants, what *residues* of humans, who lived thousands or millions of years ago, do you know of that have been extracted from the earth?

8. Think of some kind of phenomenon or event, that has taken place in your country, that can be considered an historical *blip*.

9. Think of an energy source that could provide enough power to *measure up to* the power demands used in your household. How would this energy source transmit power to your home?

Vocabulary Skill: The Root Word *mit*

In this chapter, you read the word 'intermittent,' which means 'stopping and starting at intervals.' This word is formed from the root 'mit,' also written as 'mis,' or 'mes,' which comes from the Latin word 'mittere' meaning to 'send,' 'let go,' or 'allow.' This root is combined with prefixes and suffixes to form many other words in English.

Ⓐ For each word, study the different parts. Then write the part of speech and a simple definition. Use your knowledge of prefixes and suffixes, as well as your dictionary, to help you. Share your ideas with a partner.

Vocabulary	Part of Speech	Definition
1. emission	_____	_____
2. messenger	_____	_____
3. missive	_____	_____
4. submit	_____	_____
5. missile	_____	_____
6. permit	_____	_____
7. dismiss	_____	_____
8. remittance	_____	_____

Ⓑ Complete the sentences below using the words from the chart. Be sure to use the correct form of each word.

1. After working on their project for months, it was finally good enough for the team of architects to _____ to their clients.

2. Many countries have strict regulations in order to control exhaust _____ from motor vehicles.

3. The defendant's _____, in which he apologized to the families of the victims of his crimes, was not well received; they wanted to hear a spoken apology.

4. Around the world, it is becoming increasingly common for smoking not to be _____ inside buildings.

5. Disorderly conduct led to the immediate _____ of the employee.

6. Many agree that world leaders must work together to prevent the continued development of nuclear _____, and other weapons of mass destruction.

7. Hiro will be able to pay his tuition when he receives a cash _____ from home.

8. The _____ arrived exactly on time with the envelope tucked safely under his jacket.

Think About It Discuss the following questions with a partner.

1. *Do you think that the ideas for producing alternative, renewable energy in the reading are realistic, or idealistic? Explain your answer.*

2. *What energy sources do you think people will be using in sixty years? How about in six hundred years?*

3. *Some people think that global warming is the most serious environmental issue facing humans today. Do you agree? Why or why not?*

4. *The last sentence of the reading passage states that saving the world should be a priority among nations. Do you agree with this? Explain your answer.*

Before You Read:
Alternative Energies

Discuss the following questions with a partner.

1. Name some modern inventions that are causes of environmental pollution.

2. What is the 'greenhouse effect'? Can you name any 'greenhouse gases'? Do you know what role these play in global warming?

3. What other reasons are you aware of, besides global warming, for finding alternative energy sources?

4. In the future, do you think we will be able to use the same energy source to power cars as we do now? Why or why not?

5. Look at the title of the reading. The following words can all be found in the passage:

side effects   better off   obstacles   mucking up   mass-producing

How do you think they relate to the topic of finding cleaner energy sources?

Reading Skill:
Developing Reading Fluency

Improve your reading fluency by not stopping at words you do not know. Use the reading skills you have practiced to help you read more smoothly and focus on getting the 'gist,' or general idea, of what you are reading.

Time yourself as you read through the passage. Try to read as fluently as you can. Record your time in the Reading Rate Chart on page 234.

A Long Road to Cleaner Energy Sources ___

The following reading is taken from *Facing a Long Road to Cleaner Energy Sources* by Joseph Szadkowski published March 14, 2002, in *The Washington Times*. Adapted with permission of *The Washington Times*. Copyright © 2002 News World Communications, Inc. Reprinted with permission of *The Washington Times*.

People waste energy constantly, even if unintentionally. According to the Texas Transportation Institute, drivers in the Washington area burn, on average, one quart[1] of fuel per person each workday just sitting in traffic jams. This waste has some serious side effects. That beautiful red and pink sky you sometimes
5 see as the sun sets can be attributed to clouds of nitrogen oxides,[2] and other pollutants[3] from emissions, mucking up the atmosphere. Surely better, cleaner, and more efficient alternative energy sources must exist.

What is meant by the term 'alternative energy source'?

When we think of energy, or fuel, for our homes and cars, we think of petroleum,[4] a fossil fuel processed from oil removed from the ground, of which we know there is a limited supply. But alternative fuels can be many things—the wind, sun, and water can all be used to create fuel. These alternative energies also share the distinction of being what we call renewable resources. Natural gas, propane,[5] and octane[6] can also be used to create energy, but they are not renewable in that once they are consumed they are gone.

Is the threat of running out of petroleum real?

It has taken thousands, if not millions, of years to create the natural stores of petroleum we have now. We are using what is available at a much faster rate than it is being produced over time. The real controversy surrounding the amounts of petroleum we have is how much we need to keep in reserve, for future use. Most experts agree that by around 2025, the amount of petroleum we use will reach a peak, then production and availability will begin to seriously decline. This is not to say there will be no petroleum at this point, but it will become very difficult, and therefore expensive, to harvest.

Is that the most important reason to develop alternate fuel and energy sources?

There are two very clear reasons to do so. One is that whether we have sixty or six hundred years of fossil fuels left, we have to find other fuel sources eventually, so the sooner we start, the better off we will be. The other big argument is that when you burn fossil fuels you release substances that have been literally trapped in the ground for a long time, which leads to some long-term negative effects, such as global warming and the greenhouse effect.

What are hydrogen fuel cells?

A fuel cell works like a battery in that it produces electricity. Unlike a battery, however, it does not store electricity; therefore, it needs a constant source of fuel. In a hydrogen fuel cell vehicle, for example, that fuel source is pressurized[7] hydrogen gas.

Where does hydrogen fuel come from?

Hydrogen is not a source material that you can extract, like oil. Instead, it is a byproduct of something else. One of the most readily available sources for hydrogen is natural gas. However, this leads us back to the problems associated with fossil fuels. Processing natural gas into hydrogen still creates carbon emissions (such as carbon dioxide), which are leading sources of greenhouse gases. The amount of carbon emissions created in this process is

10

15

20

25

30

35

40

45

50

significantly less than emissions created in petroleum use, though.

Does hydrogen work like fossil fuels?

Most people are familiar with the electrolysis[8] of water where electricity is
55 used to break water into hydrogen and oxygen. When children do this
experiment in a lab, they usually burn the hydrogen gas, creating a very loud
bang[9] that results from the release of energy in hydrogen combustion.[10] The
fuel cell takes that experiment, but works it backward. Instead of breaking
down water into hydrogen and oxygen, the hydrogen and oxygen are
60 combined to create electricity, and the byproducts are heat and water.

Will hydrogen work just like gasoline in our cars, and give us the same speed performance?

The power needed for our current vehicles is created when gasoline and air are
combined to create combustion. As the aforementioned experiment shows, this
65 same type of energy can be produced using hydrogen as fuel. The difficulty of
mass-producing cars powered by hydrogen fuel cells is that hydrogen is a
pressurized gas, not a liquid product like gasoline. One of the biggest obstacles
is in developing easy-to-use 'hydrogen stations,' similar to our present-day gas
stations. But because a hydrogen fuel cell car will produce zero emissions, they
70 represent a comparatively positive impact on the environment.

What is stopping the development of more hydrogen fuel cell vehicles?

One of the main issues is the cost of the technology development. It will be
some time before a hydrogen fuel cell vehicle will be available at a reasonable
price. A second issue is the problem of creating a system of accessible
75 hydrogen stations where drivers can refuel. There is also the physical problem
of developing hydrogen fuel in an easy-to-deliver form. Two possibilities are a
compressed gas, or a liquid that would need to be kept at a temperature of 20
degrees Kelvin[11] above absolute zero,[12] or minus 250 degrees Celsius. This
sounds dangerous, but work is being done to make this environmentally
80 friendly fuel as safe as gasoline.

---

[1] **one quart** a unit of liquid measure equal to ¼ gallon or .946 liter

[2] **nitrogen oxides** chemically symbolized as NOx; a group of colorless, odorless gases, all containing nitrogen and oxygen, which form as a byproduct of burning fuel, and act as environmental pollutants

[3] **pollutants** waste materials that cause harm to living organisms, and contaminate soil, air, and water

[4] **petroleum** a thick, flammable mixture of liquid, gas, and solid hydrocarbons extracted from the earth, processed, and separated into various substances and used to power cars, for heating, light, etc.

[5] **propane** a colorless gas found in natural gas and petroleum, used as a fuel

[6] **octane** a group of hydrocarbons found in petroleum and used as a fuel

[7] **pressurized** put or stored under a greater than normal pressure so as to allow a rapid, steady release

[8] **electrolysis** a chemical change caused by an electric current

[9] **bang** a sudden, loud noise

[10] **combustion** a chemical change, usually induced by burning, that produces heat and light

[11] **Kelvin** a unit of absolute temperature, each unit being equal to one Celsius degree

[12] **absolute zero** the temperature at which there is absolutely no heat; equal to -273.15°C or -459.67°F

Ⓐ How much do you remember from the reading? Choose the best answer
for each question or statement

1. Drivers stuck in traffic jams in _____ waste, on average, one quart of fuel per day.
   a. Texas
   b. the Transportation Institute
   c. Washington State
   d. the Washington area

2. An 'alternative energy source' is _____.
   a. renewable
   b. in limited supply
   c. processed from natural gas
   d. processed from oil

3. The real concern over petroleum is _____.
   a. how to replace it
   b. how to harvest it
   c. how to make it cheaper
   d. how much to keep in reserve

4. One reason for developing alternative fuel sources is _____.
   a. to use less energy
   b. to save money
   c. burning fossil fuels harms the environment
   d. fossil fuels will only last for another sixty to six hundred years

5. What are hydrogen fuel cells?
   a. Electricity sources fed by batteries
   b. Energy sources fed by pressurized hydrogen gas
   c. Batteries that are continual sources of fuel
   d. Stores of electricity

6. The most common source of hydrogen is _____.
   a. natural gas
   b. carbon emissions
   c. greenhouse gases
   d. oil

7. The advantage of using hydrogen fuel over fossil fuel is that it _____.
   a. uses water
   b. creates less emissions
   c. is a lot cheaper
   d. still creates carbon emissions

8. The development of hydrogen fuel cell vehicles is slow because of _____.
   a. money
   b. technology
   c. interest
   d. safety

Ⓑ Check your answers with a partner. Count how many you got correct—be
honest! Then, fill in the Reading Comprehension Chart on page 234.

Ⓐ Look at the list of words and phrases from the reading. Match each one with a definition on the right.

a. attain the highest level of usage or intensity
b. state of being more prosperous than before
c. pressed together so as to use less space
d. secondary effects of something, usually unpleasant

1. side effects _____
2. mucking up _____
3. in reserve _____

4. reach a peak _____
5. better off _____
6. literally _____
7. aforementioned _____
8. mass-producing _____
9. obstacles _____
10. compressed _____

e. in the strictest sense; having the most exact meaning
f. manufacturing in large quantities
g. things that prevent or hinder progress
h. for use if and when needed
i. mentioned above, or earlier
j. damaging; ruining

Ⓑ Complete the paragraph below using most of the vocabulary from A—there is one word that is not used. Be sure to use the correct form of each word.

Protect the Environment; Protect Ourselves

Have you ever considered how environmental pollution might be affecting our bodies? Pollutants in the air can _____ be absorbed by our skin, or inhaled through our lungs. The _____ of this can be very obvious, for example, pimples and skin complaints. Other people suffer from serious bronchial disorders such as asthma, especially those who live in industrial cities where smoke and gases can be seen coming out of factory chimneys, and _____ the atmosphere daily. At certain times, when emissions from these factories _____, people can become very ill, and must ensure they have plenty of medication _____. Although drug companies now _____ various medications to deal with both of the _____ conditions, many people say the only way they can be _____ health-wise is by moving out of the city, and into an area with fewer factories. Of course, this is not always possible, one obvious _____ being finding employment in another area.

Vocabulary Skill: The Prefix *ob-*

In this chapter you read the word 'obstacle' which begins with the prefix 'ob-,' meaning 'toward' or 'against.' This prefix, also written as 'op-,' is very common and is used with nouns, verbs, adjectives, and adverbs to form many words in English.

Ⓐ For each word, study the different parts. Then write the part of speech and a simple definition. Use your knowledge of word roots, suffixes, and your dictionary to help you. Share your ideas with a partner.

Vocabulary	Part of Speech	Definition
1. opponent	_____	_____
2. obstruct	_____	_____
3. optimistic	_____	_____
4. objectionable	_____	_____
5. oppression	_____	_____
6. obligatory	_____	_____
7. obnoxious	_____	_____
8. observatory	_____	_____
9. obtrusive	_____	_____
10. obviously	_____	_____

B Complete each sentence below using the words from the chart. Be sure to use the correct form of each word.

1. Francesca seemed to be unaware that her moody behavior every morning was considered to be quite _____ by everyone else in the office.

2. Misha _____ had to move to another apartment after the building she was living in caught fire.

3. Even though Sebastian was beaten by his _____ in the tennis finals, he remains _____ about his chances of winning the golf tournament.

4. Our new house will have an _____ on the top floor so we can study the stars.

5. The witness was fined for providing the police with the wrong information, and in doing so _____ the course of justice.

6. Some of Karl's colleagues find his approach to dealing with problems to be highly _____; others think it's funny.

7. In order to apply to this university, it is _____ that you attend an interview.

8. As a result of his _____ manner, Jim only lasted one afternoon working as a waiter.

9. After many years of tolerating government _____, the people voted for a leader who promised them the freedom of a true democracy.

What Do You Think?

Discuss the following questions with a partner.

1. *What do you imagine a hydrogen-powered vehicle would look like?*

2. *Can you envisage how one of these vehicles would work, and how refueling stations would work?*

3. *Do you think that the concept of using hydrogen fuel cells is a realistic one? Why or why not?*

4. *Besides burning car fuel sitting in traffic jams, what are some other ways that people waste energy? How can people reduce the amount of energy they consume, and in doing so limit human impact on the environment?*

Real Life Skill

Using a Thesaurus

A thesaurus is a vocabulary reference book that gives lists of synonyms (words that have similar meanings), and antonyms (words that have opposite meanings). It also contains groups of words related to important concepts. A thesaurus is a useful tool to help expand and enrich your vocabulary, and give more variety to your writing. However, as it does not contain definitions, you should always check the exact meaning and nuance in your dictionary before using a new word.

(A) Look at the following sentence.

> One of the biggest *obstacles* in developing alternative energy sources is the lack of government support.

Now read these entries from a thesaurus:

> **obstacle** *noun* bar, barricade, barrier, hindrance, impediment, obstruction, snag. See DIFFICULTY, OPPOSITION. *Ant:* See AID, COOPERATION
>
> **opposition** *noun* 1. resistance, renitence. See RESIST. 2. antagonism, contradiction, contrariness. *Ant:* See SUPPORT
>
> **difficulty** *noun* 1. hardship, rigor. *Ant:* See EASY. 2. clash, conflict, confrontation, contention, discord, dissent, faction, inharmony, war. See CONFLICT

(B) Use the thesaurus entries to rewrite the sentence, substituting two different words for *obstacle*. Use your dictionary to check the exact meaning and nuance of the words you choose.

1. _____

2. _____

(C) Read the following sentence, then look at the thesaurus entry beneath it.

> More investment would ensure the swift development of new sources of energy.

> **swift** *adjective* expeditious, fast, fleet, quick, rapid, speedy. See FAST
>
> **fast** *adjective* 1. brief, hasty, hurried, quick, short, speedy, swift. 2. clinging, firm, secure, tenacious, tight. See FREE, TIGHTEN

(D) Circle all the words in the thesaurus entry that can be used in place of the word *swift* in the sentence. Use your dictionary to check your answers. Share your ideas with a partner.

It's All in the Mind

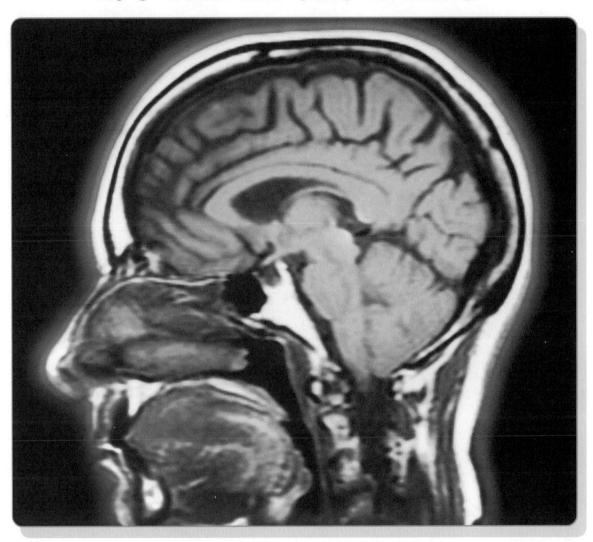

Getting Ready

Discuss the following questions with a partner.

1. *What do you know about how our brains control our behavior? Why do you think that, in certain situations, people sometimes behave awkwardly?*

2. *Have you ever been in a situation where you have been unsure of how to behave? What was the situation, and how did it make you feel?*

3. *Do you think you have a good or bad memory? Explain your answer giving examples.*

4. *Look at the following sequence of numbers for five seconds:*

   2345, 3456, 4567, 5678

   Now close your book and repeat the sequence back to a partner forwards, then backwards.

169

Before You Read:
Isn't It Funny?

Discuss the following questions with a partner.

1. What makes you laugh? Why?

2. Why do you think humans laugh? Do you know of any animal species that also laugh?

3. Have you ever laughed at something inappropriately? What happened? How did you feel afterwards?

4. Look at the title of the reading. The following words and phrases can all be found in the passage:

spontaneous   contagiousness   baffling   solidarity   triggered

How do you think they relate to the topic of the reading? Use your knowledge of prefixes, suffixes, and word roots, as well as your dictionary, to help you determine the meaning of each of these words.

Reading Skill:
Identifying Meaning from Context

> *You can guess the meaning of important but unfamiliar words in a reading passage by using the following strategy: **1.** Think about how the new word is related to the topic of what you are reading about. **2.** Identify which part of speech the new word is by looking at how it fits with the other words in its sentence. **3.** Look at how the word relates to the rest of the information in the paragraph surrounding it. **4.** Use your knowledge of prefixes, suffixes, and word roots to identify the basic meaning of the word.*

(A) The following is an extract from the reading passage. As you read through it, think about the topic of the reading, and what you already know about this topic. Pay attention to the underlined words.

> . . . laughter is an inborn characteristic. It is a universal human expression that we share with our closest animal relatives, the apes. This was known to Charles Darwin and (**1**) <u>confirmed</u> by the Dutch (**2**) <u>ethologist</u> Jan van Hooff, who set out to clarify under which circumstances apes make their laughing sounds.

(B) Decide which part of speech each underlined word is, and write them below.

(**1**) _____   (**2**) _____

How do you know this? Circle the words in the sentence that work with or affect the underlined words, and tell you the part of speech. Look at how the word relates to the rest of the paragraph. Are there any other words or phrases that give you clues to the meaning of each word? If so, circle them.

(C) Now look at the parts of the words. Does each one have a recognizable prefix, root, or suffix? Use your knowledge of these word parts to try to identify the meaning of each word. Replace each one with a word or phrase, or write a definition.

(**1**) _____   (**2**) _____

(D) Use your dictionary to check whether you have interpreted the meaning of the words correctly. Share your answers with a partner.

Ⓔ Choose five words from the list below that you do not know. Using the line references, locate each word in the passage and underline it.

intercom (line 3)	displays (line 25)	tackling (line 27)
revelations (line 29)	asymmetry (line 44)	hostile (line 51)
suppress (line 55)	chuckle (line 55)	implications (line 64)

Ⓕ Using the same strategies you practiced above, identify the part of speech of each word. Look at how each one fits into the sentences or paragraph around it. Look at the parts of each word and try to work out the meaning. Replace them with words or phrases you know that have the same meaning, or write a definition. Share your answers with a partner, and use your dictionary to check your interpretations and definitions.

Vocabulary	Part of Speech	Word/Definition
1. _____	_____	_____
2. _____	_____	_____
3. _____	_____	_____
4. _____	_____	_____
5. _____	_____	_____

Laugh and the World Laughs with You ___

The following reading is adapted from *Laugh and the World Laughs with You* by Frans B. M. De Waal. Copyright © 2002 by Scientific American, Inc. All rights reserved.

The following reading is a review of Robert R. Provine's *Laughter: A Scientific Investigation.*

One morning the school principal's voice sounded over the intercom of my high school with the shocking announcement that a popular French teacher had just died in front of his class. Everyone fell silent. While the principal went on to explain that it had been a heart attack, I couldn't keep myself from laughing. To this day, I feel embarrassed about that. 5

What is it about laughter that makes it unstoppable even if triggered by circumstances that aren't amusing? Extreme episodes of laughter, marked by loss of motor control,[1] shedding of tears, or gasping[2] for air, are positively worrying. 10 What weird trick has been played on us to make us express ourselves with such stupid "ha, ha, ha" sounds? Why don't we just leave it at "that was funny"?

These questions are old, dating back to philosophers who have puzzled over why one of humanity's finest achievements—its sense of humor—is expressed in such an animal-like fashion. There can be no doubt that laughter is an inborn 15 characteristic. It is a universal human expression that we share with our closest animal relatives, the apes. This was known to Charles Darwin and confirmed by the Dutch ethologist Jan van Hooff, who set out to clarify under which circumstances apes make their laughing sounds. He concluded that laughter is

171

20 associated with a playful attitude in both humans and apes, even though play is considerably more physical, such as tickling[3] and wrestling,[4] in apes.

Laughter: A Scientific Investigation builds on this work in that it assumes animal origins of laughter, and follows van Hooff's distinction between the laugh and the smile. The two expressions are often mentioned in the same breath yet they are
25 used quite differently in primate[5] displays, with the smile expressing affection and appeasement rather than playfulness. Robert R. Provine has set himself the task of cracking[6] the 'laugh code,' as he calls it, rather than tackling the much more complex issue of humor. The two may appear inseparable, but one of the revelations of his book is that they are not.

30 The large majority of laughs measured by Provine and his students in the shopping centers and on the sidewalks of the human natural habitat occurred in response to statements that were far from humorous. In spontaneous social contacts, people burst into laughter at unfunny comments such as "I see your point" and "Put those cigarettes away" far more often than at funny ones, such
35 as "He tried to blow his nose, but he missed." This shows that humor is not the issue: social relationships probably are.

Laughter is a loud display that much of the time seems to signal mutual liking and well-being. Some of its uses are unique to our species. When a group of people laugh, sometimes at the expense of outsiders, they show solidarity and
40 togetherness not unlike a howling[7] pack of wolves. According to Vanderbilt University psychologist Jo-Anne Bachorowski,[8] the unifying function of laughter is particularly clear among men. Provine expands on this theme with the observation that women laugh more in response to men's remarks than the reverse. The asymmetry between the sexes starts early in life, between boys and
45 girls, and seems to be cross-cultural. The man as laugh-getter also turned up in an analysis of personal ads, in which Provine found that women generally look for partners with a sense of humor, which male advertisers generally claimed to have.

Provine's well-written, often amusing, and always fascinating book presents laughter in all its complexity and with all its contradictions. He does not try to
50 sell us a one-issue explanation of laughter. He makes no secret that even after all his research he still finds laughter a baffling behavior that can be both hostile and friendly, and a response to subtle[9] humor or triggered by something banal.[10]

The amazing contagiousness of laughter even works across species. At the primate center where I work, I often hear chimpanzees laugh when they tickle
55 one another, and I cannot suppress a chuckle in response. Tickling must be the original context of laughter, and the fact that tickling oneself is notoriously ineffective confirms its social significance. Tickling and laughter are essentially play patterns, with the latter having achieved a considerably expanded meaning in our species.

60 Toward the end of the book, the author discusses disorders associated with laughter and laughing epidemics as well as the opposite: the healing power of

laughter exploited by some therapists. It is obvious that his research not only opens new avenues into human social life but also carries mental health implications.

My own reaction to the death of a teacher was only a mild case of laughter under odd circumstances compared with the clinical, and sometimes fatal, cases discussed in Provine's book. The fact that we can lose control over this expression, and that it may become tragic or sardonic[11] shows how close comedy can get to tragedy. We like to see ourselves as fully rational beings, but much of that rationality can disappear when someone makes us laugh.

65

70

---

1 **motor control** movement of the body as controlled by impulses from the brain
2 **gasping** inhaling quickly and convulsively
3 **tickling** touching the sensitive parts of a body lightly to cause laughter
4 **wrestling** fighting with someone by throwing or stopping them from moving
5 **primate** any member of the highest order of animals, including humans, apes, monkeys, and lemurs
6 **cracking** solving
7 **howling** making a long, high-pitched cry like an animal
8 **Bachorowski** /bækouɾouvski/
9 **subtle** not immediately obvious
10 **banal** boring, not interesting
11 **sardonic** mocking; hateful

Reading Comprehension: What Do You Remember?

The following sentences are all about the reading. Complete each one using information you have read. Try not to look back at the reading for the answers.

1. Laughter can be triggered by circumstances that are, and are not, _____.

2. Laughter is an expression shared by humans and _____, and is associated with _____ in both.

3. Although laughter and humor seem to be _____, Provine's book reveals that they are not.

4. Provine's research suggests that, as people often laugh at _____ comments, _____ _____ (two words) may play a larger role in laughter than humor does.

5. When people laugh as a group, they show _____.

6. Provine discovered that differences exist between _____ in the role that laughter plays in life.

7. The social significance of laughter is confirmed by the fact that _____ oneself is _____.

8. Provine's book also discusses _____ associated with laughter, and how it can be used for _____ purposes.

Vocabulary Comprehension:
Words in Context

Ⓐ Look at the following words. Using the line references, go back to the reading and locate them in the passage. Use the meaning from context strategies you practiced in the Reading Skill to try and work out the meaning of each one.

---

triggered (line 8) episodes (line 9) appeasement (line 26)
spontaneous (line 32) mutual (line 37) solidarity (line 39)
baffling (line 51) contagiousness (line 53) notoriously (line 56)
epidemics (line 61)

Ⓑ Read the paragraph below and fill in the blanks using the vocabulary items from A. Be sure to use the correct form of each word.

A Laughing Matter

Teachers at a local elementary school recently solved the mystery of a laughing _____ among the children. These _____ of laughter began a few weeks ago, and seemed to be _____ when it was raining and the children played together inside. At first, teachers thought that these _____ outbursts were caused by a young boy who is _____ for playing jokes and making people laugh. However, after the playtime laughter had continued for a few days, teachers began to suspect that this was more than a display of _____ among the children for the _____ appreciation of their fellow student's jokes. The following week, the laughter still continued, by which point teachers were _____. However, after closely monitoring the children's movements, the art teacher discovered what the children were laughing at. A small monkey was living in a tree in the school grounds. Every time a child looked out of the window the monkey would smile, wave, and jump around in the tree. The happy expressions on the faces of the young children seemed to _____ the monkey, and encouraged him to perform more tricks. As one child laughed, more and more would join in, even if they hadn't seen the monkey themselves—thus proving that laughter really is _____. It turned out that the monkey had escaped from the local zoo and found its way into the playground. Although the children wanted to keep the monkey as their school pet, he had to be returned to the zoo. In order to keep the children happy, the headmaster took a photo of the monkey and made it into large posters—enough to hang one in each classroom.

Ⓒ Now think of other examples using some of the vocabulary from A. Share your ideas with a partner.

1. As a child, did you catch any *contagious* childhood diseases? Which ones?

2. When it comes to your social life, do you like to do things *spontaneously*, or do you like to have set plans?

3. What is something—for example a topic, story, or scientific theory you have read or heard about—that you find *baffling*?

4. Is there a well-known person in your country who is *notorious* for doing embarrassing things in public? Who is it?

Vocabulary Skill:
The Prefix *epi-*

A Match each word beginning with *epi-* to a definition below. Compare your answers with a partner.

> epilogue   epicenter   epidemiology   epidermis
> epitaph   epithet   epigraph   epistle

1. A short piece of writing or poem about a dead person, especially one written on a tombstone. _____

2. The branch of medicine that deals with the study of the causes, distribution, and control of disease in populations. _____

3. An afterword, or concluding section, in a book; a short speech given directly to the audience following the end of a play. _____

4. A point of the Earth's surface directly above the source of an earthquake; a focal point. _____

5. A letter (especially a formal one); a literary work in the form of a letter. _____

6. An inscription on a building or statue; a motto or quotation at the beginning of a literary composition. _____

7. The outer, protective layer of the skin. _____

8. A descriptive term or phrase used to characterize a person or place. _____

> *In this chapter you read the word 'episode' meaning 'an event' or 'an occurrence.' You also read 'epidemic,' meaning 'affecting many people throughout an area,' or 'the rapid spread, growth, or development of something.' The prefix 'epi-' comes from the Greek word 'epi' or 'ep,' and can mean 'upon,' 'above,' 'beside,' 'among,' 'around,' or 'near.' This prefix is used with many different root words in English.*

B Now that you know the meaning of the words above, complete the chart below with some of the modern roots used.

Greek Root	Meaning	Modern Root
1. taphos	tomb	taph
2. derma	skin	_____
3. legein	to say	_____
4. graphein	to write	_____
5. stellein	to send	_____
6. tithenai	to place	_____

Think About It Discuss the following questions with a partner.

1. *Can you think of a recent joke you heard that did not make you laugh? Did anybody else laugh?*

2. *Do you think that different cultures around the world have different senses of humor? How would you describe or define the typical sense of humor in your culture?*

3. *Do you understand humor and jokes in other languages and cultures? Do you find jokes told or written in English easy to understand?*

4. *Do you agree with Provine's claim that differences exist between men and women when it comes to humor? Can you think of any other examples, besides those in the reading, that highlight this gender difference in behavior? Do you think these differences are specific to your culture?*

Unit 13

Chapter 2: Mind Like a Sieve? There's No Need to Worry

Before You Read:

Can You Remember?

Ⓐ Write the answers to the following questions. Time how long it takes you to recall the information.

1. What did you eat for dinner last night? _____

2. What is one word, phrase, or expression you learned in your last English class? _____

3. When is your best friend's birthday? _____

4. Where are your front door keys right now? _____

Ⓑ Discuss the following questions with a partner.

1. How long did it take you to answer all the questions above? Which question took the longest to answer? Why do you think this was?

2. Turn back to Getting Ready on page 169 and look at question 4 again. Did you recognize a pattern in the number sequence? Explain it.

3. Look at the title of the reading. What do you think it means if someone 'has a mind like a sieve'?

4. The following words can all be found in the reading:

reciting   atrocious   capacity

decaying   synthesize

How do you think they relate to the topic of the reading? Use your knowledge of prefixes, suffixes, and word roots, as well as your dictionary, to help you determine the meaning of each of these words.

Time yourself as you read through the passage. Try to read as fluently as you can. Record your time in the Reading Rate Chart on page 234.

Mind Like a Sieve? There's No Need to Worry

The following reading is adapted from *Forget It* by Alison Motluk. First published in *New Scientist*, October 20, 2001. Reprinted with permission of *New Scientist* © 2001.

You forgot where the car was parked at the airport yesterday. You missed your mother-in-law's birthday last week. The name of that old boyfriend or girlfriend is on the tip of your tongue[1]—but what is it? Your memory is atrocious. Or so you think. But common sense tells us that forgetfulness is vital to a healthy brain by clearing our minds of decaying memorabilia,[2] and, increasingly, so does science.

Today, a small band of scientists is trying to discover how and why the brain chooses to erase certain memories. Their aim isn't to increase our ability to remember, nor are they researching some kind of evil memory-erasing pill. What does interest them is the prospect of helping people get rid of the unwanted memories that, researchers are discovering, can contribute to mental illnesses such as depression and post-traumatic stress disorder.[3]

If they succeed, the benefits won't just be confined to clinics. Even in mentally healthy people, being unable to forget past events can dull the mind and generate misery. There is no stronger evidence of this than the life of Solomon Shereshevski, the world's most celebrated mnemonist.[4] Studied for thirty years by Russian psychologist Aleksandr Luria,[5] Shereshevski spent much of his professional life performing amazing feats of memory for paying audiences. He could memorize strings of numbers just by looking at them for a few seconds, recalling them with stunning accuracy months or even years later, and reciting them backwards or forwards.

But Shereshevski paid heavily for his talent. He remembered things by picturing them in his mind and this, it seems, hindered his intellect. "I can only understand what I can visualize," he told Luria. Unable to think in the abstract, his mental capacity never really got beyond that of an adolescent. He got muddled when a word had two meanings or an object had two names. In fact, he could barely read. "Each word he read produced images that distracted him and blocked the meaning of a sentence," wrote Luria.

Unfortunately, scientists never discovered what it was about Shereshevski's extraordinary brain that allowed him to retain details most of us would simply discard or suppress. Scientists are pretty much agreed on the basics of how new memories form. Like threads woven into cloth, memorable new experiences are essentially strengthened connections between neurons.

You might reasonably expect forgetting to be the reverse of remembering, a simple matter of the connections gradually weakening until memories vanish. But

5

10

15

20

25

30

35

there's a lot more to it than that, as scientists are starting to discover. If you can't remember what you had for breakfast, it's probably because your brain never bothered to encode the information. Also, evidence suggests that the brain naturally suppresses unwanted memories. In at least some cases, forgetting is not
40 a passive process of decay, but rather an active process of inhibiting.

Shereshevski devised elaborate ways to try to suppress his memories but found it almost impossible. He described one technique to Luria: "In my mind I erase the blackboard and cover it, as it were, with a film that's completely opaque[6] and impenetrable. Even so, when the next performance starts and I walk over to that
45 blackboard, the numbers I had erased are liable to turn up again."

And even the rest of us know there are certain memories that we can't get rid of no matter how hard we try. Sometimes it's just an annoying song in your head. But more often, it's an emotionally charged event such as the death of a loved one, or a violent attack. There's probably a good evolutionary reason for
50 remembering traumatic events: they are a threat to survival, so creatures who can remember and learn from them would have a better chance of staying alive. But not being able to forget can also have serious consequences. Studies show that people who tend to mull things over excessively experience longer episodes of depression than those who don't.

55 Moreover, it's been observed that people with lower IQs are generally more likely to suffer from post-traumatic stress disorder. "People with greater working memory capacity may be better able to suppress unwanted memories of traumatic life experiences," speculates Cris Brewin of University College in London. He says that inhibiting memories, or forgetting, uses up mental
60 resources, and can require effort. But many of our everyday memories aren't so much lost or thrown away, as merged. As time passes, the details drop away and only the broad outlines remain. You don't remember every breakfast you ate as a child, but you may well remember that you hated toast and tea and that your brother always argued with you. You remember only the gist of breakfasts past.

65 As well as being necessary for mental health, forgetfulness may also play a role in creative thinking. Here again, Shereshevski provides a telling example. He could remember the numbers 2345, 3456, 4567, 5678, for instance, in any direction and recall them perfectly after several years, but he couldn't recognize the pattern. Memory aces,[7] like Shereshevski, may recall where every detail came from, but
70 sadly, might never be able to synthesize and form original thoughts.

---

[1] **on the tip of your tongue** almost able to remember and say something
[2] **memorabilia** things that remind us of events in our lives, that we consider worthy of remembering
[3] **post-traumatic stress disorder** condition whereby one is mentally disturbed following a traumatic experience
[4] **mnemonist** /nɪmɑnɪst/ someone who has a very powerful memory
[5] **Aleksandr Luria** /ælɪgzændər luriɑ/
[6] **opaque** not see-through; not allowing light to pass through
[7] **aces** people who excel in a certain field or profession

Reading Comprehension: How Much Do You Remember?

Ⓐ The following questions are all about the reading. Use the information you have read to answer each one correctly.

1. Why are scientists interested in helping people get rid of unwanted memories?
2. Give one reason why being able to forget past events is important.
3. What was unique about Solomon Shereshevski?
4. What effects did Shereshevski's memory have on his intellectual ability?
5. How did Shereshevski try to suppress his memories?
6. What kind of events are we most likely to remember?
7. What observations have been made with regard to the relationship between IQ levels and memory?
8. As well as mental health, what other aspect of thinking is forgetfulness thought to affect?

Ⓑ Check your answers with a partner. Count how many you got correct—be honest! Then, fill in the Reading Comprehension Chart on page 234.

Vocabulary Comprehension: Word Definitions

Ⓐ Look at the list of words and phrases from the reading. Match each one with a definition on the right.

1. atrocious _____
2. decaying _____
3. reciting _____
4. hindered _____
5. muddled _____
6. capacity _____
7. elaborate _____
8. impenetrable _____
9. mull things over _____
10. synthesize _____

a. to think about something in great depth
b. detailed; planned with careful attention
c. confused
d. exceptionally bad
e. ability
f. to combine or unite things to form something new
g. gradually diminishing or decreasing
h. saying something aloud from memory
i. impossible to enter or pass through
j. interfered with the progress or development of something

Ⓑ Complete the sentences below using the vocabulary items from A. Be sure to use the correct form of each word.

1. Thomas is so nervous about starring in his first school play. He spent hours last night _____ his lines over and over.

2. Even though his teachers think his intellectual _____ is very great, Joshua doesn't get good grades as he doesn't study hard enough.

3. Look at the mess in this kitchen! How can you live in such _____ conditions?

4. By the time Ramon finally went to the dentist, his bad tooth had _____ beyond repair, and he had to have it extracted.

5. Although the guarantee that came with this tent claimed it was completely
_____ to rain, it leaked last night and I woke up in a puddle of
water.

6. Molly seems very fed up right now, but I think it has more to do with her
tendency to _____ than with having any real problems to worry
about.

7. It's obvious from the _____ way the table was laid out that Rosa
went to great lengths in planning her dinner party.

8. Blake has a really difficult time having two sets of identical twins in his class.
He's always getting them, and their work, _____ up.

9. My job with the agency involves _____ information from various
sources, then summarizing the main points for news bulletins.

10. Although being born with only one arm _____ her ability to do
certain things, Su-Hui still succeeded in becoming a world-class athlete.

Vocabulary Skill: Root Word *mem*

In this chapter you read the words 'memorabilia,' 'mnemonist,' and 'remember,' which all contain the root word 'mem,' also written as 'men,' or 'mnem,' meaning 'to remember' or 'to recall.' This root is used with prefixes and suffixes to form many words in English that relate to the subject of memory and remembering things.

Ⓐ For each word, study the different parts. Then, write the part of speech and a simple definition. Use your dictionary to help you. Share your ideas with a partner.

Vocabulary	Part of Speech	Definition
1. mnemonic	_____	_____
2. memorial	_____	_____
3. memoir(s)*	_____	_____
4. remembrance	_____	_____
5. commemorate	_____	_____
6. memento	_____	_____
7. immemorial	_____	_____
8. monument	_____	_____

*Can be used in singular or plural form

B Complete the following sentences using the words from the chart. Be sure to use the correct form of each word.

1. As _____ of our trip to Australia, I bought a boomerang and a cuddly toy koala.

2. The government is planning to build a _____ in _____ of the man who founded the town two hundred years ago.

3. One good way to learn new vocabulary is to use _____ devices, or methods. There are many good books that can show you how.

4. The name Daniel has been given to the male members of my family since time _____.

5. In order to _____ the independence of the United States from England, Americans celebrate every Fourth of July with parades, fireworks, and barbecue parties.

6. The politician's _____ not only detailed his career, but also disclosed various scandals that present members of parliament have been involved in.

7. When his wife died at a very young age, Malcolm bought a small piece of wasteland and turned it into a rose garden that serves as a _____ to her.

What Do You Think?

Discuss the following questions with a partner.

1. *Why do you think that some people have better memories than others?*

2. *The reading mentions that people with 'greater working memory capacity' may be better able to deal with memories of traumatic experiences. Do you think that people can improve their working memory capacity? How could they do this?*

3. *Do you worry about your ability to remember things? How about to forget things? If so, what is causing you to worry about these things?*

4. *In this unit the topic of mental health is discussed in relation to laughter and memory. What have you learned about how these two things affect our mental health?*

Real Life Skill

Remembering What You Read

Scientists have used discoveries about how memory works to develop mnemonic techniques for more effective study. One of these techniques, called 'SQ3R,' is a five-step method to help students understand the content of a reading, and retain it in their memory for exams. The combination of reading actively, writing, and speaking uses more areas of the brain, and processes the information more effectively.

Ⓐ Read the name of each step of the SQ3R method, then match each one with its description.

Step 1: Survey _____   Step 3: Read _____   Step 5: Review _____

Step 2: Question _____   Step 4: Recite _____

a. Using your notes with the questions and answers, go over the material within twenty-four hours of the first time you prepare it. Review it again after one week. Continue to go over your notes regularly until your exam.

b. Go through the reading again, slowly and carefully, finding and writing down the answers to each of your questions.

c. As you skim through the reading, write down a number of questions that you think it will answer. For example, if the introduction says, "Cell phones have changed our world in several ways," one question might be: What are some ways that cell phones have changed the world?

d. Skim quickly through the reading to find its main ideas and purpose. Look at any titles, pictures, the introduction and conclusion, and the first and last sentence of each paragraph.

e. After you have written the answers to all of your questions, read each question and answer aloud. This will help to fix the material in your memory.

Ⓑ Choose one of the readings in this book. It can be from this unit, from an earlier unit, or from a unit you have not studied yet. Imagine you are using the SQ3R approach to study the material in that reading for an exam. Write three or four questions you would use to help you retain the information.

1. _____ ?

2. _____ ?

3. _____ ?

4. _____ ?

Language and Life

Getting Ready

Discuss the following questions with a partner.

1. *What is the difference between a language and a dialect? How many different dialects are spoken in your native language?*
2. *In which other countries, besides your own, is your native language spoken?*
3. *What do you think are the three most widely spoken languages in the world today?*
4. *Can you name any indigenous languages spoken today? Where are they spoken?*

Before You Read:
Lost Languages

Discuss the following questions with a partner.

1. What is the relationship between language and culture? Do you think a culture can be lost if the language spoken within that culture is lost?

2. Are you aware of any endangered languages? Where is that language spoken? What is the cause of its endangerment? What are the effects?

3. Look at the title of the reading. The following words can all be found in the passage:

 revival   resurgence   converging   divergence

How do you think they relate to the topic of the reading? Use your knowledge of prefixes, suffixes, and word roots, as well as your dictionary, to help you determine the meaning of each of these words.

Reading Skill:
Identifying Cause and Effect

Words and phrases such as 'because,' 'due to (the fact that),' 'as a result,' 'so,' and 'therefore,' are used to show cause and effect relationships; in other words, they signal that one thing (the cause) makes another thing (the effect) happen. Recognizing how this language works can help you to better understand and organize the information in a reading passage.

Ⓐ Read the following statement pairs. Identify which one is the cause, and which is the effect.

1a. The Internet is an American invention.

b. Most of the information found on it is in English.

2a. Many people learn English so they can migrate to America.

b. America has the world's biggest economy.

3a. The English language is spoken differently in various parts of the world.

b. Migration of native English speakers led to a divergence of the language.

Ⓑ Look at examples of how cause and effect can be joined in a sentence.

- *Most of the information found on the Internet is in English* **because** *it is an American invention.*

- *The Internet is an American invention.* **As a result,** *most of the information found on it is in English.*

With a partner, make similar sentences using the other sentence pairs from A. Use *because* and *due to (the fact that)* to talk about the cause; use *as a result, so,* and *therefore* to talk about the effect.

Ⓒ Scan through the reading passage and find the cause or effect for each sentence below. Write the information on the line. Share your answers with a partner.

1a. The Inuktitut dialects had a common core.

b. _____

2a. Languages seem to be converging to a smaller number.

b. _____

3a. About half the languages used worldwide are endangered or on the brink of extinction.

b. _____

4a. Colloquial phrases are pleasant to the ear.

b. _____

5a. Natural disasters, war, and famine cause people to migrate to different areas.

b. _____

6a. The preservation of moribund languages, spoken only by the elderly, should be a priority.

b. _____

Now make sentences that show the cause and effect relationship between the statement pairs.

Ⓓ Now read the passage again, then answer the questions that follow.

The Exodus of Languages _____

The following reading is adapted from the article *The Exodus of Languages: How the loss of languages is much like the loss of a species* by Jessica Kwik © 1998. Reprinted from Imprint Online with permission from the author.

"I have made an impression on this first group of Inuit people. My arrival to arctic Canada was a cold one, but I'm warmed thinking of the events that will someday be stories to tell. The Inuit were surprised to see my white skin and they told rather humorous jokes about me in Inuktitut.[1] They stopped laughing though, when they heard my rebuttal in a dialect of their own tongue. I think I will enjoy 5 *this journey from Greenland to Siberia."*

It is doubtful that Knud Rasmussen[2] made such a diary entry on his travels, but these events did take place in the 1920s. Inuit communities throughout arctic Canada understood the Inuktitut spoken by the Greenland-born Rasmussen. Since the dialects had a common core that could be understood, the diverse dialects 10 show a common origin, or the same mother language. This divergence of language contrasts with the converging of languages today that is endangering languages worldwide.

Languages seem to be converging to a smaller number, as languages like English seem to eat up regional ones. The three languages used the most by first language 15 speakers today are Mandarin Chinese, English, and Spanish. English is being used more and more as the main language for business, science, and popular culture. Evidence suggests that the dominant languages are squeezing out[3] the local tongues of various regions in the world. Linguists estimate that of the approximately 6,500 languages worldwide, about half are endangered or on the 20 brink of extinction. According to some linguists, the estimated rate of language extinction is one lost in the world every two weeks. If this sounds like the world is losing a species, in a way it is.

When a language is lost, meaning no living person can teach another, a world perspective is lost. Some foreign language expressions simply cannot be translated. 25 Colloquial[4] phrases are pleasant to the ear, not only because they are familiar, but also because they reflect a unique aspect of a culture. Aboriginal languages in

Canada and other countries such as Australia have words that reflect a way of life
that is connected closely to the Earth. There are fifty different words that mean
30 'snow' in one Canadian native language, and in the Eastern Arrernte language of
Central Australia the word *nyimpe* translates to 'the smell of rain.'

These various views of the world are essential for science to help create new ways
of understanding and new connections between the human and the natural world.
Botanists[5] have discovered new species of plants by digging deeper into the
35 meaning of Aboriginal names of flora that seemed identical. Archaeologists are
also using languages to track migrations of historical cultures. University of
Waterloo Professor Robert Park knows that the ancestral origins of the present
Canadian Inuit communities can be partly explained by the language spoken by
the Inuit today. The Thule[6] culture spoke the same Inuktitut of present-day Inuit to
40 a greater or lesser degree. Dr. Park knows the prehistoric Thule migrated east from
Alaska and eventually to Labrador and Greenland by the evidence of the mutually
intelligible, living dialects of today.

Languages are much like living creatures that become endangered when numbers
dwindle. Local natural disasters, war, and famine[7] are some of the reasons
45 languages slip through the cracks[8] of history. The language that bore the different
daughter languages for the Eskimo and Inuit was almost wiped out after World
War II. The mother language, Proto-Eskimo Aleut,[9] was under siege[10] when the
Aleut people were forced to leave their land. Fortunately, some Proto-Eskimo
Aleut, which originated 6,000 to 8,000 years ago, is still spoken. Languages also
50 become endangered when they are not passed on to children or when a
metropolitan language dominates over others.

Some groups are taking action in preserving languages. Revival of languages such
as Irish is gaining ground. There is an Irish-language television channel and the
largest age group of fluent Irish speakers is now the under-twenty-fives.
55 International organizations are mobilizing for the cause as well: UNESCO[11] has
mapped the *Atlas of the World's Languages in Danger of Disappearing* in 1996.
The editor of the atlas believes the preservation of moribund languages, which are
spoken only by the elderly, should be a priority since they are on the brink of
extinction.

60 Preservation can occur in two ways. First, linguists can study moribund languages
and seek to preserve the components of the language: the sounds, the vocabulary,
the grammar, and the traditions. The second way is to teach children the language
and have linguists advise on language maintenance. An example of this latter
method is the Maori language of New Zealand. It has seen a resurgence in the
65 number of speakers from the 1960s and 1970s when there was virtually no parent
to child transmission. New Zealand has since set up 'language nests' in early
childhood centers to teach children Maori, exposing 100,000 children to their
native tongue so far.

For many linguists, preserving endangered languages is vital; a loss in global
70 languages means a loss of the diverse ideas and cultures those languages once held.

1 **Inuktitut** language of the Inuit people
2 **Knud Rasmussen** /nud ræsmusən/ Danish explorer and ethnologist who extensively researched Inuit culture
3 **squeezing out** forcing out
4 **colloquial** informal; relating to the spoken form of a language
5 **botanists** people who specialize in the study of plants
6 **Thule** /tuli/ of, or relating to, cultures of Iceland, Norway, and the Shetland Islands
7 **famine** extreme lack of food in a region
8 **slip through the cracks** pass by virtually unnoticed
9 **Aleut** /æliut/
10 **under siege** under attack from others
11 **UNESCO** United Nations Educational, Scientific, and Cultural Organization

Reading Comprehension: What Do You Remember?

The following questions are all about the reading. Answer each one using the information you have read. Try not to look back at the reading for the answers.

1. What are the three most widely spoken languages in the world today?
2. What is the approximate number of languages spoken worldwide?
3. In addition to language, what is lost when speakers of a particular language die off?
4. What examples does the reading provide of connections between language and the Earth?
5. How are languages compared to living creatures?
6. What actions can be taken to preserve languages that are endangered?
7. What role has UNESCO played in preserving endangered languages?
8. Which language has had a resurgence in recent times? How has this resurgence occurred?

Vocabulary Comprehension: Odd Word Out

Ⓐ For each group, circle the word that does not belong. The words in *italics* are vocabulary items from the reading.

1. defense   *rebuttal*   answer   praise
2. *divergence*   agreement   unlikeness   difference
3. meeting   separating   *converging*   coming together
4. *on the brink of* verging on   bordering on   hanging on
5. outlook   *perspective*   view   insight
6. fathomable   understandable   *intelligible*   incomprehensible
7. *revival*   reduction   rebirth   comeback
8. eradicated   eliminated   exhibited   *wiped out*
9. urban   *metropolitan*   municipal   rural
10. *resurgence*   reactivation   depletion   recovery

Ⓑ Now complete the sentences below using the words in *italics* from A. Be sure to use the correct form of the word.

1. As Kieron and I share the same _____ on this project, we were assigned to work on it together.

2. After many years of living in a small village, Arlen wanted a more _____ way of life.

3. Contrary to what this map shows, that road sign indicates that these two roads _____ into one about five kilometers from here.

4. Josh tried everything to _____ the bugs in his kitchen. In the end, he moved house.

5. After months of falling sales, the company CEO finally admitted to being _____ bankruptcy.

6. Jason thought he had won the argument, but Ana's _____ to his last comment really put him in his place.

7. Many years ago, overseas phone connections were so poor that only parts of a conversation were _____.

8. There is currently a big _____ in music from the 1980s. Teenagers are even beginning to wear '80s clothing!

9. A huge _____ in views on how the school should be run brought about the resignation of both the principal and the vice-principal.

10. Some say that peace protests in the United States are indicative of a _____ of political awareness among young people.

Vocabulary Skill: The Adjective Suffix -al

In this chapter, you read the adjectives 'regional,' 'aboriginal,' and 'ancestral.' These adjectives are formed by adapting the noun form of the word and adding the suffix '-al.' Many adjectives in English are formed this way. Knowing how this suffix works can help increase your vocabulary.

Ⓐ Read each definition below. Adapt the noun used, and add the suffix *-al* to form the adjective for each one. Use your dictionary to help you with spellings.

1. having to do with *history* _____
2. related to *tribes* _____
3. pertaining to the *tropics* _____
4. related to *geography* _____
5. having to do with *mathematics* _____
6. related to *biology* _____
7. related to *culture* _____
8. pertaining to *tradition* _____
9. having to do with *psychology* _____
10. related to *nature* _____

B Now complete the paragraph below using the words from A. Be careful to use the correct form of each word.

Before I started at the university, I was confused as to what I wanted to study. I've always been interested in medicine, so I thought that a good basic course for me would be in _____. However, the human mind also fascinates me, so I also considered looking into some aspects of _____ studies. In addition to my curiosity related to these fields, I enjoy reading _____ books, and I've always loved looking at maps and studying _____. I have always been fascinated by the earth and its _____ people, and imagined myself participating in a research class where we go on some kind of expedition, exploring newfound territories in the _____ regions of the world, discovering unknown _____, and their _____ ways. I've dreamed about living with the people in a remote village, learning their language, customs, and how they use their _____ environment to their advantage, while respecting and preserving it. After all, I believe that learning about how aboriginal societies live on the earth can teach us a lot about ecological preservation and conservation. Despite this wide array of interests, I ended up studying for a degree in math. I now spend my days working on formulas and _____ equations to produce new energy sources, that I hope will one day positively impact our lives.

C Think of two more examples of nouns that can be changed to adjectives by using the suffix -*al*. Write a sentence using each. Share your ideas with a partner.

1. _____

2. _____

Think About It   Discuss the following questions with a partner.

1. *What do you think the advantages would be if everyone spoke the same language? What about the disadvantages?*
2. *If you could make any changes to your language, what would you change and why?*
3. *Do you think that English will continue to be a globally dominant language, or will there be a resurgence in aboriginal languages?*
4. *What aspect, or aspects, of your culture would be lost if your language were to become moribund?*

Before You Read:

Indigenous Languages

Discuss the following questions with a partner.

1. Are there any indigenous people in your country? What do you know about them? Where and how do they live? What language do they speak?

2. Do you think that one day these people, along with their language and culture, will die out? Why?

3. Look at the title of the reading. What do you know about the Tarahumaras people? Read the first paragraph of the passage to get an idea of who they are. How do you think the following words relate to the reading topic?

isolation   literate   elusive   rugged

Reading Skill:

Developing Reading Fluency

> By reading fluently you will be able to read more; by reading more you will encounter more new words. This will help you increase the size of your vocabulary.

Time yourself as you read through the passage. Try to read as fluently as you can. Record your time in the Reading Rate Chart on page 234.

Life with the Tarahumaras _____

The following reading is adapted from *When Tarahumaras SPEAK . . . James Copeland Listens* by David D. Medina © 1996. Reprinted with permissions from Rice News.

In a remote area of the Sierra Madre[1] in northern Mexico, an indigenous group of people called the Tarahumaras live in almost total isolation. Aside from owning some cooking utensils[2] and farming equipment, the Tarahumaras exist much as they did before the Spanish arrived in the 1600s. They live in caves or in huts made 5 of stone and wood, and they eat what little they can grow on the dry, rugged land.

Ten years ago, linguist James Copeland entered the world of the Tarahumaras to study their language and culture. Since then, he has been visiting the Tarahumaras three or four times a year, sometimes spending as much as a month with them. Part of his strategy when he embarked on this lifetime project was to learn to speak 10 Tarahumara so that he could deal directly with the people. Learning Tarahumara is no easy task since it is not a written language. "There are no language police,"

Copeland says. "Children are seldom corrected by their parents. They learn by observation of speech in context and by imitation."

Copeland acquired the language through his frequent exposure to it and by analyzing the grammar. His linguistics skills and mastery of German, Spanish, French, and Russian, plus a partial knowledge of some twenty other languages, also helped. Drawing on his research, Copeland plans to produce a Tarahumara grammar book in English and perhaps one in Spanish. He is putting together a bibliography of all the linguistic research conducted so far on the Uto-Aztecan[3] languages, the group of thirty indigenous tongues to which Tarahumara belongs.

Copeland also is collecting stories and myths that have been passed down from one generation to the next. Many of the stories are being lost because they are not as well remembered. One story he has recorded is about a figure very much like the elusive Bigfoot,[4] or Sasquatch,[5] of the northwestern United States. In the Tarahumara version, the central character is either a big bear or a large hairy man who descends on a valley and steals an unmarried young woman. He hides her in a cave and they have a baby, who is half-human and half-bear. The Tarahumaras eventually kill the bear by tricking him into eating poisonous vegetables. They also kill the centaur[6]-like baby and rescue the woman.

In addition to his research, Copeland is consulting with a group of government officials from the state of Chihuahua about producing a literacy[7] program for the Tarahumaras. Most of the 60,000 Tarahumaras are not literate even though many, to varying degrees, are bilingual in their native tongue and Spanish. Copeland hopes to convince the officials that the Tarahumaras be taught to read in their native language, and in Spanish, up to the sixth grade. The Tarahumaras, unlike other indigenous peoples, are not in danger of extinction, but Copeland is not sure what effect the literacy program will have on their culture. Back in the 1600s, contact with the literate world caused some immediate changes in the culture. Since the Spaniards could not pronounce the tribe's real name, Raramuri, they called the people Tarahumaras. Raramuri means 'children of the sun god.'

The idea to study the Tarahumaras came to Copeland in 1984 when he discovered that very little research had been done on their language. He made contact with a tribe member through a social worker who worked with the Tarahumaras in the border town of Juarez,[8] Mexico. At first, the tribe member, who had taken the Spanish name of Lorenzo Gonzalez, was very reluctant to cooperate. He told Copeland that no amount of money could buy his language. But after Copeland explained to him what he intended to do with his research and how it would benefit the Tarahumaras, Gonzalez agreed to help. He took Copeland to his village and served as an intermediary. "Over a period of a year our relationship became more intense, and warmer," says Copeland. "Thanks to him, the Tarahumaras started trusting us and understood what our mission was."

Entering the world of the Tarahumaras has been an arduous project for Copeland. To reach their homeland he must drive two and a half days from Houston, Texas, across highways, blacktop[9] roads, and finally a thirteen-mile stretch of rugged trail[10]

55 that takes almost a day to maneuver. During the winter he sleeps in his truck, and in the summer next to the campfire in the way of the Tarahumaras. He loads up his vehicle with goods that the Tarahumaras can't easily get and gives them to the people as a gesture of friendship. The Tarahumaras, who don't believe in accumulating wealth, take the food and share it among themselves.

60 For Copeland, the experience has not only been academically satisfying, but it also has enriched his life in several ways. "I see people rejecting technology and living a very hard, traditional life, which offers me another notion about the meaning of progress in the Western tradition," he says. "I experience the simplicity of living in nature that I would otherwise only be able to read about. I see a lot of beauty in
65 their sense of sharing and concern for each other."

---

¹ **Sierra Madre** /siɛra madreɪ/ mountain range in northern Mexico

² **utensils** tools or instruments usually for domestic use

³ **Uto-Aztecan** /yutoʊ-æztɛkan/ related to the group of indigenous languages of North and Central America

⁴ **Bigfoot** mythical hairy, manlike beast believed to have inhabited Canada and the northwestern United States; also known as Sasquatch (see below)

⁵ **Sasquatch** /sæskwætʃ/

⁶ **centaur** type of creature from Greek mythology having the head, arms, and trunk of a man attached to the body and legs of a horse

⁷ **literacy** relating to reading and writing

⁸ **Juarez** /wɑrɛz/

⁹ **blacktop** material used to pave roads

¹⁰ **trail** a marked path through woods or dense forest

Reading Comprehension: How Much Do You Remember?

(A) Decide if the following statements about the reading are true (*T*) or false (*F*). If you check (✔) false, correct the statement to make it true.

	T	F
1. The Tarahumaras are descendents of the Spanish who arrived in Mexico in the 1600s.		
2. The Tarahumaras live in houses made of cement and wood.		
3. James Copeland has made his permanent home among the Tarahumaras.		
4. Mr. Copeland found learning the language of the Tarahumaras difficult as it is not written down.		
5. James Copeland is working to produce a grammar book of Tarahumara, as well as produce written stories and myths, in order to preserve the language.		
6. Copeland is hoping that, as many of the Tarahumaras can read, he can convince officials to teach them using his grammar book.		
7. The Tarahumaras share all the goods that Copeland takes them as they do not believe in gaining wealth only for themselves.		
8. As a result of his studies of the Tarahumaras culture, James Copeland has questioned their views on progress.		

B Check your answers with a partner. Count how many you got correct—be honest! Then, fill in the Reading Comprehension Chart on page 234.

A The following words are all vocabulary items from the reading. Using the line references, go back to the reading and use the context to work out the meaning of each one. Then, use them to complete the paragraph below. Be sure to use the correct form of each word.

isolation (line 2)	rugged (line 5)	acquired (line 14)
elusive (line 24)	descends on (line 26)	arduous (line 52)
maneuver (line 55)	accumulating (line 59)	enriched (line 61)
notion (line 62)		

Not everyone can learn a language easily. Many linguists share the (1)_____ that language skills, when taught at an early age, can be easier to (2)_____. Hence, for many monolingual adults, language learning can be an (3)_____ journey. Many adult learners make the mistake of trying to learn a new language in (4)_____. Sooner or later, they discover that (5)_____ a large enough vocabulary to enable them to converse freely in their chosen second language is impossible. However, if they change their approach to learning, what was previously (6)_____ to them can be achieved. In fact, there are just as many adult learners who manage to achieve a high level of literacy in their second language, as those who don't. Rather than giving up, these successful learners find their lives are thoroughly (7)_____ by their linguistic achievements and opportunities they previously dreamed of (8)_____ them. Perhaps learning a new language could be compared to climbing up a steep and (9)_____ mountain; it's tough to (10)_____ your way to the top, but when you get there, your view of the world is quite amazing!

Ⓑ Now think of other examples using the vocabulary from A. Share your ideas with a partner.

1. Why is it virtually impossible to learn a language in *isolation*?

2. We talk about many things being at the end of a *rugged* road. What do you think that means?

3. If you have *acquired* the necessary skills to tackle a new language, what have you learned?

4. Some adults complain that learning a language can be *elusive*. Do you agree or disagree? Why do you think this is?

5. Have you found that new opportunities in life have *descended on* you as a result of learning English? If so, give some examples.

6. Do you find learning English to be an *arduous* task? Why? What can you do to make it easier?

7. Can you think of any ways to make *maneuvering* your way through learning English grammar easier?

8. It is said that by *accumulating* a vocabulary of 600 words in a language, you can get by using that language. Make a list of the ten words that you think would be most useful to learn.

9. Do you believe the *notion* that one's life can be *enriched* by learning another language? Explain your answer.

Vocabulary Skill: Root Words *lit* and *lex*

Many words in the English language that are related to the subject of reading come from Latin root words. 'Legere,' for example, means 'read,' 'choose,' or 'gather,' and in modern English it is written as 'lect,' 'lex,' or 'leg.' The Latin word 'littera,' meaning 'letter,' is written as 'lit' in modern English. Knowing these roots and how they are used can help you build your vocabulary.

Ⓐ Study the words in the chart. Write the part of speech for each word, then match each one with a definition below. Use your dictionary to help you.

Vocabulary	Part of Speech	Definition
1. literature	_____	_____
2. literati	_____	_____
3. literary	_____	_____
4. lectern	_____	_____
5. legible	_____	_____
6. lexicon	_____	_____
7. lexicographer	_____	_____
8. dyslexia	_____	_____

a. a learning disorder characterized by the inability to read certain letters and words
b. writers, critics, and highly educated people of a place or nation
c. capable of being read or deciphered
d. a dictionary; a set of words used in a particular field
e. a tall desk or stand used by a speaker to rest notes or book on
f. a person who writes or compiles dictionaries
g. written works such as novels, plays, poetry; written information on a specific field
h. related to the field of books and writing

B Read each question below. Then take turns asking and answering the questions with a partner.

1. What is your favorite work of literature?
2. Can you name a well-known member of the literati in your country?
3. Do you know of any literary awards presented either in your country or overseas? Can you name any past winners of these awards?
4. Do professors at universities in your country use lecterns during class?
5. Do you have legible handwriting? Do you know anyone who has illegible handwriting?
6. Name another word in the English lexicon that means *understand*.
7. Do you think that being a lexicographer would be interesting? Why or why not?
8. Do you know anyone who suffers from dyslexia? How do you think people with dyslexia could be helped to learn another language?

What Do You Think?

Discuss the following questions with a partner.

1. *If you could learn to speak one other language besides English, which language would you choose? Why?*
2. *Do you find some languages easier to understand than others? Which ones?*
3. *Why do you think this is?*
4. *Do you think that there should be one dominant language in the world? Why or why not?*

Real Life Skill

Using a Pronunciation Key

An important function of a good dictionary is to provide the correct pronunciation of words, as well as meanings. Each dictionary uses a slightly different method of explaining exactly how the word should be pronounced. Some use special phonetic symbols, while others use normal letters of the alphabet with special symbols. Every good dictionary will have a key that explains the system of symbols it uses for pronunciation along with basic words that give examples of usage. It's important to familiarize yourself with the system your dictionary uses so that you can get the most value out of using it.

(A) Read this pronunciation key from a dictionary for speakers of American English.

> **PRONUNCIATION KEY**
> The consonants /b/ as in *boy*, /d/ as in *day*, /f/ as in *fox*, /g/ as in *gate*, /h/ as in *house*, /k/ as in *car*, /l/ as in *like*, /m/ as in *mat*, /n/ as in *no*, /p/ as in *pot*, /r/ as in *rope*, /s/ as in *sit*, /t/ as in *toe*, /v/ as in *vase*, /w/ as in *water*, /y/ as in *yes*, and /z/ as in *zebra*, are pronounced as they are spelled.

Vowels

/æ/ as in *bat*
/ɑ/ as in f*a*ther, c*a*lm
/ɝr/ as in g*ir*l, b*ir*d
/eɪ/ as in *age*, s*ay*
/oʊ/ as in h*o*me, s*ew*
/ɔɪ/ as in *oi*l, j*oi*n
/u/ as in s*oo*n, r*u*le
/aʊ/ as in *ou*t, h*ou*se
/ʌ/ as in *u*p, c*u*t
/ʊ/ as in b*oo*k, f*u*ll
/ə/ as in *a*go, penc*i*l, lem*o*n
/ɪ/ as in *i*f, g*i*ve
/aɪ/ as in *i*ce, r*i*de
/ɔ/ as in *o*dd, b*o*x
/i/ as in m*ee*t, s*ee*d
/ɛ/ as in *e*gg, b*e*d

Other consonants

/dʒ/ as in *j*uice
/ŋ/ as in si*ng*
/θ/ as in *th*ing, pa*th*
/ð/ as in *th*is, mo*th*er
/tʃ/ as in *ch*urch
/ʃ/ as in *sh*op
/ʒ/ as in televi*s*ion

Marks are also used to show where the primary and secondary stress in a word is:
/ˈ/ is used in front of a syllable to show primary stress: /ˈmɛnʃən/
/ˌ/ is used in front of a syllable to show secondary stress: /ˌfæsəˈneɪʃən/

(B) Read these words aloud following the key above. Then write them out alphabetically as you would read them.

1. ɪˈspɛʃəli _____
2. ˈkwɛstʃən _____
3. ɔlˈrɛdi _____
4. ˈbyutəfəl _____
5. kleɪm _____
6. ɪgˌzæməˈneɪʃən _____
7. dʒiˈɑɡrəfi _____
8. ˈdɔctər _____

(C) Using the pronunciation key above, write three new words you have learned in this unit using the phonetic symbols.

1. _____
2. _____
3. _____

(D) Now work with a partner. Take turns reading each other's words aloud using the correct pronunciation.

The Natural World

Getting Ready

Discuss the following questions with a partner.

1. *Name the animal species in the picture above. Although this animal once existed on Earth, it is now extinct. What do you know about the cause(s) of its extinction?*

2. *Can you name any animals in your country, or in the world, that have become extinct in the last one hundred years, or that are threatened with extinction?*

3. *What are some modern causes of animal extinctions?*

4. *Why should we be concerned about animal extinctions and environmental conservation?*

Before You Read:
The Threat of Extinction

Discuss the following questions with a partner.

1. What do you know about Antarctica? Name some different animal species that can be found there.

2. Are you aware of any direct effects that global warming is having on Antarctica?

3. How do these consequences of global warming affect the wildlife found on the continent?

4. Look at the title of the reading. Name some animal species that would be threatened with extinction if the world in which they live (their habitat) were melting. In what ways would a melting habitat affect them directly?

Reading Skill:
Understanding Inference

Information in a reading passage can be found in two ways: by what is stated directly and written clearly on the page, or by what we can infer. When we infer, we use the information that is stated directly to draw conclusions about events, or the writer's opinion or purpose. Knowing how to infer can help you to better understand the writer's purpose and ideas. It is a useful skill to know when reading for pleasure, and can help you better understand reading passages in exams.

Ⓐ Read each of the following questions carefully. As you scan through the reading passage think about the information that each one is asking about. Answer them based on the information you read.

1. What can we infer about the weather on Antarctica the day the penguins were observed? (e.g., foggy, stormy, etc.) Which words in the passage give you clues?

_____

2. From where do you think the writer is observing the penguins? (e.g., air, land, sea) What information tells you this?

_____

3. Describe, in as much detail as you can infer from the passage, how Adélie penguins feed their young from the time they catch food to the time they pass it to the baby's mouth. Underline the words or sentences in the passage that allow you to infer this information.

_____

_____

4. How widely can Adélie penguins be found across Antarctica? Which words or sentences in the passage tell you this?

_____

5. What does the author think will happen in the future to other Adélie colonies on Antarctica? What information in the passage tells you this?

_____

Ⓑ Share your answers with a partner. Go over the information in the reading passage that provided you with answers to the questions.

Ⓒ Now read through the passage again and complete the comprehension exercise that follows.

Caught in a Melting World _____

The following reading is adapted from *Caught in a Melting World* by Tui de Roy © 2000. Reprinted from *International Wildlife* with permission of the author.

Four little heads pop up[1] simultaneously in a pool of blue-black water surrounded by ice as far as the eye can see. They are Adélie penguins, and the ice defines their existence.

The birds—just over two feet[2] long—leap about excitedly in tight circles, going in and out of the water, perfectly at ease in this frigid sea that surrounds the shores of Antarctica. They are not only at ease, but at home. The seasonal freezing and thawing, spreading and shrinking, of the ocean's surface is the world they know. In recent years, as Earth's climate has warmed, it has also become a world in rapid and disturbing change.

Their food is tied, literally, to the frozen ocean. Within layers of sea ice, microscopic algae[3] bloom in profusion as sunlight floods in from above. When the sea ice melts with the beginning of summer, the ice algae escape into the water, where they are grazed on by dense swarms of krill—a type of shrimplike crustacean.[4] The krill, in turn, are the Adélie penguins' primary food source. To eat them, Adélies spend their entire lives on, around, or beneath the Antarctic pack ice.

As the heads appear together at the surface, they seem to hesitate, reluctant to leave the watery world through which they swim as effortlessly as fish. Then all at once, they shoot up out of the water, landing feet first on the ice. For just a few seconds they stand still. Then, as one, the little flock sets off southward across the ice, heading for the faint outline of a distant mountain range. At the base of those mountains some thirty miles[5] away lies Cape Adare, where each year at this time some 280,000 Adélie pairs get together to raise their young— the largest such colony in all of Antarctica.

The four birds recede until they are nothing but small black dots in the bright white distance. After a feeding trip that may have covered as much as 180 miles[6] of sea and ice, they are going back to their nests. Each will relieve a fasting[7] mate with which it has been taking turns incubating[8] two eggs for the last five or six weeks.

Within hours of hatching,[9] the tiny chicks are raising their wobbly heads, begging for food. They know innately that growing up is urgent in a land where summer will only last a few weeks. Their squeaks are answered by their parents with ready beakfuls of krill, dutifully carried back by the bellyful from the sea far away across the ice—that ice still firmly attached to the shore.

Should the ice stay firm for too long, requiring trips in excess of sixty miles[10] or so, the small chicks will either starve to death or grow too slowly to survive. If the ice breaks out and melts too early, the ice-driven food chain will be weakened, and the chicks will be left unattended, vulnerable to predator[11] birds, and too young to fend for themselves while both parents are off seeking food.

40 Frighteningly, this has occurred ever more frequently in the last few decades, especially around the Antarctic Peninsula,[12] which is the northernmost and warmest part of the Adélies' range. As the rest of the planet slides gradually into warmer climate trends—a change thought to be caused partly by human burning of fossil fuels—scientists working at the Palmer Station in this part of the
45 Antarctic report that average temperatures there have increased by as much as 3 to 5 degrees Fahrenheit in summer over the past fifty years, and an incredible 7 to 9 degrees in winter. That increase is at least ten times faster than for the rest of the world.

The ever-increasing ozone-hole problem, a fluorocarbon[13]-induced thinning of
50 the protective ozone layer[14] in the upper atmosphere, adds yet another unknown factor to a tricky equation. The hole is now reaching well over 10 million square miles[15] in extent. Unscreened by ozone gas, solar ultraviolet radiation strikes the surface of the Earth there and substantially reduces the productivity of the ice algae, scientists believe, and thus the krill on which the Adélies feed.

55 The combined effect of all these threats is already translating into drastic population declines in several Adélie penguin colonies. In five colonies near Palmer Station, numbers of breeding pairs have dropped from 15,200 to 9,200 in twenty-five years, while some smaller colonies have disappeared altogether. And the problem seems to be accelerating fast, with a 10 percent Adélie
60 population decline in the last two years alone. At another site farther north, a loss of about 35 percent has been measured in just ten years. It is a cruel irony that this little penguin's superb adaptations to an extremely harsh environment, and its very dependence on sea ice, could cause its undoing. Fortunately, however, there are numerous Adélie colonies around the Antarctic continent,
65 especially in the far south, where there is no hint of such drastic changes, at least not for the time being.

1 **pop up** thrust up suddenly or unexpectedly
2 **two feet** equal to 0.6 meters
3 **algae** simple plants that live in water, e.g., seaweed
4 **crustacean** animal with a hard outer shell, most often found living in water, e.g., crab, lobster
5 **30 miles** equal to approximately 48 kilometers
6 **180 miles** equal to approximately 289.6 kilometers
7 **fasting** going without food
8 **incubating** keeping eggs or an organism at optimal conditions to promote growth and development
9 **hatching** emerging from, or breaking out of, a shell
10 **60 miles** equal to approximately 96.5 kilometers
11 **predator** organism that lives by hunting for and feeding on other organisms
12 **Antarctic Peninsula** region of Antarctica extending about 1,931 km north from the main continent towards South America
13 **fluorocarbon** liquid or gas formed by a carbon and fluorine compound—fluorine being a highly corrosive and poisonous substance—used in aerosols, refrigerants, solvents, and manufacturing of plastics
14 **ozone layer** region of the upper atmosphere containing high concentrations of ozone gas (a derivative form of oxygen) that absorbs and screens the sun's harmful ultraviolet radiation
15 **10 million square miles** equal to approximately 25.9 trillion square meters

The following statements are all about the reading. Complete each one using information you have read. Try not to look back at the reading for the answers.

1. The world of the Adélie penguins is in a state of _____.

2. The Adélie's primary food source is _____.

3. Krill feed on _____, which in turn rely on _____ to grow fully.

4. Pairs of male and female Adélie penguins take turns looking after _____, and going on _____ trips.

5. The Adélies and their chicks rely on the _____ at the right time to provide them with enough krill to feed on.

6. In the last few decades, the ice has melted too _____ as a result of an _____ in temperature.

7. The problem of an ever-increasing _____ is _____ the amount of algae, and therefore _____ that the Adélies have available.

8. Environmental changes in Antarctica have led to a _____ in the numbers of Adélies, and even the _____ of some colonies altogether.

(A) Look at the list of words and phrases from the reading. Match each one with a definition on the right.

1. simultaneously _____
2. frigid _____
3. in profusion _____
4. grazed on _____
5. recede _____
6. wobbly _____
7. begging _____
8. innately _____
9. fend for themselves _____
10. undoing _____

a. downfall; ruin
b. look after or take care of themselves
c. asking for something (like food or money) in a very keen way
d. shaky; unsteady
e. to move further away (into the distance)
f. at the same time
g. fed on (usually by intermittently eating small amounts)
h. inborn; possessed at birth
i. in abundance
j. extremely cold

(B) Complete the sentences below using the vocabulary from A. Be sure to use the correct form of each word.

1. Theft and fraud among his accountants led to the eventual _____ of Steve's finance company.

2. The _____ winter weather of Alaska creates a beautiful landscape, but prevents many tourists from visiting in January and February.

3. This beach is amazing. At low tide when the water _____ you can find all sorts of unusual shells and marine creatures.

4. When goats are born, they have the _____ ability to walk, even though their legs are quite _____ at first.

5. Although the offspring of many mammals cannot _____ when they are first born, unlike humans they grow to become independent very quickly.

6. A good dog owner will train his or her pet not to _____ for food.

7. Amanda's garden looks so beautiful right now. There are roses blossoming _____.

8. In order to work as a language translator for the United Nations, you must be qualified as a _____ interpreter.

9. When his lawnmower broke, instead of buying a new one, Albert bought a goat to _____ the grass to keep it short.

Vocabulary Skill:

Roots of Life Processes:

nat/viv/bio/gen

In this chapter you read the words 'innately,' meaning 'inborn,' and 'survive,' meaning 'to remain alive' or 'to live longer than.' Both words include root words that relate to life and life processes: 'nat,' meaning 'life' or 'birth,' and 'viv' (also written as 'vit'), meaning 'life.' Two other root words that also mean 'life' are 'bio' and 'gen.' These roots are combined with prefixes and suffixes to form many words in English.

Ⓐ **Study the words in the chart. What do you think they mean? Use your knowledge of prefixes, suffixes, and the roots *nat, viv, bio,* and *gen* to match each word with a definition.**

Noun	Verb	Adjective
biosphere	degenerate	supernatural
symbiosis	revive	vivacious
nationality		convivial
vitality		biodegradable
genealogy		congenital

1. lively; very cheerful _____

2. to give new energy to something _____

3. identity based on citizenship of a country _____

4. the Earth and its atmosphere in which living things exist _____

5. capable of breaking apart and being absorbed by nature through natural processes, without harming the environment _____

6. relationship between two or more different organisms that can be of benefit to each other _____

7. relating to something that exists beyond the natural world _____

8. the study of the history of one's family and ancestry _____

9. to fall into a condition worse than its original state; to deteriorate _____

10. of, or related to, a condition that is present at birth but is not inherited _____

11. energy, strength, and health that one possesses _____

12. friendly; sociable _____

B Complete the following paragraph using some of the words from A. Be sure to use the correct form of each word. Not all the words are used.

News in Brief

Water supplies were shut off in a small coastal town yesterday after an environmental scare. It seems that a chemical powder which was thought to be _____ was buried in soil near the source of the town's water supply. Instead of breaking down into harmless particles, the powder leaked into the water supply and contaminated it. Scientists have warned everyone in the neighborhood not to drink any tap water, especially pregnant women, as the side effects of drinking water containing the chemical can include stomach problems, skin complaints and, if consumed by pregnant women, _____ birth defects.

On a lighter note, a woman of Irish _____ claims to have researched her family name and _____ through _____ methods. The woman is reported to have contacted her deceased father, grandfather, great grandfather, and great-great grandfather by using her psychic powers. In a recent interview she told us she had made discoveries about her family history, *and* about characteristics of the male family members she contacted, too. She revealed that while her great-great grandfather was a very kind _____ man who loved to entertain, her great grandfather was the opposite—a complete introvert. And although her grandfather was a lively, _____ man, her father was renowned for being miserable. The woman concluded that this family characteristic explained her own son's enormous _____ and spirited nature—a trait he inherited from his grandfather.

Think About It Discuss the following questions with a partner.

1. *Describe the food chain of the Adélie penguins. Draw a diagram to illustrate each element of the chain, and put arrows on it to show how each part of it relates to the other.*

2. *Can you name any other animal species that have had their food chain threatened by environmental problems? Where in the world is this threat taking place? What is causing it?*

3. *Go back to the reading passage and look at the statistics cited on the decline in the Adélie populations. Based on these figures, do you think the Adélie penguin will become extinct in your lifetime? Explain your answer.*

4. *If your answer to the above was 'yes,' what measures should or could be taken to protect this animal species from extinction?*

Before You Read:
Exotic Ecosystems

Discuss the following questions with a partner.

1. Name some native species of plant or animal that your country is famous for.
2. Do you know of any plant or animal species that exist in your country, but are not native species? How or why were these species introduced to your country?
3. Have these introduced species caused any problems for the native species in your country? If so, what problems have they caused?
4. Look at the title of the passage. What do you understand the term 'alien species' to mean? What issues might the reading discuss in terms of an alien species fitting in to a new or different environment?

Reading Skill:
Developing
Reading
Fluency

> *Reading fluently means using your reading skills to get the main idea of what you are reading without slowing down to look up words in a dictionary. If necessary, go back through this book and read through the Reading Skill sidebars to remind yourself of the reading skills you have learned.*

Time yourself as you read through the passage. Try to read as fluently as you can. Record your time in the Reading Rate Chart on page 234.

Alien Species: Fitting In _____

The following reading is adapted from *Alien Species Often Fit in Fine, Some Scientists Contend* by Mark Derr. Copyright © 2001 by the New York Times Co. Reprinted by permission.

Governments, private groups, and individuals spend billions of dollars a year trying to root out non-native organisms that are considered dangerous to ecosystems, and to prevent the introduction of new interlopers.

But a number of scientists question the assumption that the presence of alien
5 species can never be acceptable in a natural ecosystem. While applauding efforts to banish harmful organisms—like the brown tree snakes that have destroyed most of Guam's[1] native species of forest birds, or the star thistle (a prickly[2] weed that is toxic[3] to horses, and has invaded much of the West)—they say that portraying introduced species as inherently bad is an unscientific approach.

10 "Distinctions between exotics and native species are artificial," said Dr. Michael Rosenzweig, a professor of evolutionary biology[4] at the University of Arizona, because they depend on picking a date and calling the plants and animals that show up after that 'exotic.' Ecosystems free of species defined as exotic are, by

default, considered the most natural. "You can't roll back the clock and remove all exotics or fix habitats," Dr. Rosenzweig said. "Both native and exotic species can become invasive, and so they all have to be monitored and controlled when they begin to get out of hand."

At its core, the debate is about how to manage the world's remaining natural ecosystems and about how, and how much, to restore other habitats. Species that invade a territory can harm ecosystems, agriculture, and human health. They can threaten some native species or even destroy and replace others. Next to habitat loss, these invasive species represent the greatest threat to biodiversity[5] worldwide, many ecologists say.

Ecologists generally define an alien species as one that people, inadvertently or deliberately, carried to its new location. Across the American continents, exotic species are those introduced after the first European contact. That date, rounded off to A.D. 1500, represents what ecologists consider to have been a major shift in the spread of species, including crops and livestock, as they began to leapfrog[6] with humans from continent to continent.

"Only a small percentage of alien species cause problems in their new habitats," said a professor of ecology and evolutionary biology at the University of Tennessee. "Of the 7,000 alien species in the United States—out of a total of 150,000 species—only about 10 percent are invasive," he pointed out. The other 90 percent have fit into their environments and are considered naturalized. Yet appearances can deceive, ecologists caution, and many of these exotics may be considered acceptable only because no one has documented their harmful effects. What is more, non-native species can appear innocuous for decades, then turn invasive.

One example is the Brazilian pepper, which landscapers introduced into South Florida in the late nineteenth century. It started to spread widely in the 1950s and has now crowded out native vegetation throughout the Florida Everglades.[7] Once a species begins to run amok,[8] it is extremely difficult to eradicate.

Faced with such uncertainty, many ecologists argue for strong steps to be taken, stressing the need to actively take precautions to prevent exotic species from becoming problematic. Their approach is to remove exotics from natural ecosystems. But a number of experts question the scientific wisdom of trying to roll back ecosystems to a time when they were more natural.

"Defining which species belong in an ecosystem is based less on science than on historical, cultural, moral, geographic, and theological[9] arguments," said Dr. Mark Sagoff, who studies the issue at the University of Maryland's Institute for Philosophy and Public Policy. "Science cannot judge an ecosystem with exotics to be worse, or less natural, than one without them," he said, "without also taking into account [all] the effects of those species on their environments."

Even many ecologists who would like to rid ecosystems of all exotics admit that

55 this goal is impractical. According to the director of conservation programs at a nonprofit group called Nature Conservancy, a return to pre-settlement ecosystems simply cannot be accomplished. "For one thing," he said, "many exotic species have become so integrated into ecosystems that [other] animals, some endangered, rely on them for food and shelter."

60 "This is not the only problem that can result from the removal of exotics," Dr. Rosenzweig said. In Australia's Northern Territory, for example, the eradication of the non-native water buffalo that were ravaging vegetation led to the explosive growth of a little-noticed plant—the giant mimosa—which was introduced from Central America in the 1890s. This shrub[10] has been more 65 destructive and harder to remove than the water buffalo.

In an issue of the science journal *Evolutionary Ecology Research*, Dr. Rosenzweig, the editor, challenges the prevailing view that invasive alien species reduce biodiversity. The exotics increase the number of species in the environment, he wrote. Even if alien species cause extinctions, the extinction 70 phase will eventually end, and new species may then begin to evolve, he explained.

"Ecologists should focus on managing the environments that include exotic immigrants," Dr. Rosenzweig said, "and creating new ones where necessary to enhance species' survival and biodiversity."

---

[1] **Guam** /gwɑm/ an unincorporated territory of the United States; one of the Mariana Islands in the western Pacific Ocean

[2] **prickly** having spikes or thorns

[3] **toxic** poisonous

[4] **evolutionary biology** the science and study of the evolution of living organisms

[5] **biodiversity** variety of plants, animals, and other living organisms found in a given geographic area

[6] **leapfrog** to move from one place to the next with the help of a second party

[7] **Florida Everglades** subtropical area of southern Florida state noted for its wildlife

[8] **run amok** to spread in an uncontrolled manner

[9] **theological** of, or relating to, the study of religion

[10] **shrub** a low, woody plant having several stems growing from its roots

---

Reading Comprehension: How Much Do You Remember?

(A) How much do you remember from the reading? Choose the best answer for each question or statement.

1. How much money is spent each year trying to eliminate non-native organisms from ecosystems?

   a. hundreds of dollars   **c.** thousands of dollars

   b. millions of dollars   **d.** billions of dollars

2. Some scientists view the assumption that all non-native organisms in an ecosystem are bad as _____.

   a. unscientific   **c.** correct

   b. false, since no data support it   **d.** admirable

3. Distinguishing between natural and exotic species is seen by some as _____.

   a. out of control

   b. controlled by science

   c. impossible to determine

   d. artificial

4. The debate about alien species centers on _____.

   a. how to manage ecosystems

   b. managing agriculture

   c. how to protect human health

   d. worldwide habitats

5. Alien species were first introduced to new ecosystems as a result of _____.

   a. crossing the American continent

   b. human travel

   c. contact with Europeans

   d. movement of livestock

6. The number of alien species that actually cause problems in new habitats is about _____.

   a. 7%

   b. 50%

   c. 10%

   d. 90%

7. When judging an ecosystem with exotics, scientists should take _____ factors into consideration.

   a. historical

   b. geographical

   c. moral

   d. all

8. Dr. Rosenzweig believes that managing environments that include exotics can _____.

   a. enhance biodiversity

   b. reduce biodiversity

   c. result in their eradication

   d. cause extinctions

(B) **Check your answers with a partner. Count how many you got correct—be honest! Then, fill in the Reading Comprehension Chart on page 234.**

Vocabulary Comprehension: Words in Context

(A) **Look at the following words. Using the line references, go back to the reading passage and locate them in the text. Use the meaning from context strategies outlined on pages 58 and 86 to try and work out the meaning of each one. If necessary, go back to those pages and review this skill before you begin.**

root out (line 2)	interlopers (line 3)	applauding (line 5)
banish (line 6)	portraying (line 9)	get out of hand (line 17)
inadvertently (line 24)	innocuous (line 37)	eradicate (line 42)
impractical (line 55)		

(B) **Complete the paragraph below using some of the vocabulary items from A. Be sure to use the correct form of each word.**

My Not-So-Green Thumb

Anyone who has ever planted a garden knows that often, while things appear to be under control, they can (1)_____. This is what happened to me when I planted mint. It all started with a rather (2)_____ beginning. My neighbors were very impressed with my planting, and even (3)_____ my creative use of the fragrant herb; I incorporated it into everything from cocktails to ice cream. I thoroughly enjoyed (4)_____ myself as a creative farmer, but soon realized that I had (5)_____ planted more than I could ever use. My thriving crop suddenly seemed to be invading my garden, and the smell overpowered my kitchen. As much as I tried, I couldn't use up the stuff! No matter how much I gave away to friends and neighbors, by the end of the summer, my house was filled with an (6)_____ amount of mint. By this point I was ready to (7)_____ it completely from my diet, and (8)_____ it from the house and garden forever! Luckily my aunt-in-law, who is usually an awful (9)_____ when it comes to household matters, offered me some friendly gardening advice. She even managed to (10)_____ some old gardening books from her attic and gave them to me. From those, I've figured out how much to plant, and how much not to. So next time I decide to plant mint I'll be sure to grow just enough. For now, though, mint is noticeably, and thankfully, absent from my garden.

C Now think of other examples using the vocabulary from A. Discuss your ideas with a partner.

1. Do you ever let the amount of study assignments you have to do *get out of hand*, or do you tend to keep on top of things?
2. What moral values or principles do you *applaud*, especially in friends?
3. If you could be any character in a movie or play, who would you like to *portray* and why?
4. If you bought something in a shop, and the cashier *inadvertently* gave you too much change, what would you do?
5. Think of examples of diseases that have been *eradicated* over time by vaccines or other medical developments.
6. Name a modern gadget or machine that you consider to be *impractical*. Why do you think it is *impractical*?
7. Is there any trend, gadget, or device that you think should be *banished* from society? What is it and why do you dislike it so much?

Vocabulary Skill: The Prefix *non-*

In this chapter, you read the words 'non-native' and 'nonprofit.' These words begin with the prefix 'non,' meaning 'not.' This is a common negative prefix that can come before nouns, verbs, adjectives, and adverbs to form many words in English. Some of these words are hyphenated, others are not.

A Look at the words in the box below. What do you think they mean? Use your knowledge of prefixes, suffixes, and word roots to match them to the definitions.

fiction	_____	committal	_____	flammable	_____
discriminatory	_____	stop	_____	existent	_____
scheduled	_____	violent	_____	conformist	_____

a. forcible or rough; severe
b. prejudiced; unfairly treated
c. capable of burning quickly
d. someone who behaves according to a group's usual expectations and standards
e. to pause or stay in place
f. being real; present in the world
g. the act of promising or pledging oneself to a particular view or position
h. type of story or writing that is about imaginary characters and situations
i. planned

B Complete the sentences below by adding the prefix *non* to the correct words from A.

1. My favorite form of literature is _____. I especially love reading autobiographies.

2. The Bay Theater often has _____ events at the weekend; they can sometimes be more entertaining than the plays that are showing.

3. Gregory tends to have very _____ opinions about marriage and society.

4. By taking the _____ flight to Sydney, I'll get there two hours earlier than the flight that stops in Brisbane.

5. Our company is highly regarded by others in the industry in terms of its _____ policies on gender, race, and religion.

6. Tamara's _____ attitude toward the project was what led her boss to fire her.

C Now use the remaining words to write three more sentences of your own. Share your ideas with a partner.

1. _____

2. _____

3. _____

What Do You Think?

Discuss the following questions with a partner.

1. *Do you think that the amount of money spent each year on managing ecosystems is justified? Explain your answer.*

2. *The reading states that one consequence of invading alien species is a harmful effect on agriculture. Can you think of any specific examples of this? How does this affect the human food chain?*

3. *In terms of everything that is happening in the world right now, how important would you rate the issue of global warming and environmental conservation? Give reasons for your answer.*

4. *Every day, people transport animals and plants from their native country to a country where they are considered exotic. After reading this passage, do you think there should be tighter restrictions on the numbers of these animals and plants that are allowed to pass through customs?*

Real Life Skill

Animal Terminology

English names of animals are very old, and their usage dates back hundreds of years. Many have irregular plural forms, and the names of offspring often bear little or no resemblance to that of the adult. For example, a baby penguin is called a chick (as seen in the chapter one reading). A group of the same animal also has a special name that again, bears little or no resemblance to the name of the animal, for example, a 'flock' of penguins. This vocabulary is important to know when reading about nature.

A Work with a partner to match the names of these animals with their young. Use your dictionary to check any that you are not sure of.

1. cat _____	**a.** fawn
2. dog _____	**b.** kid
3. horse _____	**c.** calf
4. cow _____	**d.** lamb
5. bird _____	**e.** foal
6. frog _____	**f.** chick
7. hen _____	**g.** tadpole
8. deer _____	**h.** puppy
9. sheep _____	**i.** kitten
10. goat _____	**j.** nestling

B Now write the plural form of each of these animals. Use your dictionary to help you.

1. a mouse; two _____

2. a goose; many _____

3. a fish; ten _____

4. an ox; a pair of _____

5. a puppy; three _____

6. a wolf; several _____

C Groups of very different animals can share the same name. When we use these terms the plural form of the animal name is always used. Look at the group names below and write the plural forms of the correct animals on the appropriate line.

kitten	wolf	bird	ox	cow	fish
horse	seagull	puppy	shark	sheep	bat

1. A herd of _____

2. A flock of _____

3. A school of _____

4. A pack of _____

5. A litter of _____

6. A colony of _____

Music: Influence and Innovation

Getting Ready

Discuss the following questions with a partner.

1. *Do you recognize any of the bands or artists in the photos above? How would you describe the music and the image of each one? Would you say you are a fan of any of these bands or artists?*

2. *How would you define your taste in music? Which musical genre or genres do you listen to the most?*

3. *Is there any one person or event in your life that has influenced your musical preferences? If so, what or who was it?*

4. *What innovations in music have taken place over the last few years? Do you think they have benefited music artists and bands, and the average music buyer? Explain your answer.*

Before You Read:

Ancient Sounds of Music

Discuss the following questions with a partner.

1. Are there any types of music you have heard that sound unusual or extraordinary to you?

2. Do you ever listen to blues music? Can you name any blues artists or bands?

3. Are there any bands or artists in your country that produce any type of 'alternative' or noncommercial genres of music? Who are the bands or artists, and what kind of music do they play?

4. The following words can be found in the reading:

   > droning   fiddling   trembling   twangy

   Which of them describe sound, and which are movements? Use your knowledge of word roots, as well as your dictionary, to help you determine the meaning of each word.

Reading Skill:

Identifying Meaning from Context

You can guess the meaning of important but unfamiliar words in a reading passage by using the following strategy:
1. *Think about how the new word is related to the topic of what you are reading about.* ***2.*** *Identify which part of speech the new word is by looking at how it fits with the other words in its sentence.*
3. *Look at how the word relates to the rest of the information in the paragraph surrounding it.* ***4.*** *Use your knowledge of prefixes, suffixes, and word roots to identify the basic meaning of the word.*

(A) The following is an extract from the reading passage. As you read through it, think about the topic of the reading, and what you already know about this topic. Pay attention to the underlined words.

> The film follows Paul Pena, a blues musician from San Francisco, on a voyage to Central Asia, where he participates in a contest celebrating the ancient art of throat-singing. Witnessing that (1) <u>high point</u> in Pena's otherwise difficult life—he's blind, in (2) <u>shaky</u> health, and prone to depression—is one of the film's major pleasures; another is encountering Pena's (3) <u>exuberant</u> friend and (4) <u>mentor</u>, the master throat-singer Kongar-ol Ondar.

(B) Decide which part of speech each underlined word or phrase is, and write them below.

(1) _____   (3) _____
(2) _____   (4) _____

How do you know this? Circle the words in the sentence that work with or affect the underlined words, and tell you the part of speech. Look at how the word relates to the rest of the paragraph. Are there any other words or phrases that give you clues to the meaning of each word? If so, circle them.

(C) Now look at the parts of the words. Does each one have a recognizable prefix, root, or suffix? Use your knowledge of these word parts to try to identify the meaning of each word. Replace each one with a word or phrase, or write a definition.

(1) _____   (3) _____
(2) _____   (4) _____

(D) Use your dictionary to check whether you have interpreted the meaning of the words correctly. Share your answers with a partner.

(E) Look at the list of words opposite. Using the line references, locate each word in the passage and underline it.

Vocabulary	Part of Speech	Word/Definition
1. call into question (line 3)	_____	_____
2. sidled up to (line 29)	_____	_____
3. triennial (line 30)	_____	_____
4. spirited (line 41)	_____	_____
5. despondent (line 43)	_____	_____
6. frantic (line 48)	_____	_____

(F) Using the same strategies you practiced above, identify the part of speech of each word. Look at how each one fits into the sentences or paragraph around it. Look at the parts of each word and try to work out the meaning. Replace them with words or phrases you know that have the same meaning, or write a definition. Share your answers with a partner, and use your dictionary to check your interpretations and definitions.

(G) Now read through the passage again, and complete the comprehension exercise that follows.

Genghis Blues _____

The following reading is adapted from *Genghis Blues* by Daniel Mangin © 1999. Reprinted from *Salon.com* with permission of the author.

Andy Warhol[1] once observed that film is, first and foremost, about personality. "People are fantastic. You can't take a bad picture," he said in the '60s. Although some of today's television calls this view into question, the documentary *Genghis Blues* proves that if you put fantastic people in front of the camera, something memorable is likely to happen.   5

The film follows Paul Pena, a blues musician from San Francisco, on a voyage to Central Asia, where he participates in a contest celebrating the ancient art of throat-singing. Witnessing that high point in Pena's otherwise difficult life—he's blind, in shaky health, and prone to depression—is one of the film's major pleasures; another is encountering Pena's exuberant friend and mentor, the master 10
throat-singer Kongar-ol Ondar.

Fiddling with his short-wave radio[2] early one morning in 1984, Pena stumbled across some strange sounds. What seemed at first like electronic oscillations[3] turned out to be human voices capable of producing two or more notes at the same time. "Now that's for me," Pena said to himself. Some notes were high- 15
pitched, twangy, and whistle-like; others had the guttural[4] quality of a bullfrog's droning, which reminded Pena of the blues singer Howlin' Wolf.[5]

It took Pena seven years to ascertain that the sounds he'd heard were created in Tuva, a small Russian republic along the northwestern border of Mongolia.[6] Only a brief outline of the history of Tuva is supplied in the opening section of 20
the documentary. The country was settled centuries ago by Turkic people who became allied with Genghis Khan.[7] After spending the eighteenth and nineteenth centuries under Chinese rule, Tuva was absorbed first into czarist Russia[8] (the

documentary doesn't state this), and allegedly became independent before
25 officially joining the Soviet Union in 1944.

Within a few weeks of purchasing a Tuvan CD, Pena was able to reproduce those
sounds and had started integrating them into his music. While Ondar was
greeting his fans after a concert in San Francisco during the early 1990s, Pena
sidled up to the master and began vocalizing in the lower-pitched *kargyraa*[9] style.
30 Ondar was so impressed he invited Pena to Tuva's 1995 triennial throat-singing
competition.

For its first half-hour, *Genghis Blues* unfolds more or less like a conventional
documentary as director, Roko Belic,[10] who produced and shot the film with his
brother, Adrian, introduces Pena and the engaging eccentrics who either
35 accompany him on his Asian adventure, or help make it happen. Among Pena's
supporters are Ralph Leighton,[11] a founder of the California-based Friends of
Tuva, and the late Mario Casetta, a wisecracker[12] who for years played world
music on Los Angeles public radio.

Shortly after the group's arrival in Tuva, however, *Genghis Blues* evolves into an
40 intimate portrait of two sentient artists. The eminently likable Pena, a Creole-
American[13] who traces his familial and musical roots to Cape Verde,[14] is a spirited
bundle of emotions. At various moments he's jolly, petrified,[15] confident, and
despondent, though onstage he consistently wows the audience. The Tuvans call
him 'Earthquake' because he's from San Francisco and because he's able to hit
45 notes so low they sound like the earth trembling. Belic told me recently that he'd
been under pressure from some of the musician's friends not to show Pena's less
self-assured moments—he admits to despair over his blindness and becomes
frantic after losing his depression medication—but the director wisely included
them.

50 The drama in *Genghis Blues* revolves around Pena's participation in the contest,
but the most poignant sequences occur when Ondar, who veritably radiates joy,
takes Pena and his pals on a tour of Tuva's countryside. Though the documentary
doesn't directly mention it, one paradox about the contest, which grew out of its
founder's zeal to preserve a cultural tradition, is that it presents throat-singing in
55 a wholly artificial milieu.[16] The Tuvans were nomadic herders,[17] and some still
are; throat-singing, which lone herdsmen did to relate to the land and to
communicate with compatriots who were sometimes far away—the sounds
apparently carry through the air very well—was never intended as performance
per se.[18] Tuvan songs tend to be about rivers, grassland, and other aspects of
60 nature, and it's only after the camera traces the areas that inspire the music that
the connection between form and content is fully made. The on-the-road footage
also underscores the Tuvans' embrace of life, despite poverty and other
challenges, which in turn shows how deeply intuitive Pena was in incorporating
throat-singing into blues music.

65 At one point, Pena stands where the Dalai Lama had stood a few years earlier,
and rues[19] his inability to express the timelessness he's sensing about the place. "I
don't know if you can get such a thing on camera," he says, as it focuses on a
nondescript monument. That the Belics left in this acknowledgment of their

documentary's limitations reflects the overall integrity of their endeavor. Watching *Genghis Blues*, I sometimes got the feeling that there was more to the story. But Pena and Ondar are highly compelling, and the film captures the combination of sensitivity and serendipity that underlies artistic expression.

70

---

1. **Andy Warhol** American artist and leader of the pop art movement who lived until 1987
2. **short-wave radio** a radio capable of receiving at wavelengths of approximately 20 to 200 meters
3. **oscillations** the act of vibrating or moving back and forth with a regular, uninterrupted motion
4. **guttural** of, or related to, a low sound produced in the throat
5. **Howlin' Wolf** American blues singer (1910–1976) whose career peaked in the 1950s and 1960s
6. **Mongolia** ancient region of east-central Asia inhabited by Mongol people
7. **Genghis Khan** tribal leader of the Mongol people who united the different tribes to form a great empire
8. **czarist Russia** /zɑrɪst/ Russia at a time when the government was ruled by a male emperor (up to 1917)
9. **kargyraa** /kɑrgirɑ/
10. **Roko Belic** /rɔkɔ bɛlɪk/
11. **Ralph Leighton** /rælf leɪtən/
12. **wisecracker** a person who has a tendency to be sardonic or mocking
13. **Creole-American** a person descended from European or African settlers of the United States who has American citizenship
14. **Cape Verde** /keɪp vɜrd/ an island country situated west of Senegal in the Atlantic Ocean
15. **petrified** terrified; paralyzed with great fear
16. **milieu** /mɪlyʊ/ environment; surroundings
17. **nomadic herders** people who have no fixed home but continually travel around, driving and tending herds of livestock
18. **per se** by itself
19. **rues** feels regret or sorrow for (something)

Reading Comprehension: What Do You Remember?

The following questions are all about the reading. Use the information you have read to answer each one. Try not to look back at the reading for the answers.

1. What is the author's overall view of contemporary television?
2. What does the author consider to be the two main highlights of *Genghis Blues*?
3. How did Paul Pena first come across the art of throat singing?
4. How did Paul Pena meet Kongar-ol Ondar?
5. Where does most of the documentary take place?
6. Why do the Tuvans call Pena 'Earthquake'?
7. For what purpose did Tuvan nomadic herders sing?
8. What are some common themes of traditional Tuvan songs?

Vocabulary Comprehension: Odd Word Out

(A) For each group, circle the word that does not belong. The words in *italics* are vocabulary items from the reading.

1. determine	divulge	discover	*ascertain*
2. fascinating	boring	*engaging*	charming
3. oblivious	sensitive	aware	*sentient*
4. *eminently*	extremely	emotionally	exceptionally
5. touching	*poignant*	dull	moving
6. questionably	doubtfully	*veritably*	arguably

7. contradiction	parallel	*paradox*	inconsistency
8. *intuitive*	insightful	unaware	instinctive
9. fraud	*integrity*	honesty	morality
10. enlightenment	catastrophe	*serendipity*	self-discovery

B Complete the sentences using the words in *italics* from A. Be sure to use the correct form of each word.

1. Most artists and musicians are _____ people, probably as a result of having such creative minds.

2. Jo's many years of editing experience made her _____ qualified to handle the job of publisher.

3. What makes Phillipe such a talented entertainer and host is his _____ manner; people seem to be instantly drawn to him.

4. Luis likes to think of his painting of women at war as a _____ of human behavior.

5. There are some people who base all of their life decisions, no matter how big or small, on their _____.

6. After seeing all the cuts and scratches on his legs, Nina quickly _____ that it was the boy next door who was climbing over her garden fence to steal her apples.

7. Though her husband passed away years ago, Margaret still wears her wedding ring as a _____ reminder of her life with him.

8. Christa's decision to quit her executive position after only two months, and take a higher paying job, shows a distinct lack of _____.

9. The experience of writing and recording their first album left the band with a strong sense of _____ and personal growth.

10. I don't know anyone who has such a _____ run of good fortune like Eliza has. She won the lottery jackpot and a new car in the same month.

Vocabulary Skill:
The Prefix *ad-*

In this chapter, you read the words 'aspect,' 'ascertain,' and 'admits.' These words all begin with the prefixes 'ad' or 'as,' meaning 'to,' 'toward,' and 'next to.' These common prefixes are used with nouns, verbs, adjectives, and adverbs to form many words in English.

A For each word, study the different parts. Use your knowledge of prefixes, suffixes, and word roots to write the part of speech and a simple definition for each one. Use your dictionary to check your answers. Share your ideas with a partner.

Vocabulary	Part of Speech	Definition
1. adjoining	_____	_____
2. adhere	_____	_____
3. adjacent	_____	_____
4. adverse	_____	_____
5. adverb	_____	_____
6. assimilate	_____	_____
7. assertively	_____	_____

Vocabulary	Part of Speech	Definition
8. assign	_____	_____
9. assistant	_____	_____
10. ascribe	_____	_____

(B) Complete each sentence using the words from the chart. Be sure to use the correct form of each word.

1. As Seow Lin only returned from New York last night, I think we can _____ her bad mood to a classic case of jet lag.

2. Due to the _____ weather conditions our flight has been delayed.

3. Now that we're in senior high school, our teachers seem to be _____ us more and more homework every week. I can't keep up!

4. An _____ is a word that can be used in English to modify many other words.

5. Although Takuji is a very intelligent child, he can't seem to _____ written words as readily as other children his age do.

6. Sulinko has decided to take a job as a teaching _____ for a year to help her decide if she really wants to become a trained teacher.

7. I've heard there's a great coffee shop in the _____ building. Let's try it out later.

8. After so many years of ignoring his doctor's advice, Karl now has to _____ to a strict diet in order to maintain his health.

9. Samuel, who is usually so quiet, shocked everyone when he objected so _____ to the proposed changes in company policy.

10. Although we plan to extensively remodel our new house, every bedroom will still have an _____ bathroom, as they do now.

Think About It Discuss the following questions with a partner.

1. Look back at the opening paragraph of the reading. Do you agree with Andy Warhol's point of view about film? Explain your answer giving examples.

2. Can you imagine what Tuvan throat singing sounds like? Have you heard any other music that is similar?

3. Does your country or culture have any kind of unique music, or musical instruments, not widely heard of in the rest of the world? Do you like to listen to this music?

4. Do you think Genghis Blues would be an interesting film to watch? Why or why not?

Before You Read:

Art of Music Video

Discuss the following questions with a partner.

1. Do you ever watch MTV? If so, how often? Do you watch any particular MTV shows regularly? If not, do you watch any other music programs on TV?

2. What do you like or dislike about music programs on TV?

3. Do you have a favorite contemporary song? What makes it your favorite? Have you seen the music video for this song? What do you think of it?

4. How do you think music videos have changed in the last few years?

5. The following phrases can all be found in the reading:

   (**down-and-out (line 7)**)   (**hook up with (line 8)**)   (**hole up (line 52)**)

   Using the line references, locate each phrase in the passage. Using the meaning from context strategies outlined in the previous chapter, identify what these phrases mean.

Reading Skill:

Developing Reading Fluency

Time yourself as you read through the passage. Try to read as fluently as you can. Record your time in the Reading Rate Chart on page 234.

MTV: Secrets in the Sauce _____

The following reading is adapted from *Secrets in the Sauce (MTV Networks Inc's Successful Programs)* by Alan Waldman. Used by permission from *Multichannel News*, a Reed Business publication © August 2, 2002.

A beautiful young woman recoils in horror at the news she's just gotten from a fortune-teller. Her best friends have drawn cards for 'success' and 'wealth,' but Carmen's future has even the soothsayer[1] in a funk.[2] The only thing ahead for her, he says, is 'death.'

Carmen, played by pop music megastar Beyonce Knowles,[3] runs from the fortune-teller's ornate parlor, determined to avoid her fate. In the next few hours, she'll abandon the handsome but down-and-out man she loves and hook up with Blaze, a hugely successful rap star, only to be shot dead by a corrupt cop. The scenes are hip, studded with music industry stars and reminiscent of Bizet's[4] famous opera, *Carmen*. Only in this production, the characters aren't singing their lines, they're rapping them.

MTV's Hiphopera, *Carmen*, topped the ratings for viewers aged twelve to thirty-four the night of its premiere, and captured the second largest audience ever for an original film on MTV. It also typified the kind of programming left turns[5] that have kept the network out front in the art of creating new forms of TV entertainment.

MTV created its first reality show, *Real World*, a decade before the reality TV craze emerged. It also sparked a boom in bent-humored[6] animation aimed at adults and changed forever the way awards shows are presented with its annual, hugely successful showcase of the best in music video.

Behind all this innovation is a never-ending need to stay ahead of what's happening in the world of entertainment. "MTV has to keep reinventing itself, because its audience is always evolving and becoming disenchanted with what was cool last season," says *TV Guide* senior critic Matt Roush. "Because each new MTV audience rebels against the previous one, each program burns out and has to be replaced by something newer, cooler, funnier, and more outrageous. MTV can never rest on its laurels,[7] because that is antithetical[8] to what the network is."

The countdown of MTV's programming breakthroughs is long. Its first original program, 1985's *Remote Control*, "was the first show to turn TV on its ear and make fun of the medium itself," recalls Brian Graden who has, as programming and production president for MTV, been responsible for many of the channel's innovations since 1997. The list of groundbreaking MTV original programs goes on and on, while the network has launched more personalities into pop culture than any other cable outlet, including Jenny McCarthy,[9] Ben Stiller,[10] and Cindy Crawford.[11]

Yet despite such a track record, the quest to 'stay fresh' and come up with new ideas has never gotten easy, says Van Toffler, president of MTV and MTV2. A big part of the way MTV operates, in fact, is geared towards keeping the entire company searching for what's next. Top executives like Toffler, and Judy McGrath, encourage department heads to identify the brightest young minds on their teams, singling them out to attend 'brainstorms'—gatherings of key staff members—to address issues.

The 'brainstorm,' in fact, is part of what McGrath calls 'MTV secrets in the
sauce.' It is a gathering of people that can involve staffers from across all the
MTV networks, and a dozen or so can be going on at any given time.
Currently, one brainstorm is looking at interactive TV while another is
examining MTV itself, its 'tone and attitude,' and "what it tells people when
making decisions about new videos, shows, or on-air talent," McGrath says.

An important brainstorm takes place every year in June, when sixty or so
MTV executives and staffers head to a run-down resort on the tip of Long
Island, to hole up for three days and consider new programming ideas. This
event gets individuals to describe their ideas, and leads the group to build on
them and agree on which projects will go forward. "We leave having
greenlighted[12] fifty projects, everything we need for a year," McGrath explains.

The atmosphere at MTV also encourages creativity, insiders say. "The
environment here is everybody talking at once and interrupting each other,"
McGrath says. "For me, and for a lot of us—the senior executives, if you
will—it's an opportunity to hear from people deeper within the organization.
You walk the halls and see these great-looking, interesting people and you
want to hear what they have to say."

MTV staffers hit the clubs regularly, looking for what's new. A number of the
network's executives make a habit of hanging out with viewers standing in line
at events like the Movie Awards, or assembling daily out front of the
company's Times Square headquarters.

Behind the whole process, says Toffler, is MTV Networks chairman Tom
Freston, who makes it clear that creativity comes first. "The business side is
important, of course," Toffler says, "but you can see his eyes light up when he
hears a good idea, and you know that he knows the profits don't come
without the ideas." McGrath adds that what keeps the innovations coming is
Freston's credo,[13] followed at MTV since almost the beginning: "Try not to let
people realize that this is a business."

---

1 **soothsayer** fortune-teller

2 **in a funk** in a state of worry or fear

3 **Beyonce Knowles** /biyɑnseɪ noʊls/

4 **Bizet** /bizeɪ/ classical music composer Georges Bizet (1838–1875); best known for his opera *Carmen*

5 **left turns** moves away from the mainstream

6 **bent-humored** comedy that has a tendency to be twisted or perverted

7 **rest on its laurels** stop making efforts to improve as a result of being satisfied with achievements so far

8 **antithetical** directly opposed

9 **Jenny McCarthy** American ex-model turned actress, TV show host, MTV host and VJ (video jockey)

10 **Ben Stiller** American comedy actor best known for roles in *There's Something About Mary* and *Meet the Parents*

11 **Cindy Crawford** American supermodel turned MTV show host

12 **greenlighted** approved; given the go ahead

13 **credo** system of beliefs or principles

A Decide if the following statements about the reading are true (*T*), false (*F*), or not mentioned (*NM*). If a statement is false, correct it to make it true.

	T	F	NM
1. MTV's *Carmen* achieved very high viewer ratings on its premier night.			
2. MTV showed a reality TV program a year before the reality TV craze began.			
3. MTV needs to keep reinventing itself so it can keep up with evolutions in music.			
4. MTV is continually searching for new business ventures.			
5. Top executives at MTV encourage the development of the brightest young staff members.			
6. An annual brainstorming session takes place every year in December.			
7. The working environment at MTV encourages staff to be creative.			
8. The main belief driving the success at MTV is to conceal the fact it is a profit-making business.			

B Check your answers with a partner. Count how many you got correct—be honest! Then, fill in the Reading Comprehension Chart on page 234.

A Look at the list of words and phrases from the reading. Match each one with a definition on the right.

1. recoils _____
2. corrupt _____
3. disenchanted _____
4. burns out _____
5. outrageous _____
6. turn on its ear _____
7. make fun of _____
8. groundbreaking _____
9. singling out _____
10. run-down _____

a. in bad condition

b. picking someone or something out from others for special attention

c. shake up and provide something radically different

d. original and innovative

e. shrinks back in fear or adversity

f. to tease or ridicule someone or something

g. becomes worn out or jaded

h. disillusioned; bored

i. unrestrained or shocking; going beyond what is normally acceptable

j. dishonest and immoral

B Complete the paragraph below using most of the vocabulary from A. Be sure to use the correct form of each word. Not every word is used.

One Eye on the Audience

Going to the movies is always good fun, and not only because of the movie. Sometimes watching the audience can be even more entertaining! Recently, I've become rather (1)_____ with a number of kids' movies—they just seem to recycle the same (2)_____ old plot—so I took my children to see *Spy Kids II*. Although this movie wasn't exactly (3)_____ in terms of its special effects, it was refreshingly different. However, what I enjoyed the most was watching the children. I (4)_____ a few children to our left to observe, as well as my own son and daughter. During the scary parts, they (5)_____ in joyful fear, covering their faces with candy-covered fingers. They screamed and tried desperately to bury themselves in their parents' arms. They laughed hysterically when the (6)_____ daddy was discovered, and when the Spy Kids (7)_____ him. Again, though the movie certainly didn't wow the audience, it provided an amount of distraction that was engaging enough, and I was able to watch my favorite show: the audience.

C Now write three sentences of your own using the words that are left over from A. Share your ideas with a partner.

1. _____

2. _____

3. _____

Vocabulary Skill:
Phrasal Verbs with *up* and *out*

In this chapter, you read the phrasal verbs 'hook up,' 'hole up,' 'single out,' and 'burn out.' In English, many verbs can be combined with the prepositions 'up' and 'out' to form phrasal verbs that are used in a wide variety of contexts.

A Look at the verbs in the box below. Write them in the chart depending on whether they fit with *up*, *out*, or both prepositions. Use your dictionary to help you. Compare your answers with a partner.

take	think	draw	cheer	hurry	save
pull	split	tear	hang	burn	point
set	keep	ask	let	give	cut

Up	Both	Out
_____	_____	_____
_____	_____	_____
_____	_____	_____
_____	_____	_____
_____	_____	_____
_____	_____	_____

B Now use some of the phrasal verbs to complete the story below. Be sure to use the correct tense of each verb. Share your answers with a partner.

The Club

When I was just nine years old, my friend Noah and I (1)_____ a great club. Our idea was to (2)_____ to build a place where we could (3)_____ by ourselves—just us, no parents, siblings, or anyone else disturbing us. When we told my mother about our plan she (4)_____ that we had a big old box in the basement that we could use, if we wanted. We (5)_____ plans on how we could design our hangout. First we decided to paint the box, so we (6)_____ all our paints and decided on a color scheme. We (7)_____ and Noah went back to his house to look for things to put on the outside of the box. We (8)_____ pictures from lots of different magazines—photos of our favorite pop stars, actors, and actresses, pictures of animals, and photos of our favorite foods. We (9)_____ two flaps on the box for an entrance so that we could easily go in and out. We also (10)_____ our pocket money to buy things for our little hideaway. Needless to say, the club was a great success. In summer, we would (11)_____ the box outside to the back yard, and in winter we would bring it indoors to the basement. We would invite friends over, and many of our most long-lasting friendships were formed in that box. To this day, my father keeps threatening to (12)_____ the box and throw it in the garbage, but my mom, knowing how much it still means to me, always persuades him to leave it right where it is—in a cozy corner of our basement.

C Use four phrasal verbs from the chart in A, not already used in the passage above, to write four sentences of your own. Share your ideas with a partner.

1. _____
2. _____
3. _____
4. _____

What Do You Think?

Discuss the following questions with a partner.

1. *What influences you into buying CDs or music videos?*
2. *Name one personality who you would like to see host an MTV program. Why would you choose this person?*
3. *What ideas would you like to contribute to an MTV brainstorming session?*
4. *After the development of MTV, the invention of the CD, the MD, and the MP3, what do you think the future holds for innovations in music? Explain your answer.*

Real Life Skill

The Orchestra

Advertising for an orchestra concert generally gives information about the music that will be performed, and the conductor or musicians. Often, the descriptions refer to the different sections (or types) of instruments in the orchestra. If you are looking for a concert in which you will hear a particular type of instrument, you need to be familiar with these terms.

Ⓐ Read the following definitions of the sections of instruments in an orchestra.

strings—instruments that are played by using a bow on strings
brass—metal instruments that are played by blowing into them
woodwinds—wooden instruments that are played by blowing into them
percussion—instruments that are played by striking or hitting them

Ⓑ Match these orchestra instruments to the correct category by writing them on the appropriate line. Use your dictionary to help you as necessary. Add any other instruments that you know.

French horn	cymbals	cello	violin
trumpet	clarinet	tuba	drum
oboe	bass	harp	trombone

strings: viola, _____

brass: baritone, _____

woodwinds: flute, _____

percussion: kettledrum, _____

Ⓒ Discuss these questions with a partner.

1. Which of these types of instruments do you enjoy listening to? Are there any that you dislike? Explain your answers.
2. Can you play any of these instruments? Are there any that you would like to learn to play?
3. Which instrument do you think is the easiest to learn to play? Which do you think is the most difficult?

Vocabulary Index

Skills Index

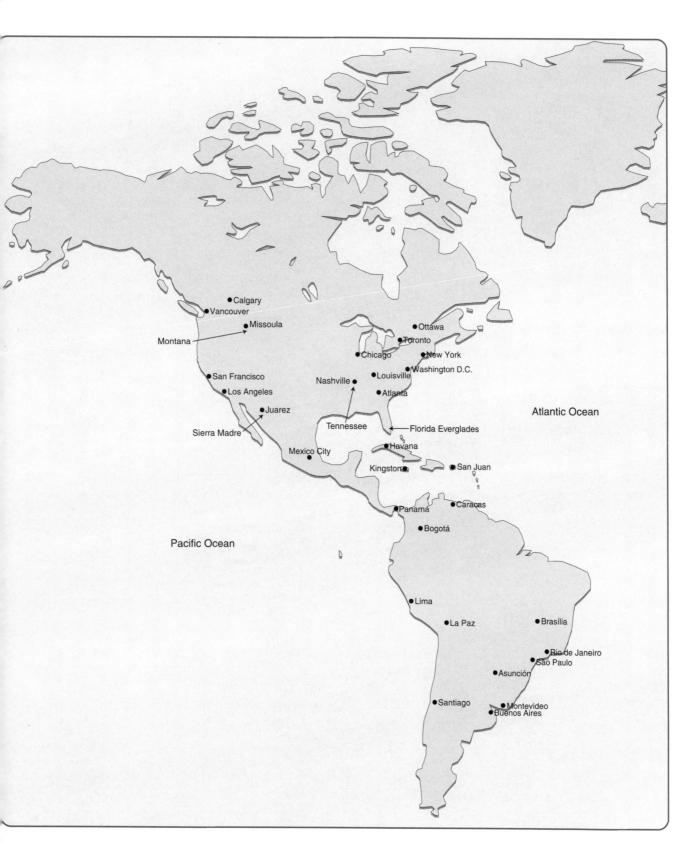

Calgary
Vancouver
Missoula
Montana

Ottawa
Toronto
Chicago
New York
Washington D.C.
San Francisco
Louisville
Los Angeles
Nashville
Atlanta
Juarez
Sierra Madre
Tennessee
Florida Everglades
Mexico City
Havana
Kingston
San Juan
Panamá
Caracas
Bogotá

Atlantic Ocean

Pacific Ocean

Lima
La Paz
Brasília
Rio de Janeiro
São Paulo
Asunción
Santiago
Montevideo
Buenos Aires

Greenland

Iceland

Oslo● ●Helsinki
●Stockholm

Edinburgh●   Moscow●

Dublin●   Copenhagen●
London●   Amsterdam● ●Berlin ●Warsaw
           ●Brussels ●Prague
       ●Paris   Vienna● ●Budapest
              Belgrade●
                 ●Bucharest
Madrid●   ●Rome   Istanbul●
Lisbon●   Athens● ●Ankara

Mediterranean Sea ——→ Algiers● ●Tunis
●Casablanca   Tripoli●

North Atlantic
Ocean

Cairo●

Cape Verde Islands
●Dakar

●Khartoum

●Monrovia   ●Djibouti
                 ●Addis Ababa

        Kampala●   ●Mogadishu
               ●Nairobi
●Kinshasa   ●Dar es Salaam

South Atlantic
Ocean   Indian Ocean

        ●Pretoria

Cape Town●

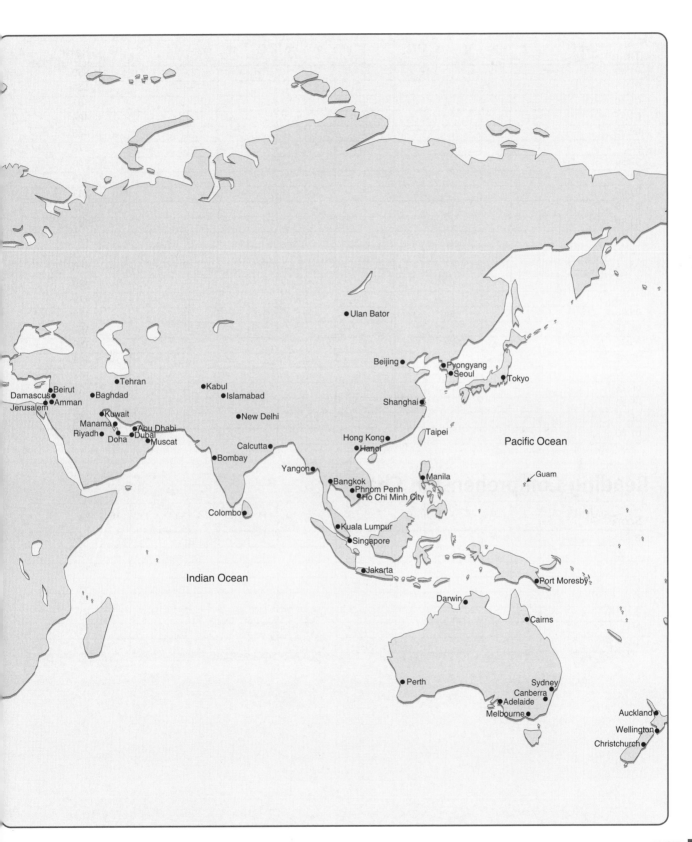

Ulan Bator

Beijing
Pyongyang
Seoul
Tokyo

Damascus
Beirut
Tehran
Kabul
Amman
Baghdad
Islamabad
Shanghai
Jerusalem
Kuwait
New Delhi
Manama
Abu Dhabi
Riyadh
Doha
Dubai
Muscat
Hong Kong
Taipei
Pacific Ocean
Calcutta
Hanoi
Bombay
Yangon
Manila
Guam
Bangkok
Phnom Penh
Ho Chi Minh City
Colombo
Kuala Lumpur
Singapore
Jakarta
Port Moresby
Indian Ocean
Darwin
Cairns
Perth
Sydney
Canberra
Adelaide
Auckland
Melbourne
Wellington
Christchurch

Charts

Reading Rate Chart

Time \ Unit	1	2	3	4	5	6	7	8	9	10	11	12	13	14	15	16	Rate (words per minute)
01:00																	850
01:15																	680
01:30																	567
01:45																	486
02:00																	425
02:15																	378
02:30																	340
02:45																	309
03:00																	283
03:15																	262
03:30																	243
03:45																	227
04:00																	213
04:15																	200
04:30																	189
04:45																	179
05:00																	170
05:15																	162
05:30																	155
05:45																	148
06:00																	142
06:15																	136
06:30																	131
06:45																	126
07:00																	121

Reading Comprehension Chart

Score \ Unit	1	2	3	4	5	6	7	8	9	10	11	12	13	14	15	16	%
8																	100
7																	86
6																	75
5																	63
4																	50
3																	38
2																	25
1																	13